Perspectives
on a
Century

Perspectives on a Century

A Compendium *of* 100 Years *of* THE Christian Community Journal

Foreword *by* Tom Ravetz

This selection first published in 2022 by Floris Books
© 2022 Floris Books

All rights reserved. No part of this publication may
be reproduced without the prior permission of
Floris Books, Edinburgh
www.florisbooks.co.uk

British Library CIP Data available
ISBN: 978-178250-788-8
Printed in Great Britain by Bell & Bain Ltd

Floris Books supports sustainable forest management by printing this book on materials made from wood that comes from responsible sources and reclaimed material

Contents

Foreword *Tom Ravetz*	9
1920s	
Christ *Friedrich Rittelmeyer*	13
From Buddha to Christ: Repeated Earth Lives *Hermann Beckh*	19
An Easter Revelation in the Old Testament *Emil Bock*	24
1930s	
Creation *Oliver Mathews*	31
The Name 'Michael' *Rudolf Frieling*	35
Tobit: An Easter Story *Leo Baker*	38
Human Nature and Morality *Eduard Lenz*	42
1940s	
The Quaker-Catholic *Eileen Hersey*	47
The Two Jesus Children *Alfred Heidenreich*	52
God and the Devil *Oliver Mathews*	55
1950s	
The Tragedy of Judas *Alfred Heidenreich*	61
Making Friends with Time *Adam Bittleston*	66

Billy Graham and the Religious Situation in Britain
   Alfred Heidenreich — 68

True and False Vision *Evelyn Francis Derry* — 74

Urizen and Los *Adam Bittleston* — 80

The Problem of Community *Kalmia Bittleston* — 86

1960s

Shakespeare and the Realm of the Dead *Adam Bittleston* — 91

The Two Messiahs *Ormond Edwards* — 98

The Trinity *Evelyn Francis Derry* — 101

1970s

Abraham Lincoln: Servant of Michael *Donald Perkins* — 111

The Origins of Celtic Christianity *Michael Tapp* — 119

1980s

Our Relationship with Those Who Have Died *Stanley Drake* — 127

The Voice of Conscience in William Wilberforce *Stanley Drake* — 133

Freud's Picture of Man *Tony Brown* — 138

The Mystery of Rebirth in an Esoteric Gospel *Andrew Welburn* — 146

1990s

The Body and Its Redemption *Pearl Goodwin* — 155

Is Religion Useful? *Tom Ravetz* — 159

Market Forces and Ethics *Baruch Luke Urieli* — 162

Counselling and Sacramental Consultation *Tom Ravetz* — 167

Forgiving is More Than Amnesia: Reconciliation in South Africa
   Julian Sleigh — 173

Finding Stillness in Chaos, Renewal in Decline *Elizabeth Roberts* — 178

2000s

On the 150th Anniversary of Darwin's *Origin of Species*
   Pearl Goodwin   185

In Search of the Divine Feminine: The Re-emergence of Sophia
   in Our Times *Martin Samson*   189

2010s

Mary, Sophia and the New Advent of Christ *Patrick Kennedy*   197

Fighting the Stigma of AIDs in Uganda *Deborah Ravetz*   204

The Spiritual Hierarchies and Our Relationship to Them
   Michael Kientzler   208

Homosexuality and the Bible *Paul Corman*   214

Why Did God Create Moths? *Yaroslava Black*   219

Seize the Day: Reflections on Brexit *Luke Barr*   223

Bursts of Light in the Darkness: Violence in the Light
   of Anthroposophy *Michael Chase*   226

2020s

Paul and Christ *Cynthia Hindes*   235

Transforming Evil : Understanding, Confrontation,
   Redemption *Bastiaan Baan*   240

Is the Earth a Living Body? (And If So, Whose Is It?)
   Peter Skaller   24.

Sources   251
About *Perspectives*   253

This book reproduces a selection of articles as they were originally published from the early twentieth century onwards. The language used in each article is reflective of the time in which it was written. We recommend reading this book with an understanding of the cultural context in which these articles first appeared.

Foreword

Tom Ravetz

The Christian Community was founded in 1922 partly in response to what some of its founders – many of them former or aspiring students of Lutheran theology – saw as the decline in theological scholarship and, with it, church life. They wished to return to the vitality that we can still experience in the writings of the first theologians of the early church, a vitality drawn from an encounter with the living Christ. And just as those theologians drew freely on the spiritual resources of their day, so, too, the authors of many of the articles in this important book found in anthroposophy the help they needed to articulate their experiences. These articles were not intended to become fixed dogma, but rather a living library of insights, a stimulus to further thinking and a means of exploration for their readers.

The journal of The Christian Community began life in 1923. It was originally published in German, with the English edition following in January 1932, around two years after The Christian Community was founded in Britain. Over the century that followed, a considerable body of work grew up, covering a wide range of subjects. Inevitably, a centenary collection such as this can only present a selection of this writing. Still, it showcases some of the variety. Some of the articles shed light on the events of their day, such as Billy Graham's visit to the UK in the 1950s, or the Truth and Reconciliation process in South Africa in the 1990s. There are articles that tackle difficult and controversial subjects, such as the stigma of AIDS, or the question of homosexuality and the Bible. The more traditional, theological topics are also covered, presented by different authors through the decades and often with refreshingly different viewpoints – for example, the different perspectives on the infancy narratives in the Gospels of St Matthew and St Luke. Some articles, such as those on the spiritual hierarchies and evil, draw directly from anthroposophy itself, using the concepts found there to enrich our thinking. In a world where nothing is outside the circle of divine working, puzzling over the existence of moths feels as essential as fathoming the mysteries of the Trinity. In this approach we see an expression of The Christian Community's mission to heal the divide between the sacred and the profane.

As an author and the current editor of *Perspectives*, I am always surprised and delighted when I meet people in Christian Community congregations and beyond who have drawn inspiration from an article that we published, perhaps years ago. It serves as a reminder that what is contained in this collection is only one part of the conversation that goes on between authors and their readers. What cannot be documented is the way ideas resonate and continue to develop in the souls of those who have read them. We are now able to send the journal around the world digitally, and the rapid uptake of that option in recent years has been a wonderful affirmation of our work.

In this centenary year of the founding of The Christian Community, we face a great challenge: how to communicate our message in such a way that new generations will be able to find their way to the healing power of the sacraments. This core aspect of our mission is what the journal seeks to serve, and this book is a wonderful celebration of how it has been achieving its aim for over one hundred years.

1920s

Christ

Friedrich Rittelmeyer

Friedrich Rittelmeyer (1872–1938) was Germany's most famous Lutheran preacher. He met Rudolf Steiner in 1911 and became a firm supporter of his work. Along with a group of mainly Lutheran priests and theology students, he founded The Christian Community in 1922 and became its leader. This opening article of the first issue of The Christian Community's journal, initially called Tatchristentum *(Christianity of deeds), still has the flavour of a Lutheran preacher, a quality Rittelmeyer overcame and transformed in subsequent years.*

The first essay in our new journal can bear no other name than this. And yet how can we take the responsibility of speaking of Christ, given all our frailty, darkness and misguidedness? Is the mirror to reveal all its defects and flaws by letting the sunlight shine fully upon it?

In spirit we seek out those human beings for whom in past centuries the name of Christ was most sacred. We look to the apostle Paul who, after the Risen One had spoken in his soul as the new, holy power of life, henceforth was led by a super-earthly power, allowing himself to be cursed and maltreated, tormented and stoned. Despite enemies left and right, above and below, he succeeded in planting the Christ seed into the degenerating culture of the West. We look to the evangelist John, who absorbed the Christ into the depths of his being as the purest, most tranquil light that now shines luminous in him through the millennia in sublime, peaceful joy as only the high stars in the firmament can shine, except that in comparison with him the stars themselves appear cold and dead. In spirit we seek Francis of Assisi who rose to become song through Christ, who took poverty from him and the stigmata, but who transformed himself within into such jubilation that rowdy Italy paused to listen, its poets taking up the sublime song of Christ-blessedness and letting it reverberate on through the centuries in artworks and human deeds. We also greet Luther who, as German warrior, received from his 'Master Christ' a sacred strength and the christening of his sensibility, who broke the thousand-year chains of Rome and helped the spirit towards freedom. Under the gaze of all of these, and under that of many nameless ones for whom he became the highest name of earth existence, we must shoulder the responsibility for what we say of Christ.

We take this responsibility not only towards them but towards all those yet to come, those not yet born. For if those touched by Christ are sure of anything it is this: that the history of Christianity is only just beginning, despite all the saints and heroes, despite all missionaries and martyrs. The most spiritually potent sermons on Christ have not yet been given, the most sacred Christ music still slumbers unborn, the mightiest Christ deeds still await those capable of accomplishing them. And if we think of these, and also of the invisible spirits of all who may dwell in higher realms and whose clear spirit gaze is capable of resting upon the Christ being in deepest vision, then the ultimate responsibility we must take is towards Christ himself, the miracle of whose being is the very highest reality that the human spirit can approach in divining intimation, and to which the human soul can open and surrender itself.

Should we keep silent? Our era stands in a huge Christ-crisis, and the lack of Christ is its greatest distress, all the greater in that humanity scarcely apprehends it.

Here already we meet a contradiction. Why do we speak of Christ and not of God? Why always this dangerous detour through history? Is the divine mystery of existence not inherently available to human beings? Did not Jesus himself seek to lead us to the Father? And, as Fichte stressed, would he not be contented even if his work was fulfilled though his name was never mentioned? Whoever says so is hopelessly at odds with reality, even if he is called Fichte. The truth is that human beings will lose the divine Father-Ground of existence altogether if they lose Christ, and we have already taken many steps down this path as should be apparent to any of clear vision. Certainly, for a while, one could continue to speak of the divine in general terms for another generation or two. But this god will increasingly turn into one in far more need of our redemption than he would be capable of redeeming us, and, after a little while, humanity would bury this god without so much as a song or a dance. This is what will happen if human beings no longer hear the divine Word of life that spoke so strongly and clearly to us in Christ, spoke directly to human ears and human souls, through a human nature and a human life: the divine Word of revelation that so deeply imparted to us what Man is and how he should become.

If we try to make clear to ourselves the nature of our contemporary, spiritual-historical Christ-crisis, we could begin with Friedrich Schleiermacher's famous Christology. Back then, when Kant brushed aside an old foundation of religion with his famous critique of proofs of God, it could be felt as an extraordinarily beneficent deed that the greatest theologian of Protestantism found a new foundation for belief in God in the historical appearance of Jesus. Roughly, in Schleiermacher's thesis, Jesus exists, and anyone who regards him needs no other proof of God. How this Jesus lives within God and dies for God is sufficient proof of God. The truth and clarity with which one who is fully alive becomes a witness in his whole life and being to the divine, living Ground of all existence, the world Father, is itself directly compelling and convincing. This message was heard in a hundred auditoria, from a thousand pulpits, and certainly not without justification or blessing. But it was not unlike the famous painting by the recently deceased Max Klinger, *Christ in Olympus,* in which as Zeus delights above in his own divine glory, untroubled and unknowing, the Titans below are already at work mercilessly hacking the foundations of his throne to pieces. The work of the New Testament scholars was indeed titanic and merciless enough. One need only have experienced this at first hand as an evangelical theologian in those decades, how one sustaining saying of Christ after another was stolen from our hands: the whole of the Gospel of John, the words of Christ on the Cross, the Lord's Prayer. If one wished to preach, one often had the feeling of walking upon ground that had been undermined, upon which no safe step could be taken, let alone a house built. It was understandable if many evangelical theologians refused to know anything of this whole destructive thrust of academic scholarship, and simply clung instead to the 'simple Gospel'. But no enemy has ever been overcome by a failure to see him coming.

The hour will surely come when we must inform our readers in full detail how we believe we can combat all these scholarly attacks upon the Christ event arising from new studies in the fields of mythology and astrology: how we can do so in such a way that from all this, in fact, only greater knowledge of Christ can be won. But all that is the task more of theology than of religion. Our great question is this: how can modern people come to experience Christ once more? How can they come to a new, inward, fully authentic and profoundly powerful relationship with Christ that accords with a modernity that they must inevitably affirm?

Allow me to offer a personal account here, since an individual destiny can often mirror the broader developments of an era. Brought up in 'the old faith', like many others I first had to discard all I had learned and seek my own path. Having gained a first access to the personality of Jesus and theses about the 'kingdom of God' (for which I have to thank 'liberal theology') the strong impression made on me by the words of Jesus gave rise to a heartfelt desire to write a book about Jesus. But I also knew immediately – I was about twenty-five at the time – that such an undertaking would have to be the work of a lifetime. 'You must spend many, many years finding your way into the sayings of Jesus – perhaps until you are around forty – and at the same time you must work your way towards him externally by studying precisely those minds who are most opposed to him!' Thus I read Nietzsche and allowed him to affect me to the full through every line he had written; then also Buddha, who has been called the 'other great religious founder'. After this I studied significant promulgators of Christianity: Tolstoy, Meister Eckhart, and from our own era Johannes Mueller. At the age of forty I did then actually write my little volume on Jesus, and I was pleased that readers responded by saying it could only have been written after twenty years of preaching on Jesus.

Yet I discovered to my great surprise that despite all my efforts I had only just begun to tackle the problem. This Jesus is not Jesus! I saw this quite clearly now. This Jesus is a mystery! How can a person live and die as he did? How can someone speak and live out of God as he did? How can someone say 'I' in the way he did: 'But I say to you…', 'I am come', 'I forgive you', 'I am your resolve'. How can this 'I' stand in the world so purely and surely, so clearly and with such grandeur, without trembling or fear, with such majestic humility? Those who believe they can solve the problem of Jesus with their historical scholarship have no inkling at all of the seriousness and gravity of these questions. Nor do our young friends often sufficiently recognise the grandeur of these questions and the reality surging beneath them: they speak all too easily and self-evidently again today of the Christ who came to us in Jesus. At the time it felt to me as if all my endeavours had led me only to a brick wall and that I could go no further. But it is good fortune to have seen this Christ-wall before you at least! What is needed then is to start all over again with studying and questioning. If someone can say of themselves that the battles of their era are mirrored in their own long struggles, then surely they may invite others' attention when stepping before them and saying: I have found a path that leads further, and it is called meditation!

It was not anthroposophy that first showed me this path. If, for instance, you read in our first book of sermons, *God and the Soul*, the sermon on 'Being Alone' given in around 1904, you can clearly see what was already present beforehand but which then, through the clear, practical counsels of anthroposophy, was formed into a quite different, living fruitfulness. For instance, what always kept me on sure ground at the time of the disputes about the 'Christ Myth', especially as propounded by Arthur Drews in his book of the same name, was not some idiosyncratic or fixed dogma of an historical or metaphysical kind, nor any uninformed shallowness that shies away from tackling real questions. But simply remembering my meditations on the words, 'I have come to cast a fire on the earth...' For me it was beyond denial that these were the words of someone, whoever he may have been, to whom the inmost soul hearkens, asking: who is this? He speaks with a purity and grandeur like no other before him.

And this now was the way forward that could lead us up the steep ascent of the Christ-wall to the heights of Christ. We can earnestly endeavour to penetrate the words of Christ with all the powers of our being and our life – first choosing those sayings we find most accessible and incontrovertible, leaving aside everything else that might obstruct our understanding. And then, seeking to bring this figure to life, if we ask, what kind of man is this who can speak such words? What sort of spirit do his words express? What kind of being and life stands behind them? What kind of person would I have to be to speak in such a way? – we will gradually gain a very clear impression of the completely distinctive Christ spirit, of the wholly unique, incomparable Christ being, of the divine stream of Christ power that is beyond all we have known. There is no need to believe from the outset in a risen Christ or in a living presence. We can leave this all to one side, even for instance the question of the true origin of the words in the John Gospel. The decisive thing is that we gain a really life-filled sense of the inner glory of Christ. And for this purpose the gospels have been given to us. In them lives the glory of Christ, a glory 'full of grace and truth'. And if we do not discover this in the gospels, then for us they were written in vain. Perhaps the first thing is to behold redemption as it were flowing from this Christ, the power of redemption for millions upon millions of human beings, for thousands upon thousands of millennia. Let us feel the breath of an unimagined, inexhaustible rejuvenation of the world, one that would signify its complete transformation if only we will accept it – albeit with our whole will! If the world as a whole were as Christ was in a single human being, then the world would be divine!

Upon this path we can continually progress. In as natural and sure a way as we perceive the sun, we perceive that this Christ is not an abstract power or someone who belongs to the past. He is alive today, more alive than a thousand things we think are alive. He is still real today, indeed, he becomes more and more a reality for us, 'the truth' as the evangelist says. It becomes ever clearer that Christ is here. He is invisibly present and spiritually potent at every moment in which we can raise our soul to him: a world of brightest purity, purest self-surrender and healing sanctity, a world and a personality, at the same time transpersonal and closer to us than our own soul, as clear and clearer than the sun, as glorious and more glorious than we have conceived heaven to be. Yes, he is truly a heaven: the heaven we can enter at any time and from which we can draw what we need in the way of strength and tranquillity, wisdom and love. And no one need fear that they in any way dishonour their own uniqueness when they open themselves to this Christ. On the contrary, in Christ's spirit our hidden, true I first finds the air in which it can truly breathe, the light within which it can truly awaken. Those familiar with the New Testament will know that living Christians have said this from the very beginning.

To find the Christ in this way means to rediscover Christianity anew out of the present moment: a Christianity that is absolutely undogmatic, free, completely unconstrained by historical context; that is not in the least muddled but clear as sunlight; that is not withering away but alive in the core of our being. The very same Christianity that stands before us in the New Testament and in the words of St Paul: I live – yet not I but Christ lives in me! Of course, to understand how this Christ lives in Jesus, how he may have lived previously, and how today he can be a close and living presence, how we can perceive him, what the capacities of our soul are through which we can sense him, and what of us lives on in him beyond death – to understand all this in an entirely contemporary way, we need a new theology, indeed, a new philosophy. It is not too hard to see that the old theology and philosophy cannot get much further on their chosen paths. But with all this we have only spoken of how each individual can wrestle their way through to Christ. Will all be able to pursue this path? Precisely those who have Christ can open up for others another path to Christ in communal life, in the life of social action. This can happen everywhere in life, but happens above all in acts of worship.

From Buddha to Christ: Repeated Earth Lives

Hermann Beckh

Hermann Beckh (1875–1937) studied Sanskrit, Tibetan, Egyptian and other ancient languages, and became 'extraordinary professor' and lecturer on Buddhism in Berlin. When he heard of the preparatory meetings for the founding of The Christian Community he decided to go along. Upon arriving, he announced: 'Now I'm here, I'm part of this.'

At the centre of Christianity is an event, a deed: the deed of life and death accomplished on Golgotha. At the centre of Buddhism is a system of knowledge. Through enlightenment the Bodhisattva is set free from reincarnation and becomes a Buddha. But the knowledge imparted to the world by Buddha was not to be merely accepted in faith. With the knowledge was combined the way along which the soul could approach the healing truth discovered by Buddha. Both knowledge and the way which leads to knowledge are comprised in the teaching of Buddha; the mere acceptance of a creed is far removed from it. This forms an important distinction between Buddhism and other religions – even that which passes in many circles for Christianity and the Christian confession of faith.

The knowledge gained by Buddha under the sacred fig tree is always, in legend and doctrine, represented as threefold. The first and second parts of this knowledge (the order varies) concern the destiny of beings in the circle of rebirths. It is concerned with the knowledge of karma, the great law of destiny, and of reincarnation, of repeated earth-lives. The third part is the knowledge of suffering, its cause and its conquest. It is dealt with in the teachings of Buddha, which include the 'four noble truths' and the 'list of the twelve causes'.

Belief in karma, the law of destiny, and in reincarnation is universal today in India, and already was so in the age of Buddha. But with Buddha – and this is emphasised everywhere in the sacred tradition – it is not merely a matter of accepting a creed or dogma, but of a knowledge and a direct vision that any disciple who followed the Path could make their own. As from a high watchtower one may see people walking in streets and squares, going into and out of the houses, so it is said that the Buddha saw in meditation, under the sacred fig tree, how beings ('people' are never directly mentioned) after the dissolution of physical death take either the 'evil path' or the 'good path'. Because their actions are determined by their concepts, those who are led by a false world-concept, by a lack of reverence, and by evil thoughts, words and deeds, are set in dark places of torment, while those who are led by a right world-concept, by reverence for the sublime, and by good thoughts, words and deeds, reach the heavenly worlds of light, from which they return into earth-life; although from the Nirvana accessible only to a Buddha, there is no return. Similarly, of the knowledge of repeated earth-lives it is said that under the fig tree the Buddha had a perfectly clear recollection of his own earlier earth-lives, and that his disciples in meditation also recalled theirs to consciousness, though not with the same clarity as the Buddha himself. Mystics of all kinds, it is said, have these life-memories, but theirs are as dim as the glint of a glow-worm, while with the Buddha's disciples they are as clear as the light of a lamp. With the elect they shine like the morning star. With the Buddha who has found illumination for himself alone without imparting it to the world, they shine like moonlight; but with a world-redeeming Buddha, they are as bright as the light of a thousand suns.

Legend relates that when the Bodhisattva awoke from meditation to Buddha-enlightenment in the first watch of the night, he saw with his supersensible eye beings wandering through the light and dark regions on this side and the other, each according to his karma; then, in the second watch of the night, he turned his gaze to the vision of his own earlier earth-lives. With his supersensible eye he saw these earth-lives and those of other beings through countless cosmic ages past, with all their various joys and sorrows, their high and lowly destinies. As he saw them, he remembered the name he bore in each of these incarnations, he remembered his sex, his caste, the circumstances and duration of his life in each. Just as those who wake from sleep can recall the dreams of many nights, so the Buddha, wakened from the long sleep of human consciousness, recalled the dreams of many earth-nights. But only they who, like the Buddha, have stripped themselves of everything personal in this present earth-life see how not only this one earth-life becomes strange to them, but the whole chain of their incarnations.

The two branches of knowledge, that of karma, the law of destiny, and that of repeated earth-lives are very closely connected. Their recognition modifies the whole balance and feeling of life. It makes all the difference if a man regards himself as a plaything of external powers which determine, without choice or justice, his birth and the conditions of his life, or if he recognises himself as part of a great cosmic scheme in which everything is rationally harmonised. Karma is one of those truths of which man gains a living understanding through a new orientation of his life. The feeling of moral responsibility with which the soul confronts its earthly task acquires a more solemn significance. The disciples of the Buddha were able to acquire the knowledge of karma and reincarnation as a genuine supersensible fact when, in their meditative exercises, they achieved control of *sanskara*, the formative forces of existence, in the depths of their own consciousness.

What becomes of such knowledge in the light of Christ? Could it ever happen that in the soul's progress from Buddha to Christ this knowledge would no longer be needed? No; but in the light of Christ it will be transformed and its value altered in many ways. For Buddhists, karma is a personal matter only. He who has fathomed the lore of karma in the Indian sense, will not see it as his special task even to try and create a favourable karma for himself. For such a karma would also, in the course of time, like any other, hold the soul fast in the circle of rebirths which the Indian wishes to eliminate. To the Indian, any karma represents a debt which he desires to pay off as speedily as possible, a burden of which he desires to rid himself. For the individual who has succeeded in getting quit of his individual debt to existence by the settlement of his karmic account, the further fate of earth and humanity is without interest. This attitude which, from a higher point of view is undoubtedly an egoistic one, was, in those last stages of man's descent, justifiable; but it could not stand against the light in which, for the spiritual eye, the earth again began to shine when the Christ-sun-being was united with it in the Mystery of Golgotha. The earth became henceforth the Body of Christ, and earth destiny and human destiny his immediate concern. But the destiny of earth could be fulfilled according to the mind of Christ only if each soul were united in individual freedom with the ego-impulse of Christ. This cannot be done if the soul tries to settle its karma, its own personal reckoning, in the Buddhist way, by considering only the significance for itself of its former deeds. The soul indwelt by Christ considers also the consequences which its deeds may have for the earth as a whole. The soul becomes conscious of the burden laid upon the karma of the whole earth by its individual karma, and feels its share of responsibility in the karma and future of the planet. Looking upon the earth and humanity in this way, the soul sees also the being who is united with the soul of the earth and who controls its future and that of humanity: Christ. The soul sees that Christ has taken upon himself that which the soul's deeds have wrought upon the earth, so that all discord caused by human karma may, in future ages, be restored to harmonious balance by him. And therein the soul sees the deep meaning of Christ's forgiveness of sin.

The individual soul is not relieved of anything for which a higher feeling of responsibility would make it accountable. Had the Christian forgiveness of sins such a personal, egoistic meaning, there would be no progress in it, but rather a retrograde step towards the Buddhist knowledge of karma. But when Christian forgiveness is rightly understood, then knowledge of karma is embraced in its widest scope. Nothing is deducted from this knowledge as Buddha saw it under the sacred fig tree. But when the Buddhist knowledge is placed in the light shining from the Cross of Calvary, there flows from it a will-impulse that is entirely new. In this new impulse Christ is the ruler. Under its influence, people will no longer desire only to free themselves as rapidly as possible from the burden of their personal karma. They will consent to their destiny, taking it upon themselves through the power of Christ. People will no longer desire that any part of their destiny should be personally remitted; rather it will be the wish of their hearts to bring harmony into all that their deeds have done to the evolution of the earth, not that they may be freed from the necessity of further incarnations, but that the human prototype darkened by sin may, in future ages, rise again in a more perfect and pristine purity. People will bear their destiny throughout their incarnations in order to collaborate, in the light of Christ, with the restoration of the divine human type, to work willingly with Christ at the new earth, and to help in the building of humanity's future. And therein lies the true forgiveness of sins, that the soul – when thus it boldly takes upon itself its personal destiny and resolves to collaborate in building the temple of humanity – can be assured that through Christ it is relieved from the oppressive consciousness of having irreparably spoilt something in this temple-building by its past deeds. Just because the soul has courage to bear its destiny, to take the personal result of its deeds upon itself, a higher power is thereby enabled to take on the objective significance of those deeds, which extends beyond the personal over the whole earth. The sun-power of Christ, now become the Spirit of the earth, can do this.

When the soul has united itself with the light of Christ, impulses that do not seek, like Buddha's, to annihilate existence but which are in the highest sense of the word creative, flow from the knowledge of karma. This is the fundamental revaluation through Christ of the Buddha's Law of Destiny (Karma), which is of such deep significance for all mankind. The knowledge itself is not in any way changed by this revaluation, but the will-impulse flowing from it to the Christ-filled future of the earth, flows into the souls of those who have attained true union with the Christ.

An Easter Revelation in the Old Testament

Emil Bock

Emil Bock (1895–1959) came across Rudolf Steiner's work while serving as a wartime postal censor in Berlin, examining packages of books being sent to Switzerland. He also heard Friedrich Rittelmeyer preaching and was later to succeed Rittelmeyer as leader of The Christian Community. Bock's series of books on the Old and New Testaments reflect his intense study of the Bible, anthroposophy and the geography of the Holy Land, which he visited twice.

The book of the prophet Isaiah, thundering with the storms of the Last Judgement, luminous with the hopeful rays of future world renewal, has long been an enigma in theological discourse. Between chapters 39 and 40 it so clearly splits asunder into two parts that people nowadays usually think that these are two different books brought together under the same prophet's name. Behind the first 39 chapters, it is thought, stands the figure of Isaiah, but behind chapters 40 to 66, there instead stands a great and nameless figure. This is known as the second, the other Isaiah, the Deutero-Isaiah.

Those who have been moved by the wisdom and wonderfully rigorous lawfulness that holds sway in the structure of the Bible's holy scriptures, cannot accept such an unconnected juxtaposition of two prophet figures and two prophets' books, of Isaiah and Deutero-Isaiah. If the Bible, which knows no caprice or random accident, joins two books so intimately together, we must ask what the bridge is that leads from the first to the second Isaiah.

The key to solving this riddle is given in chapters 38 and 39 of Isaiah, directly preceding the beginning of the second great book. In these chapters a mighty drama unfolds, albeit in hidden and inconspicuous fashion, which could be entitled 'The Death and Resurrection of a King'.

King Hezekiah falls ill. Isaiah stands beside him announcing the impending death.

> The time had come when Hezekiah fell ill, with a sickness unto death. And Isaiah, the son of Amos, the prophet, came to him and said: 'This says the Lord, "Conclude life in your earthly dwelling, for you will die and have no further strength of life."' (38:1)

But the king's soul is great and strong. In death it raises itself to clear spirit experience, and complete dedication to God. The Old Testament text, both in the Hebrew and the Greek, allows us to feel the real soul experience a person undergoes in death when seeing the whole memory tableau of their life spread around them at once. This great panoramic vision of life is meant when it is said that Hezekiah turned his face to 'the wall'. In the retrospective gaze of a soul departing from the body, Hezekiah can look upon a life of truth and a truth-sustaining heart. He passes the trial at the threshold of death. The pain that now floods through him is a pure one. The tears he weeps are those of an eye that suddenly gazes into bright light.

At this point Isaiah, who before had announced his death to him, must bring the king the message of new life. He places a paste or plaster of figs upon Hezekiah, thus giving life back to him. Already immersed with part of his being in the world beyond the grave, Hezekiah is now called upon to return into his body, to climb the steps of this sacred temple again and to live once more within it (38:22).

The death and resurrection of King Hezekiah is not due to an illness of an ordinary, corporeal kind. The sickness that leads him to death is a trial of the soul, a stage on a path of consecration, of rebirth: a path of initiation. The prophet Isaiah stands as hierophant beside his royal pupil in the mysteries. It is he who, at the command of God, first guides the king into death and then to rebirth. Like the book of the prophet Jonah, who spent three days inside the whale, that is, the grave of earth, but was then released to new life, these two chapters of Isaiah describe an initiation that passes through death and rebirth. Jonah and Hezekiah in the Old Testament are like a prefiguring shadow cast by the future light of Christ's death and resurrection.

From the lips of King Hezekiah, as from those of the prophet Jonah, a psalm pours forth that we could call an 'initiation psalm' for it describes the real spirit experiences of the soul in its passage through death and rebirth:

> The book of the revelations of Hezekiah, king of the Jews, when he fell sick unto death and rose again from his mortal illness:
> My I, in the heights, whence it looks back upon all my days, speaks thus: I enter the gates of Hades. The future stages of my way are lost to me. No longer may I behold the divine light of salvation upon the earth amongst the living; no longer may I behold on earth the holy goal of Israel, and no longer does man stand before me. I am taken away from human circles to which I belonged, I have lost the rest of my life. I have departed from myself and am carried off, my being is like a tent that has been dismantled. My spirit is spread out before me like a cloth and the tailor comes to snip off the thread. On this day I am given up to the lion as his prey until the hour of awakening and all my bones will be broken. I am given up to perdition in the whole sphere between night and day. Like a swallow my cry rings out, like a dove I mourn. My eyes fail from gazing upward into the heights of heaven where is enthroned the Lord who raises me and takes away the travails of my soul.
> Lord, I called upward to you for the sake of my soul and you have awakened my spirit, and I won a new life through your awakening call. You sustained my soul so that it should not go under, you cast all my sins behind me. Those who praise you are not in Hades; those who bless you are not in death; those who hope for salvation are not shades. The living will bless you. And I am one of them. Henceforth all that I do and undertake shall announce your world of goodness. God of my salvation, I will not cease to praise you with psalms through all the days of my life. I will live always before the countenance of the temple of God. (38:9-20)*

On receiving the message of Hezekiah's mortal illness and rebirth, the king of Babylon dispatches letters and gifts to Jerusalem. Thus one initiate greets another who has now stepped also into the circle of those who have received initiation. Hezekiah opens all his treasure chambers to the messenger: 'And there was

---

* Translated from the Greek, which always renders initiation aspects with more clarity than the Hebrew.

nothing that Hezekiah did not show him in his house and in the whole realm of his dominion' (39:2). What kind of treasures are these that Hezekiah reveals to the messenger of the king of Babylon? In his passage through the trial of death, he has gained citizenship in the worlds of spirit. In his hand he holds the key to the worlds that his soul entered in death. The spirit world now opened to him is the treasure chamber whose glories he shows his guests.

Isaiah comes. He had announced the death and then brought the rebirth, and now he must ask a question: he asks about the treasures and the guests who saw them. And he must reveal a tragic future fate: Israel and all its treasures will one day be carried off to Babylon into exile.

Hezekiah replies to the prophet: 'The word of the Lord is good that you have spoken. I know that my days must lead into the kingdom of peace and the existence of the good.'

With this we arrive at the end of chapter 39 and of what is thought to be the Book of Isaiah. If we simply read on, overlooking the caesura that is always regarded as occurring here before chapter 40 starts – 'Be comforted, comforted, my people... Hear the voice of one preaching in the wilderness: "Prepare the way of the Lord... The glory of the Lord will be revealed..."' – then all this appears as a continuation of what Hezekiah says. He has passed through death and resurrection. In his reborn state he can set against Isaiah's prophecy of disaster, which looks ahead to the Babylonian exile, a far-future prospect of salvation. He has opened his treasure chambers to the messenger from Babylon. Now he does the same to Isaiah himself. The revelation of these treasures is the message of salvation in chapters 40–66. Hezekiah is Deutero-Isaiah, but can be so only after passing through his own Good Friday and Easter. Isaiah beholds Israel's captivity in Babylon (chapter 39). Deutero-Isaiah sees Babylon's downfall and Israel's liberation by the great conqueror, Cyrus (chapters 45–47). It is because Hezekiah/Deutero-Isaiah tasted the suffering of death to the full that he can prophesy the great sufferings of the Son of Man on behalf of humanity: 'Truly, he bore our sickness...' (chapter 53). It is because Hezekiah was awoken to new life that he can proclaim the world-Easter message of the new Jerusalem, the new earth and the new heavens: 'Behold, I will fashion a new heaven and a new earth, such that none will remember the one that is past' (65:17).

Death and rebirth of the king becomes the key to the book of Deutero-Isaiah. And now it is easy to see that 38:9, which is seemingly only the heading for the psalm of consecration, in fact concerns the whole second part of the Book of Isaiah: 'The book of the revelations of Hezekiah, king of Judea, when he fell sick unto death and rose again from his mortal illness' (In the King James version: 'The writing of Hezekiah king of Judah, when he had been sick, and was recovered of his sickness...'.)

The problem of Deutero-Isaiah is not merely an academic matter. If we understand its solution, which is basically so clearly apparent in the Bible itself, it is an Old Testament foreshadowing of Easter. Each of us is Isaiah, gazing ahead to the storm of the Last Judgement until, in the passage through Good Friday and Easter day, we behold the dawning rays of a new sun-earth, the earth of Christ.

1930s

The Christian Community

The Christian Community

EDITED ON BEHALF OF
THE CHRISTIAN COMMUNITY IN ENGLAND BY
LEO BAKER.

Vol. 1.   JANUARY, 1932.   No. 1.

EDITORIAL

We are presenting this monthly paper at a time of the greatest significance. Already the words "world crisis" are becoming devitalised by journalistic repetition, although the perils of crisis still show us their faces and not their backs.

Today we all live dangerously. The present is uncerta[in] and for millions of humanity the future holds no hope at without violent disruption. For the darkness and turbulence of the world, the coldness of our own hearts, the sickness of [our] bodies, we desire not palliatives, but transformation.

This paper exists to serve the renewal of the religious [life] [hu]man of our time. The vital connection between subject [and]

Creation

Oliver Mathews

Oliver Mathews (1900–1988) was ordained in 1931 and was one of the first English-speaking priests in The Christian Community. He worked for most of his life in the Midlands, England, and wrote many articles on various aspects of the Bible. In this article he looks at scientific and traditional religious views concerning the creation of the universe.

It sounds rather ambitious to head an article with the title 'Creation'. Nevertheless, all that is attempted here is to put forward some ideas that may lead to a more conscious understanding of what is meant by 'Creation'. For this word, derived from the Latin *procreo,* which originally meant the procreation of children, is often used in a way that shows the user has a confused idea of its meaning.

It would be interesting to find out from a number of people what the creation of the world meant to them. Traditional religious thought regards the creation as a magical act of God, whereby something comes into being out of nothing. This is opposed by the idea of the world coming into being that precludes any conscious act of will altogether: creation is a long process whereby an indestructible primeval substance gradually evolved into the world we know today through the natural working of cause and effect. The holders of this view prefer, indeed, not to use the word creation at all; they speak of evolution. These are two extreme views, and there are numerous others in between leaning more or less to the one side or the other.

Of these two extremes, the first dispenses with matter and the second with the Creator. The first is a magical conception and places the whole event beyond hope of understanding through any process of reason. The second takes us a long way with our thinking but brings us up against the impassable barrier of the First Cause. Moreover, the evolutionary theory does not account for any other forces at work besides gradual development. 'Evolution' does not account for the apparent jumps from matter to life, from life to consciousness and so on. Something is continually appearing in the process that cannot be found in the preceding conditions, and which therefore cannot be said to be caused by the conditions. The cornerstone of this theory is the indestructibility of matter, a theory which has been badly shaken, if not as yet quite destroyed, by the discovery of the spontaneous disintegration of matter in connection with radioactive decay.

We only come to a reasonable understanding of creation if we combine these two views and think of the primal existence as being the Ground of the World himself, through whose outpouring of being the world has come into existence.

At the beginning of the Affirmation, which corresponds to the Creed in The Christian Community, are the words: 'An almighty divine being, spiritual-physical, is the ground of existence of the heavens and of the earth, who goes before his creatures like a Father.' In this almighty divine being spirit and substance are one, the true physical is indestructible, but it is not 'matter': the material has come into existence from the physical. Matter exists, the spiritual-physical 'subsists'.

It is about this coming into existence that the first chapter of St John's Gospel speaks: 'In the beginning was the Word ... All things were made by him and without him was not anything made that was made.' This is the Christ of whom the Trinity Prayer says:

> He holds sway through the world as Spirit Word.
> He creates in all that we create,
> Our existing is his creating,
> Our life is his creating life.

The idea of the shaping word can be related to phenomena that are familiar to us in this world. The shaping power of sound, for instance, is well known to science. Iron filings subjected to the vibrations made by drawing a bow across the strings of a violin, will form patterns. Everyone knows that all matter has three states: the gaseous, the liquid, and the solid. These are represented for us in everyday life by earth, water and air. It is generally agreed amongst scientists that the earth had a gaseous origin and has gradually condensed into the solid. Beyond the gas the scientists do not go, because the next stage is beyond that which is recognised as material. Yet there is no logical reason why, if one can trace matter through a liquid to a gaseous state, one should stop there.

The 'Word' is the connecting link between the subsisting physical being of the Father-Ground of the World and the created 'existing' world that we experience.

We can form some kind of picture of the unity of primal being from which and with which the Word went forth, shaping and forming in cosmic harmonies, magnifying and intensifying. The Father-Ground of the World underlies all existence as the Trinity Prayer says:

> He is in all that we are,
> Our substance is his substance,
> Our being is his being.

In matter spirit sleeps, it lies as it were enchanted. Gradually the spirit is released and matter passes away.

Though we talk of the creation of the Word as a thing of the past, and the disintegration of the world as a thing of the future, the process of coming into being and of disintegration is continuous.

The trouble has been that in recent times the Church has considered it blasphemous to speak about such matters as creation in scientific terms, while science has attempted to explain away the theological view, and when faced with problems that have no material explanation, has remained agnostic.

The possibility and the necessity now exist for bridging the gap between religion and science, and we can say that in the Act of Consecration of Man we find an aid to a new scientific understanding. It can be a means of leading science beyond the realm of matter into a clear and accurate knowledge of the spirit. Thus can the scientific table of the future become more and more like an altar.

The realm of the Word lies in all that has to do with the leading over into existence, all that has to do with the birth and growth of human beings, and also with their truly creative work. Art is the leading over of that which exists eternally in the spiritual world into a physical existence. The works of man are art only in so far as they are an expression of something supersensible. It is the unseen that is the heart, the source of life of man's creating.

The process of human birth and human art are closely allied. Art is the revelation of a spiritual fact through a material medium. It is the fashioning of a body for a spiritual reality – a process of incarnating the spiritual in the material – and so is human birth. It is a process whereby an eternal spiritual being enters into the material world and expresses itself therein.

Man can make all that he does a work of art, into a revelation of the spirit, and thereby spiritualise the earth and transform it. The Act of Consecration of Man is a work of art, and a training for artistic working. In the sacrament the spiritual world speaks to man through the medium of the senses.

Christ revealed himself in a human form; he entered into the earth to transform it. He speaks to us in the Act of Consecration of Man. He enters into the bread and wine. This is an act of sacrifice in which we join ourselves with Christ, and because creation only comes about through the sacrifice of the creator, so we learn to see the creation of the world as an act of sacrifice. We learn that as creatures – as created beings – we are destined to become creators when we are able to sacrifice ourselves. This is the hardest thing to learn. When we have really learnt what sacrifice is then all our actions will be acts of sacrifice, all our actions will be creative. And so we rise through the Act of Consecration of Man into the reality of creation: in our thinking to an understanding of creation, in our feeling to an artistic impulse, and in our will to an act of sacrifice. It is by this path that the creature learns to be a creator.

The Name 'Michael'

Rudolf Frieling

At the age of 21, Rudolf Frieling (1901–86) was one of the youngest founding priests of The Christian Community. He had a remarkable talent for languages, both ancient and modern, as was evident in his writings on the Old and New Testament, and the many services and lectures he gave in Czech, English and French.

It is often forgotten that the Hebrew names for the archangels, as passed down by tradition, have a very specific meaning. Thus, for instance, Rapha-El means 'God heals', Uri-El means 'God is my fire', and Gabri-El means 'God is my strength'.

The name of Michael, however, is quite distinctive in not conveying a simple attribute like the others do. Rather, Micha-El is a question: 'Who is like God?'

Such a name, consisting of a questioning phrase, has a quite different effect upon the hearer than a straightforward declaration. A declaration stands there. One can approach it more closely if one feels an interest in it, or one can simply leave it be. But an interrogative clause asks something of the hearer. It directs itself towards us and concerns us.

The name of Michael concerns humankind. 'Who is like God?' The appellation 'like God' touches us in the depths of our nature. A primordial, tragic memory of humanity is here invoked. Who was it, after all, who once spoke in these terms to the still childlike human being in paradise? Lucifer, the snake. 'You will be like God.'

Lucifer was cunning: precisely with these words, if at all, he might hope to wrest the human being from obedience to God. 'Like God' – with this he hit the bull's-eye, the deep, darkness-shrouded core of human nature.

The human being had been created to become God's likeness. 'Let us create the human being in our own image.' 'Like God!' This sublime thought of the Creator was sealed within us, and for this reason we felt that Lucifer had invoked our own most intrinsic name: a name that we suddenly became aware of, and which was here raised in an instant out of the slumbering depths of the soul into bright light. It was only because this name touched the very core of the human being that he could overcome his horror of the alien and sinister serpent and find the sacrilegious courage to disobey God.

The adversary had taken possession of God's conception of the human being, undermining the plan of the Godhead. He hung this image – 'like God' – before the spiritual vision of a human nature that was still immature, and it glittered like a star with a dangerously beautiful, illusory radiance.

Thus, the human being was 'delivered' from the delicate bonds of a paradisal dream and grew onward in independence, becoming the 'little god of the earth'. And yet this was a distorted image, led and governed by the adversary.

Michael opposes this adversarial power of the 'ancient serpent' of the Fall. He hurls his mighty being against it in the full vehemence of the question, 'Who is like God?' He casts it down from divine resemblance, from its arrogant supposition of proximity to God – he 'casts it out of heaven'. He is the guardian of the unapproachable majesty of God. 'Who is like God?' All presumption of likeness to God falls into the abyss, judged by the sacred gravity of this question, along with that deceptively glittering, dangerously beautiful star. 'How have you fallen from the heavens, you beautiful star of morning?'

But is this really the last and final word on humanity – that the radiant star of promise of being 'like God' has fallen from heaven? Has the adversary really succeeded in wresting the Godhead's great plan from it, even compelling it to step in and destroy this plan for ever?

No. For Christ came and prised the words 'like God' from the enemy. He redeemed the Devil's promise that 'you will be like God'. He fulfilled and perfected what the adversary forestalled with a distorted image. He took up and took new hold of the divine idea of the human being, he re-sanctified human existence. 'Be perfect as your Father in heaven is perfect.' He brought the true I, which is independent, individual and in the highest sense free, yet also loyal and devoted to the will of the Father. 'Behold, the human being!'

If we try to take up this Christ into us, if we try to say, 'Not I, but Christ in me' as St Paul did, then we are on the way towards our true likeness to God. Then we become 'like God'.

But this self-permeation with Christ does not happen by itself like a natural process. Our will must be involved. We must call the Christ into our house, for otherwise he passes by. Human beings do not become 'like God' unless they themselves earnestly intend it.

Just as Adam possessed a sacrilegious courage, so there also exists a false humility that in truth is only laziness and cowardice, which thinks this goal of 'being like God' is too lofty, which seeks to render us small so that we do not dare to reach for this crown that God intended for us.

And now this name of Michael has another resonance. 'Who is like God?' In the Christian context this phrase is an awakening call, something that inspires and raises us. The name of Michael was a crushing judgement on the presumption of being like God, but for the Christian seeker it becomes a raising invocation. Having woken our humility, he now addresses our courage. Who dares to reach for the crown of our divine humanity? Who dares to become a Christian?

The star of 'like God' stands once more in the heavens. Christ himself purified and purged it. Now it is in truth the brightly radiant, sacred and beautiful morning star of a promise without which we cannot live.

Tobit: An Easter Story
Leo Baker

Born in London, Leo Baker (1898–1986) was an actor who had wide links with the arts world and was on the fringes of the Inklings, the literary group that included J. R. R. Tolkien, C. S. Lewis and Owen Barfield. He was ordained in 1931 and was one of the first English-speaking priests in The Christian Community. He later became the editor of The Christian Community Journal. *In 1943 he left his work as a priest and broke off all contact with the Community.*

Often a great painter shows by his treatment of a story from the holy writings that he knows more about it than most theologians. This is partly because in his preparation, when he wants to fix his subject in his imagination so that the whole is a harmony and the details are exact and clear, he must follow a process akin to meditation. He permits his soul to bathe in the *pictorial* quality of the story and thus he sees it more truly than those who only have thoughts about it.

Therefore, one can turn with some eagerness to the picture of Botticelli in which he shows the boy Tobias with his fish and his little dog, to provide a comment on the Book of Tobit in the Apocrypha. One is surprised to see that while only the archangel Raphael appears in the story, in the picture there are three angelic beings walking as companions along the road with the youth. The other two – witness the sword and the lily in their hands – are clearly the archangels Michael and Gabriel.

The archangel Raphael appears both in the story and the picture as the *teacher* of Tobias. The youth is too young to walk by himself alone, and yet he is just reaching the age of marriage. Raphael is his teacher and guides him through the time of puberty, so that under his care Tobias passes from boyhood to manhood. This is one of the three great periods of 'growing up', from birth to the formation of our second teeth, from then to puberty, and from puberty to adulthood. Botticelli sees that the Book of Tobit is partly about the passage through a major crisis in growing up. From one point of view he says, 'If the teacher wants to know how to teach let him take at one age Gabriel for his guide, at another Raphael, at the third Michael.' From another point of view he says, 'Tobias at one time was taught by each of these three archangels, now you must understand he is the disciple of Raphael.' This has an importance for everyone when they can see that Tobias and his father, Tobit, belong to those whose personal history touches the universal, that the story of this Jewish family is preserved and has so long spoken to many hearts because it is a story of the human family.

The story purports to be written towards the end of the eighth century before Christ, but actually it must have been written very much later, perhaps nearly 400 years later. Whenever it was written, the historic scene belongs to the more distant date. The story truly belongs to the new age that dawned for the world during the eighth century BC, and which lasted until the fifteenth century AD. It is a story that essentially belongs to the central period of the history of humanity. It is told, figuratively, at the beginning of the period as though it were a prevision of the great event that would change the destiny of the whole world: the Easter event.

The whole course of the story belongs to Easter. Death and resurrection are the theme. The healing commission for the powers of death is brought from the throne of light by Raphael, the Easter archangel, and reaches humanity through the help of the 'youth' who is also an initiate. We will refer to this initiation later.

We are shown two related families, each of three persons. The first consists of Tobit with his wife, Anna, and their only son, Tobias. Tobit is a great Hebrew. His whole being is immersed passionately in the fulfilment of the Law. Even in captivity, in the position of a slave with no rights and no redress against the officers of the Law, he alone treasures the fulfilment of the Law as his will. It is his will. He has, for the best reasons, and as we say 'justly', identified his will with the Law. But the great lesson that the Hebrews had to learn during this period was that with the coming of the Christ there came a new dispensation. The Law was then no longer enough. Not justification by Law, but justification by the individual's free *sight* of the light of Christ, which Paul calls 'faith' – this is the change brought about at Easter.

Tobit tries to live justly, but he is serving a dying cause and therefore his course leads to disaster. When he is blinded, it is not only physical blindness that falls upon him.

As head of the family, he is the representative of Yahweh. Anna, the mother, is the representative of the race spirit, the spirit of the Hebrew nation. Out of their union a true Hebrew child can be born. The understanding of this dual representation is very strong in the ancient Hebrew literature.

Yet when he is blinded, Tobit becomes divided from Anna, he no longer believes her word. Even the spirit of his nation, which he has served so wholeheartedly, becomes separated from him. Truly he cannot see any longer. For this he is not to be blamed, any more than Raphael blames him. It lies within his fate to suffer so long as he is the servant of the past. His sickness lies in the fact that he belongs to a past – or passing – stream; his healing comes when the leap forward into the future is made possible through his son, Tobias, when he no longer serves the generations of the old Adam but turns his face towards the path of the new Adam.

Sarah, the abandoned member of the story's second family, suffers from a different sickness. She cannot properly incarnate. The soul that cannot find her 'husband', cannot find the ego with which she can make the unity of life. Sarah and Tobit, with Tobias between them, remind us of the Easter picture of Christ between the two thieves of life, between the power which longs to draw man below the earth, and the power whose hope is to hold man out of incarnation. From the central figure healing can come to both. And, at Easter time especially, the two thieves draw near to humanity hoping to snatch away its life forces. We find the power to remain rulers of ourselves if we stand beneath the central cross, if we choose Christ.

The initiation of Tobias is almost, one can say, post-Christian. Compare the details with the pre-Christian Jonah initiation. Jonah enters into the darkness of the fish for three and a half days: he is overcome by the unconscious trance. When the fish approaches Tobias, he fears the death that seems to threaten him, but Raphael gives him the courage and the knowledge to awaken his will. He seizes hold of the fish and casts it up on the land, then he and the archangel together celebrate a holy meal with the fish for food.

This reminds us of the Easter story at the end of St John's gospel. The disciples, through the courage and knowledge given to them by the Risen Christ, bring fish out of the dark sea to the land, and then with him receive part of the fish for food.

When the Christian disciple, in the sacraments or in meditation receives spiritual treasure that he can bring to the shore of life, the gift comes at Christ's hand, and the use of the gift, when it is taken in to nourish life, is Communion.

The one who can receive the Communion, who awakens to the Christ within, can then carry that precious gift into the world. They can be the servant and the helper of the angels; they can be the vehicle of healing.

So does the beautiful story of Tobias show how at Easter time, when from one side the Devil and from the other side Satan attack, then Raphael, the archangel of healing and the messenger of Christ, draws near to help humanity awaken to a deeper knowledge of the Easter event. To the young disciple, the one who can be a companion of angels, the power of healing is entrusted. This power streams out first to create the new social order based on union out of freedom, and then to bless the old social order, the community of blood. From the Easter of the world a light shines forth that humanity can lift up from the darkness of the grave to build the New Jerusalem as a dwelling place of light.

> For the sons of Light shall be gathered together,
> And Jerusalem shall be built with sapphires and emeralds and precious stones,
> Her walls and towers and battlements with pure gold,
> And all her streets shall say, Hallelujah, and give praise.
> Hallelujah! Amen. (Tobit 13)

Human Nature and Morality

Eduard Lenz

One of the founding priests of The Christian Community, Eduard Lenz (1901–45) worked in Germany and in Prague. When the Community was banned under the Nazis, he joined the German army. At the end of the war he was captured and died as a German prisoner of war in Russian captivity. In this article he looks at the conflict between 'moral duty and natural tendencies' and how they can be resolved through a love that freely wills the good.

Since time immemorial philosophy has endeavoured to bring the demands of society into harmony with human nature – so far with little success. It looks as though moral law is destined always to be in conflict with the stirrings of the human heart. Moral instruction knows no more than to demand the total suppression of anything that contradicts imperative conscience. Kant said in fact that only what is joyless can be moral. In the last analysis then all morality assumes the form of ascetic demands. Is there really no way out of this conflict between moral duty and natural tendencies?

St Luke's Gospel (7:36–50) offers a solution to this problem, which has so far been quite overlooked, and which could form the foundation of Christian morality. The gospel relates how Jesus was one day invited to a ceremonial dinner at the house of one of the Pharisees. On hearing of this, a certain woman also made her way there. She had the reputation of being a great sinner. As soon as she saw Jesus, she fell on her knees before him, kissed his feet and sprinkled them with her tears; then she dried his feet with her hair. The Pharisee saw this, and thought to himself, 'If he were really a prophet he would know what sort of a woman is touching him.' But Jesus sensed what he was thinking and drew the Pharisee's attention to the fact that he had not paid his guest any such devoted attention, had not anointed him, had not kissed him as he entered his house. But the woman had done all this. He then told the Pharisee a story of two debtors whose debts were forgiven. This woman too would be forgiven for she had loved much. Then, turning to the woman, Jesus said, 'Your sins are forgiven, go in peace. Your faith has led you to salvation.'

This significant anecdote serves to illustrate the enormous contrast between strict morality and the demands of the human heart. The Pharisee represents the iron upholder of moral order. The woman stands for all those people whose actions are still uninhibited. The gulf that separates them is unbridgeable. The Pharisee had only scorn for this woman. He was without doubt a worthy man, but he lacked one thing: that which Christ pointed to as the warmth and tact that spring from the heart. The Pharisee thought morally; he acted entirely in accordance with the Law. But his heart remained untouched by enthusiasm for the Good. In strong contrast, the woman is moved by passionate love, although it is not under strict spiritual control. It is quite possible that she had obeyed all her natural desires since her youth. But she was beginning to experience what Plato described when he talked about human desire: Eros. Eros is a wanderer; he is never satisfied by the beauty of one body, he must enjoy the beauty of everything that Nature has to offer. But one day he discovers how beautiful and virtuous a soul is when it is filled with wisdom. Even now he cannot remain still. Desire is infinite and can only be brought to rest by the beauty of an infinite Being. Not until the soul reaches the border of the spiritual world and beholds the eternal beauty of God can its desire be fulfilled. Every love seeks God, fundamentally. This is the wisdom of Plato. St Augustine, one of the Church Fathers, says the same when he writes, 'Our heart is restless until it rests in God.'

This woman's love often led her astray. Her searching heart lost itself deeply in things unworthy. But never losing herself completely, she always went on searching, until one day she found him to whom she could open herself entirely, for he was infinitely beautiful and at the same time infinitely good: Jesus, in whom the divine beauty and goodness of Christ was revealed.

Moral law, with its merciless veto, could never make any impression on this woman's heart. One can obey the law, but one cannot love it. The Christ was the embodiment of divine Goodness which was become Man. He could be loved with all one's heart. For him this woman's soul could burn in humble devotion purged of all the confusion of her passion.

With this narrative the Gospel shows how man can bring the voice of conscience into harmony within himself with his heart's desires. Love for Christ in whom was revealed on earth the beauty and goodness of the divine spheres, makes humanity good. The human heart can love Christ deeply, without danger. This love is morally pure and good, for it is directed towards the highest of ideals, the God become Man. Love for Christ unites in the disciple the voice of conscience with the needs of the human heart.

Only love can form the foundation of Christian morality. All previous moral codes are really pre-Christian, ascetic, and only widen the gulf between morality and Nature. Love for what we know is good leads both to true morality and inward freedom, for then we do what is right not just because the law demands this, but because our whole being wills it.

The Gospel has something to say to up-to-date humanity too. It conceals answers to many questions that are asked nowadays. It can be the mission of a new understanding of the Bible to bring to light such hidden treasures in the Gospels.

1940s

CHRISTIAN COMMUNITY MONTHLY LETTER. 3.
(temporarily in place of the Christian Community Journal).
MICHAELMAS NUMBER.
October, 1940.

1001, Finchley Rd.
London, N.W.11.

THE ISLAND OF MICHAEL.

Stanley Drake.

  Off the South Coast of Devon is a small and little known island. The landward side is a steep grassy slope climbing up more than a hundred feet. On the seaward side, wind and waves have carved a jagged wall of rock full of holes and fissures. On the highest point stands a small brick look-out post where once, according to local legend, a chapel dedicated to Saint Michael once stood. The island is reached by a sandy causeway from the mainland during the greater part of each day. Only at high tides is it completely an island.

  In all its main characteristics it is thus related to the St. Michael's Mount of Cornwall and the Mont St. Michel of Brittany, where according to many legends the Archangel Michael, Leader of the Hosts of Heaven, performed wonderful deeds on earth against his adversary the devil.

  There are many more of these "Michael Islands" - which are not completely islands, and they may be a picture of what our spiritual life should be today. We do not withdraw entirely from the workaday world and bury ourselves as hermits on a long-

The Quaker-Catholic
Eileen Hersey

Eileen Hersey (1901–86) was active in Quaker social work before teaching in a Christian-Arab girl's school in Jerusalem. On returning to London in 1935, she began working for The Christian Community and was ordained in 1944. After Alfred Heidenreich's death, she became editor of The Christian Community Journal.

In the course of his correspondence with Anglican priest Dick Sheppard, recently published under the title *What Can We Believe?*, the playwright Laurence Housman wrote:

> What I hanker after is an impossible combination – the Quaker-Catholic; Quaker principles and spiritual liberty, add Catholic presentation and sacramental symbol.

One cannot help wondering for how many modern men and women the author of *The Little Plays of St Francis* is speaking, when he expresses this longing for a church that would combine clearness and strength of moral vision and spiritual freedom on the one hand, with a wide philosophy and an approach to the material world that is both scientific and redemptive on the other. Realising how deep is the need of modern humanity for a rediscovery of Christianity that would fulfil just these particular demands, one is moved to ask: 'Is such a church really impossible?'

Outwardly, the gulf between Quakerism and Catholicism is so deep that it would appear quite impassable; inwardly, it is as narrow as it is deep. It is like one of those apparently bottomless crevasses in an alpine glacier, over which it is possible to pass from one sharply defined edge to the other in a single determined leap. For the apparent contradiction is resolved in the fundamental need of the human soul for a basis of authority in matters of belief and conduct, and in the need for a method by which it may overcome its sense of isolation from the universe around it: to the Catholic, the Holy Spirit offers all that a person needs in both these spheres through the vehicle of the visible Church on earth; to the Quaker, it is the 'Light of Christ within', the 'seed of God' in the human soul, that can alone inspire true faith and action, and awaken that love in the individual that can reunite them with the surrounding world.

The historic significance of the Quaker witness against all outward creeds and sacraments was that it was first given at a period in human development when differences in forms of creed and worship were still a cause of bloodshed between groups and nations. The Quakers proclaimed the complete dependence of the individual soul on its immediate experience of the divine working of the spirit. At the time the ink was scarcely dry on the Treaty of Westphalia, which divided the peoples of Europe into confessional 'blocs' on the principle of *cujus regio, ejus religio*' ('whose realm, their religion'). Just at the moment when Christianity was being reorganised on a national basis, and Protestant churches were being formed in varying degrees of dependence on the new-born national states, there were thousands of individual men and women, both on the Continent and in England, to whom the direct appeal of George Fox to 'that of God in every man' came as a clear call to throw off every form of religious attachment that seemed to lessen individual responsibility and restrict individual freedom. It was the logical extreme of Protestantism to which Fox pointed, and every other aspect of Quakerism followed from it: the absence of a special order of priests, the equality of men and women in the ministry, and a fundamentally democratic form of church government.

Fox says in his *Journal*: 'Now the Lord God opened to me his invisible power that every man is enlightened by the divine light of Christ, and I saw it shine through all.' The Friends' denial of all outward forms of sacramental worship, and their emphasis on the silent waiting for the voice of God to speak in the souls of worshippers, was the result of painful experience in churches where the divine spark had been smothered by the dogmatic utterances of 'reformed' preachers, and the divine voice drowned out in the flood of formal prayers whose original inspiration belonged to the past. It seems that by the middle of the seventeenth century, the spiritual forces that had kept the medieval church alive had really passed away at last. The church as a body had really died, but it was only mystics like George Fox and his followers who saw that it was dead and desired to give it decent burial. Most of the reformers tried to preserve this or that decaying limb or organ, retaining here a certain form of the creed, or there the bare bones of a sacrament. Jakob Böhme and others of the continental mystics had spoken of the inner life as the source of all true religion, but perhaps it required the peculiar genius of the English nation to produce a community of individuals who felt an overwhelming need to translate this inward experience into outward action and organisation. It was this emphasis on the necessity of obedience to the inward Guide that led the Quakers into their practical witness against war, slavery and other social evils. They became friends of all people, even the lowest, because they felt they held the secret of communion with Christ and they were a society of 'Friends in the Truth'.

In his longing for the 'spiritual liberty' of the Quakers, Laurence Housman is representative of the modern man who can bear far less with creeds and dogmas and outworn ritual than the man of the seventeenth century. But the thinking man of the twentieth century is hampered not so much by ecclesiastical formulas as by a deadweight of 'scientific' dogma, whose validity he is unable to test by his own experience. Whether he likes it or not, he cannot help being impressed by the various 'ideologies' which are 'in the air' around him. And while he would scornfully repudiate religious ceremonial based on tradition as superstitious, he is now forced to adopt new forms of 'ritual' ordered overnight by political pontiffs, who are as aware of the compelling influence of such corporate practices as any Renaissance ecclesiastic.

Where are the spiritual forces that will suffice in the long run to withstand the increased pressure of materialism in modern life? Human beings today are thirsting for a *knowledge* of themselves not merely as a part of the natural world, or as members of a social or national group, but as that part of nature and as organs of a spiritual body whose task is to help in the actual work of creation, to assist in 'making all things new'. They need to know themselves as conscious spiritual beings whose task it is to transform themselves and, in so doing, to share in the redemption of the earth.

This need of the human soul for what Laurence Housman calls 'Catholic presentation and sacramental symbol' is the need for a form of worship based on a knowledge of spiritual *facts* in all their richness and diversity, as well as in their full relationship to the life of the earth. The stream of mystical Christianity, which during the Middle Ages had run parallel to the life of the Church (though it sometimes led away from it), ran underground in Quakerism. It moistened the hard earth of rationalistic thinking in the eighteenth and nineteenth centuries, so bringing forth rich fruit of moral insight and social helpfulness. That, after nearly three centuries, this stream should spring once more into sight and sound is surely the answer of the divine world to a spiritual hunger of humanity that is greater now than ever before.

The Act of Consecration of Man, the communion service of The Christian Community, is a new birth upon earth of that spirit which once lived in the ancient form of the Christian sacrament. It comes, as a living parable of divine events, to meet the free, awakened consciousness of the individual soul. It includes in its spiritual activity, representatives of the world of 'matter': metal and wood, bread and wine, linen and silk. Nature, and what humanity has made of nature, are here united with the individual's own striving after the divine, and so the long, slow process of the earth's redemption is continued, through the deed of humanity's consecration.

In every detail of the Act of Consecration of Man, full freedom is given to the individual: there is nothing in which he is forced to take an active part, no singing of hymns, or prayers spoken by the congregation. The priest, who acts as leader, removes that part of his vestments – the stole, which indicates his office – when he speaks the words that express the fundamental facts of Christianity, the 'creed'. By doing so, he shows that he is now speaking as an individual and not for the congregation, who are free to express their faith in their own way through their own consciousness. Similarly, when the priest addresses the congregation from out of his own thinking (that is, in the sermon), he places the biretta on his head as a sign that what he is saying carries only its own authority and forms no part of the ritual. The server, who helps the priest and speaks words of response to the prayers, does so as a representative of the whole congregation; yet each individual member of it is still responsible for the degree and quality of the inward activity that they bring to the total act of worship.

Seen from this aspect, the congregation taking part in the Act of Consecration of Man consists as much of 'silent worshippers' as does a Friends' Meeting. Only there is now added a focus-point of worship that is independent of the moods or particular stage of spiritual development of any member of the congregation. From the Quaker point of view, this might seem to take away from individual freedom and responsibility, but seen as a *historic* development, this is not the case. For the original revolt of Quakerism was against a dead or dying ritual, and the living power of their form of worship, based on silence, lay in the new freedom that it gave for the utterance of inspired messages to those gathered together. It was a form of worship based on the free recognition by the congregation, individually and corporately, of the word of Christ, spoken through a soul sincerely dedicated to their work on earth. In the same way, the share of the individual worshipper in the Act of Consecration of Man depends just on this ability to recognise 'where words come from'. Nothing rests on tradition, and the fact that in many modern minds actual prejudices often have to be overcome before full freedom and openness can be attained, means that a real inward effort is required, making in the end for a more fully awakened sensitiveness to spiritual values than before. In other words, the religious life of The Christian Community, like that of the Friends, is based on *experience* of the workings of the spirit, and corresponds to the fundamentally 'scientific' attitude of modern individuals that will not accept a religion handed out by authority.

It was said by an early Quaker of the scriptures: 'As by the inward testimony of the spirit do we alone truly know them, so they testify that the spirit is that guide by which the saints are led into all truth.' It is just because people of today so greatly need, in the darkness of their souls, a focus-point at which their inward eye can meet the sunlight of the spirit, that the question has been asked, 'Can spiritual liberty be combined with sacramental symbol?' The answer of The Christian Community is to say, like Nathaniel of old, 'Come and see.'

The Two Jesus Children
Alfred Heidenreich

Of the founding priests of The Christian Community, Alfred Heidenreich (1898–1969) was the most cosmopolitan, his experience and interests extending far beyond his native Germany. In 1929 he moved to London where he founded The Christian Community in Great Britain. After the Second World War he visited North America, then South America and later South Africa, helping found congregations on each of these continents. In this article Heidenreich helps us make sense of the differing nativity stories of Matthew and Luke.

The Christian Community, which publishes this journal, owes a deep debt of gratitude to the late Dr Rudolf Steiner. One must go far to find anything like the original and penetrating light that he throws on the problems of Christian history and Christian doctrine. The number of people who find great help through his works increases daily. But there is one stumbling block where many draw the line: his contention that the two different stories of the birth of Jesus (Matt. 2 and Luke 2) refer to *two different children*.

If one is prepared to get over the first shock, and looks afresh at the two gospels, one cannot fail to see that the difference between the stories is very striking and indeed irreconcilable. First of all, we are faced with two genealogical trees (Matt. 1 and Luke 3). It is unlikely that they differ simply through carelessness. The genealogy of Jesus was public property. He was a scion of the house of David which was, in spite of having been deposed, the true royal family of the Jews. To put it in relatively more modern terms, in his generation Jesus was the Pretender. His family tree would be zealously preserved and defended.

But apart from the genealogies, the two nativity stories are completely different in every respect; so different that many old masters painted two

Christmas pictures, often on the same altar piece, side by side. Luke's story has all the lovely, simple charm of youth, gentleness and nature, and of the shepherds and the holy angels. This Mary has been painted as a young maiden in a white garment, holding her baby and surrounded by the ox and the ass in the poverty of a natural grotto. Matthew's story, however, is full of pomp and circumstance. It contains no reference to a weary journey from Nazareth, and none to an inn which had no room. The Wise Men enter 'into the house', and it is said that 'all Jerusalem' is disturbed by the child expected to be born at Bethlehem. The painters in their artistic vision have represented this Mary as a royal lady (often with a wedding ring) receiving guests. There to the townhouse of the royal family, the 'Three Kings from Orient' come with their train and treasures. Unlike the event in Luke, everything happens in the blazing light of history. No wonder that Herod, the usurper on the throne, threatens the life of the child. The whole setting and atmosphere could not be more different from the lowly and sacred event in the stable. The contrast is overwhelming.

Those who have made it their task to compare the gospels with other historic documents, have met with another hitherto insurmountable difficulty concerning the birth of Jesus. According to existing records King Herod the Great, whom Matthew mentions, died before the census was taken (under Cyrenius, governor of Syria) which Luke mentions. All kinds of ingenious ideas have been put forward to square the discrepancy, and historians have now generally acquiesced in the theory that Christ was born several years 'BC'. But this tricky problem solves itself naturally if Rudolf Steiner is right and what we are really dealing with is the story of two births. If we assume a period of about one year between them, all difficulties of historical chronology disappear. Are the festivals of Epiphany and Christmas related to each other in the opposite sequence to that generally assumed? Epiphany, celebrated on January 6, has always been associated with the three Magi. Perhaps this tradition preserves the ancient truth that the Matthew child was born on January 6 and the Luke child on the following December 25?

However, if we are ready to consider these facts, which are as illuminating as they are astonishing, we have still to face the greatest difficulty of all. How do the two children become eventually the one Jesus who at the Baptism in Jordan becomes the Christ? The Gospel of Luke both reveals and conceals the mysterious union in the story of the twelve-year-old boy in the Temple. Like so many stories of the gospel, it comprises many layers of meaning and significance. The child is drawn away from the earthly father into the house and 'business' of the Heavenly

Father. But the astonishing change in his nature, which causes pain and fear to his parents, has its deepest cause in the fact that – as Rudolf Steiner describes it – the mature individuality of the royal child of Matthew's gospel has passed over into the heavenly soul-nature of the Luke child.

No one who lives for a time with these strangely potent thoughts can fail to see how they form a lens through which the light of revelation and understanding sends its beams into the distant past and farthest future. The whole dramatic story of human evolution, as the Bible presents it, contains the leitmotif of these two polarities. From Cain and Abel onward the two elements flow through all of human history: innocence and experience, town and country, magi and shepherds, revolutionaries and conservatives, East and West. In shaping the earthly vehicle of the Christ the wisdom of earthly experience and the innocence of heavenly humility unite. Cain and Abel become one again and are redeemed in each other.

Looking into the future, the rediscovery of the mystery of the two Jesus children can sound a bell. It opens a sphere of spiritual fact long lost to humanity. This sphere is of absorbing interest and will draw souls into its orbit who have lost the Christ because he has become too simple, too common, too suburban in the teaching of tradition. At the moment this may be understood by only a few, but the signs of the times show that humanity stands at the threshold where it must absorb the new revelation of the Being of Christ or go from catastrophe to catastrophe.

God and the Devil

Oliver Mathews

Oliver Mathews (1900–1988) was one of the first English-speaking priests of The Christian Community. He was particularly interested in social questions. Here he looks at different forms of society that lead to impersonal forces dominating our lives – occasions, he says, when the Devil rules. He argues that a social structure is needed that allows for individual initiative while limiting the extent to which it can be exploited by others.

The Christian rule for a God-filled life is 'Love the Lord your God with all your heart' and 'Love your neighbour as yourself'. A concise description of a life in which the Devil holds sway may be found in the proverb 'Needs must when the Devil drives'.

The first is a command, but a command that can only be fulfilled in freedom. No one can love God or their neighbour out of compulsion. This command puts before us an ideal which we only realise gradually and at the cost of much sorrow and pain. It demands the utmost not only of our good will but of our intelligence. The second is no command, it is the statement of a fact. The Devil-ruled life is a determined life. No place for freedom here! The first is personal. It is addressed to each individual human being. But it is more than that, for it is a command to transcend our personal limitations. We may therefore describe it as super-personal. The second is impersonal. The Devil can only drive when human initiative is surrendered. It may be described as sub-personal.

We may say then that God never enforces his rule. He is able to rule, when man recognises his divine power and makes himself its instrument. The Devil rules when man surrenders all personal responsibility and initiative and recognises only impersonal laws and forces. It is not difficult to see which has the upper hand today. If there is one thing that has put its stamp on the whole structure of society in modern times, it is the machine. Anyone who does not blindfold himself can see the crying evils of our social order, but where will you find the human beings who are really responsible for these evils? We are rushing headlong towards war, but if you were to question the leaders of any nation they would all say that they were doing their best to prevent it. Even in democratic countries we are ruled by laws and regulations that have often been discussed inadequately or not at all. This is not the intention and wish of Parliament or the government, but there is not time to do all that requires to be done. And so it is all the way through, 'Needs must when the Devil drives'!

The truth is that we are all guilty in so far as we have surrendered our conscience and our individual responsibility to something that works in an impersonal way, be it a limited liability company, a trades union, a political party, or a church. That does not mean that these organisations should not exist, but that in so far as they obliterate, instead of directly or indirectly adding to, the *freedom* and *initiative* of the individual human being, they are serving the Devil. But let it be said straight away that it is by no means a question of eliminating the Devil, but only of eliminating his control over *us*. He can be a very useful member of society if kept in his proper place, and his proper place is in the mine, the factory and the scullery, in every place where material forces and material knowledge is needed to serve our purely earthly needs. It is not a question of trying to escape from the Devil, but of *recognising* him. Once we have recognised him and begun to understand how he works, we can put him in his right place.

It is one of the curious tragedies of modern times that a Christianity that has ceased to believe in the Devil has lost its God, and a society that does not reckon with either has become Devil-ridden. This was however inevitable, for if you thrust the Devil out of your conscious mind, he works in the subconscious, where he much prefers to work because he works entirely without hindrance. Any psychoanalyst could confirm this statement, though they may describe it in a different language. One of the pathetic sights of the present age is to see the dear pious materialists trying to make the world better by getting rid of human responsibility. They place the Devil still more securely in his seat. And as for war! Let us have done with illusion and hypocrisy. Let us face the stark fact that we do not win wars by praying to God, but by using the Devil. Well, if we do use him, let us use him with our eyes open and no pretence that it is God who wins wars. The tendency towards collectivism and the resultant elimination of freedom, forced upon us by war organisation, and the apparent economic necessities of post-war society, are further steps away from a God-filled society.

What can we say?

Only that needs must when the Devil drives! Long ago, we allowed the Devil to take the helm and he is steering civilisation in the only direction he can steer it – to destruction.

There is one thing, however, that he cannot do if we do not will it, and that is kill our souls. Whether in the midst of a war of weapons or the chaos that war brings, we can see to it that we do not lose our sense of proportion. Let the great difference between ourselves and those who put their *whole* trust in planning and organisation, whether for peace or war, be this: that, whereas they are not only using the Devil, but have made him their God, we will use him, recognising him for what he is and realising that our true aims lie elsewhere, namely in the loving service of God and Man, and in the building up of a social order in which God has a chance to work.

If this is our true aim, then we should begin here and now to do something about it. I say 'do something', because I do not think God works except through our freely willed deeds. Prayer should be much more a listening to God, a striving to find out what he wants us to do. Worship should be an act of sacrifice. It is probable that many people have left the churches and have ceased to pray today, because they feel it is hypocritical to direct requests to God to do for us what we should be doing for ourselves. We should have outgrown the religion of childhood and adolescence. We should be standing on our own feet. It is an adult's religion we need today. The Christianity of Christ is certainly an adult's religion, but neither the churches nor society have yet grown to it. It is for you and me to see that they do. But what can we do? Is there not something we can begin here and now, as a guarantee to ourselves and the world that our real aim as a people is to found a social order that really expresses the love of God and Man?

I can only indicate briefly what I believe is required. We have sought the solution of our social problems in recent years in some form of system or organisation, in something in which the responsibility of the individual tends to be eliminated. Thus the development of what we describe as the capitalist system has made an impersonal, economic necessity the virtual ruler of our lives. Socialists would substitute nationalisation and a vast bureaucracy of officialdom. Fascism makes a fetish of the state in which all organisations are 'nationalised' and must take their orders from the centre. All these give the rule to the Devil and leave little room for God. What is needed is an organism flexible enough to allow the maximum opportunity for individual initiative while leaving the minimum opportunity for exploitation.

I have three suggestions as something to start on. I can only state them and leave it to my readers to think out what they imply – and they imply a great deal:

1. Put a time limit to the life of all invested capital or eliminate interest and rent except for the repayment of debt. Encourage private enterprise to the full. Let our economic life be discussed and replanned by those taking part in it and by representatives of the consumers.
2. Build up a political life in which Parliament is more representative of the people. The unit of the political structure could be the weekly meeting of the inhabitants of a street or group of streets. This meeting could send its representative to a ward or parish meeting, and this again to the urban or rural district council. Councilors of so many years' standing would be eligible for parliamentary election by the votes of the whole constituency.
3. Encourage a vigorous free development of the cultural life – the religious, philosophical, scientific, artistic, musical, literary, dramatic and educational – by the founding of numbers of small local societies, which could then be linked into larger associations.

Through these three suggestions, the way would be opened for the development and expression of individual initiative and genius. Energies would be released that could transform society. On these lines individuals and society could make themselves the channel for a creative impulse. In other words it would open the door to God. These suggestions will involve sacrifices from us all, but they will rob no one of what is needed to get the best out of life. They will take from us only those things that enable us to serve the Devil. They will put authority, necessity and determinism in their right place. They will encourage liberty, equality and co-operation. They will need a very real love of God and our neighbours to carry through.

We can begin to work for these aims here and now, wherever we are. It need not interfere with our other tasks. It must occupy such spare time as we have. Aims of this nature might be the means of avoiding war if they began to take shape soon, for they contain the kind of solution for which all the world is seeking. I am not suggesting that the government should initiate these things. It is better if they start from the initiative of a few enthusiastic individuals and grow from there. We are still a free people. Alongside the frustration we cause and are compelled to suffer, let us begin to build.

1950s

The Christian Community
A JOURNAL FOR THE NEW AGE OF CHRISTIANITY
PUBLISHED BY THE CHRISTIAN COMMUNITY
IN GREAT BRITAIN

VOLUME IV (NEW SERIES) NOS. 1, 2.   JAN.—FEB., 1951

As they continued their journey, he went into a certain village. A woman named Martha received him into her house. There was also a sister named Mary. She seated herself at the Master's feet, to listen to his words. But Martha was distracted by attending to many needs, and she came up and said : Master, does it not seem wrong to you that my sister has left me all alone to do the work? Come, tell her that she should help me. The Master answered her : Martha, Martha, you are worried and anxious about many things. But our needs are small ; indeed only one thing is necessary. Mary has chosen the good thing, which shall not be taken away from her.

Luke 10, 38—42.

How many a woman has been half ashamed because she thought that she was a "Martha type"! Let us be clear that Luke's story does not condemn the Martha type at all. Where would we all be without the Marthas? Where would the essentials of life, the food, the clothes, the housing come from, if not from the care and the skilled, untiring hands of "Marthas", be they men or women ? Where would, on a deeper level, that service come from which Nature expects from Man, for its share in the deliverance of the creation ? No, there is nothing wrong with being a Martha. The "laborare" is as essential to the Christian life as the "orare", as the first Benedictines knew when they adopted the famous motto for their Order.

But when the Christ calls at the house, external activities must come to rest. Martha must learn *when to stop*. This is the secret of the story. When the Christ calls, the active life must change into the contemplative. Activities can be poisons, all the weak more

The Tragedy of Judas
Alfred Heidenreich

Born in Germany, Alfred Heidenreich (1898–1961), one of the founding priests of The Christian Community, worked for most of his life in Great Britain, becoming so English that one would not have guessed he had been born in Germany. In this article he looks at how Judas was admitted into the circle surrounding Christ.

In the central story of human history, the life of Christ, a great problem is presented in the personality and conduct of Judas. How did Judas ever come into the intimate circle of Christ? The Middle Ages simply accepted him as a traitor, an arch villain, greedy, vain, ambitious, disloyal. In more recent times he has been explained more 'psychologically'. Goethe, in a sketch for a proposed poetical treatment of the Legend of the Wandering Jew, threw out the suggestion that Judas did not really want to betray Christ, but wanted to force him into a position where at long last he would have to show his hand as the real Messiah. This explanation has been put forward again quite recently by Leslie Weatherhead in *Personalities of the Passion* (Hodder and Stoughton, 1942):

> And here [Christ] is fleeing from one place to another, talking about this mad idea of love, babbling about a cross, saying that he must suffer. Why doesn't he act?

So ran Judas' argument, according to Weatherhead, and with this impatience in his soul he tried to force Jesus into action. But this rationalisation of Judas is a concession to our intellectual minds. It is clever, but not on the level of cosmic tragedy on which the life of Christ moved.

The cosmic measure of Christ's life is apparent when he appoints his disciples: 'Jesus went up on a mountainside and called to him those he wanted, and they came to him. He appointed twelve.' (Mark 3:13–14). Nothing was left to chance in this choice; he did not select according to human preference. 'He appointed twelve', or 'He created a twelvehood' would be an even better translation of the original. With the necessity of a cosmic pattern Judas, too, was called to his place. Among the twelve signs of the zodiac that the sun passes through is Scorpio, the region of death and destruction. Among the twelve months of the year November, with its darkness and foreboding of death, has its appointed place. So has Judas in the circle that surrounds the Son of Man. Jesus said: 'Have I not chosen you, the Twelve? Yet one of you is a devil!' (John 6:70). A more explanatory translation might be: 'And one of you must be a vehicle for the Being of Evil.' This is a cosmic necessity. If the twelvehood of the disciples was to show how Christ was to be proclaimed to humanity in twelve different ways – just as the sun sends its rays from twelve different stations – one of them had to show where human life would lead without Christ.

In Leonardo da Vinci's *Last Supper* an internal splendour seems to irradiate the face of Christ, but an inward darkness emanates from Judas. It is one of the artistic marvels of that famous picture that Leonardo has succeeded in portraying the two figures quite naturally and realistically while at the same time he makes them transparent for the cosmic polarity of Light and Darkness. The gospel account carries us one step further in that it describes how Christ himself draws the darkness finally into Judas. Christ dipped a piece of bread into the wine and put it into the mouth of Judas. Judas swallowed it, and in that instant Satan took possession of him. Christ treated Judas like a lightning conductor for the evil of the whole world. He made him, at this moment, the very incarnation of the sin of the world. But not in order to destroy him but in order that he might become the agent through whom Christ might come to grips with evil and redeem it.

Few mysteries resist more strongly every attempt to put them into words. But when Lent and Easter come round in the course of the year, our souls are invited to dwell on the sacred story and to ponder it in reverent thought. We may grasp that the pattern of the Messianic redemption of the world was preordained. It had been described and proclaimed by the prophets of Israel. It had been foreshadowed by the sacred rites of the ancient mysteries. It included a betrayal into the hands of death. Christ entered into this redemptive ritual in full knowledge and fulfilled it in perfect freedom. As St Paul writes in his letter to the

Philippians, 'He humbled himself, and became obedient unto death, even death on the cross.'

Was Judas then only a victim without freedom, a pawn in the game? Early Christianity approached this awful mystery by allowing the Judas story to grow into a legend. Nothing less than the figure of King Oedipus, the universal hero-victim of evil in the classic plays of the great Greek dramatists Aeschylus, Sophocles and Euripides, provided the material for the Judas legend. According to the legend, Judas, like King Oedipus, is born under fearful signs and portents. His terrified parents abandon him in a little basket which drifts to the island of Icaria. The queen of the island adopts him as her son. But the curse of Cain is upon him, and full of envy for the queen's real son, Judas murders him: Judas must flee. He comes to Jerusalem where he enters the service of Pontius Pilate. One day Pilate lusts after the apples in his neighbour's garden. Judas offers to procure them for Pilate, but the neighbour resists. In a fit of rage Judas kills him not knowing that he kills his own father. In order to reward his loyalty, Pilate acquires the house of the neighbour for Judas and gives him the widow as his wife. It is Ciborea, Judas' own mother. One day Ciborea speaks to him of the child whom she abandoned. Now Judas realises his guilt and ghastly history. Despair seizes him. Is there any hope left for a creature of such appalling evil? His mother thinks of Christ whom she has met. In his compassion, Christ accepts Judas as a disciple.

It might seem as if this legend set out to paint Judas as a lost individual from the beginning. In reality, it exonerates him. For it is not the alleged life of the historic Judas that it means to tell, instead it presents the biography of Man. The crimes of Judas in the legend are the symbolic stages of the progressive fall of humanity. The historic Judas of the gospels is the last stage. He is one from our midst whose lot it was to carry to the very end what Adam had begun. Through him the Serpent struck once more and met his conqueror and Redeemer. And to Judas, as an individual soul in deep contrition, went out the love of Christ who asked the Father to forgive those who do not know what they do. Rudolf Steiner gives a very guarded but unmistakable indication that allows us to believe that the soul of Judas was permitted to serve the advance of Christianity in another life.

If we try to come to terms with the tragedy of Judas religiously, we must take Judas as the man in whom we see portrayed our own potential wickedness. Goethe was· honest enough to confess that he never heard of a crime which he could not have committed himself. Do we not feel the same? Do we not even project ourselves sometimes onto the screen or into a novel and enjoy, actually enjoy, vicariously, the wickedness of the villain? Judas is the epitome of this vicarious wickedness that is ours. And insofar as we see our kind in him, his picture calls us to repentance. He is, also, the victim and bearer of the evil in us.

In some of the medieval Passion Plays the death of Judas is followed by the appearance on stage of St Augustine who warns everybody to conquer 'the Judas within himself' with contrition and repentance:

> *By Judas sij uch kunt gethan*
> *das ir alle sullet ruwen han.*
> (By Judas all of you are taught
> that repentance must be sought).

So speaks St Augustine in the Frankfurt Passion Play of 1493. Conscious acknowledgement of evil, and repentance, are the means whereby we may join in the process of redemption. With the picture of Judas before our eyes this realisation can become very vivid. He in us and we in him have had our share in the betrayal of Christ. But the cool and conscious realisation of this fact by our head, and the humble act of repentance in our heart, integrates us into the process of redemption.

In the tragic destiny of Judas a universal and ultimate question is powerfully posed. Why was evil ever allowed? Why was all this tragic suffering necessary? Evil has a profound significance in the making of humanity.

> For Man to develop the consciousness of self in earth-life, he must
> become much more thoroughly detached from the divine spiritual world
> which gave him his origin, than can be done by that world itself.

In these dispassionate words Rudolf Steiner wrote in the last months of his life from his sickbed about the mission of evil. The divine world cannot through its own powers detach man sufficiently from itself for him to develop an adequate 'consciousness of self'. This necessary detachment can only be brought about by other forces, the forces of evil. Man gains consciousness of self through them, but pays for this gain with suffering. Christ, by accepting freely the fullness of suffering, helps man to outgrow evil and suffering without losing its gain, the consciousness of self.

The unique Event of Golgotha is the free, cosmic act of Love within earth's history; it is to be comprehended and seized on, too, only by the Love that Man brings to its comprehension.

In this process Judas holds a unique place, both as a real factor and as a representative symbol.

This meaning and mission of evil, though seemingly unfathomable to the purely argumentative intellect, has been time and again divined by the higher vision of the poetic mind. English poetry in particular contains marvellous instances. Well known are Pope's lines in his 'Essay on Man' where he describes, 'All discord, harmony not understood; / All partial evil, universal good.'

But while Pope's treatment of the problem remains somewhat rationalistic, James Stephens' poem 'The Fullness of Time' is perhaps the most beautiful example in English literature of a full, Christian comprehension of the mission of evil and its redemption. It is a triumphant message of Easter:

> On a rusty iron throne
> Past the furthest star of space
> I saw Satan sit alone,
> Old and haggard was his face;
> For his work was done and he
> Rested in eternity.
>
> And to him from out the sun
> Came his father and his friend
> Saying, now the work is done
> Enmity is at an end:
> And he guided Satan to
> Paradises that he knew.
>
> Gabriel without a frown,
> Uriel without a spear,
> Raphael came singing down
> Welcoming their ancient peer,
> And they seated him beside
> One who had been crucified.

Making Friends with Time
Adam Bittleston

Adam Bittleston (1911–89) was a brilliant and wise individual, at home in the realm of ideas. He was ordained in 1935 and worked in Leeds and Edinburgh. His final years were spent in Forest Row, Sussex, teaching at Emerson College. As well as his love of Shakespeare, he had a keen interest in astronomy.

To wake up in the morning is one of the most mysterious of all the familiar things we do. What power has brought us back again into our eyes and ears and all our senses? What great Ferryman has rowed us safe across, and helped us gently on to land? We are too occupied with the next steps to thank or think of him. Hopes and wishes, tasks and problems of the day rush to meet us, and only a few shreds of dream still hang about us to remind us of the crossing.

On the other side, we had spoken with our angel. For him our lives, and time itself, have quite a different aspect. What we each remember is only a fragment, broken off at the beginning and the end, reaching only from some moment in early childhood to the present. It is broken off at the edges too, for we see very little of the real causes or effects of our actions. Our angel watches with patient, profound concern how our lives, leading down from realms before birth and on towards a death the time and circumstances of which are in the main already appointed, are interwoven with the world's life. The angel sees in full reality our connections with those we know and those we have still to meet, but he sees too how we are part of the life of the earth.

When we wake up, it is good if we can think of time not only in relation to the clock, but also in relation to the life of the earth. For if we can form vivid, spiritually true ideas about the season of the year, for example, we raise towards consciousness something that our angel has already laid in our hearts. He knows the opportunities that are ours because it is spring or summer or autumn or winter, or even this particular day. Far more than we might realise we can be strengthened by trying to make friends with the mysteries of time. In our bodies, it is the beat of heart and lung that is the most tireless, and most essentially healthy, of our inner processes – a rhythm that is in accord with the great, regular movements of the earth, sun and stars through the ages. This rhythm of our bodies we receive as a gift. But our minds and feelings are at odds with time, unless we do something to bring about harmony.

The spiritual patterns of the day, the year, and of human life from birth to death, are all more complex than they appear. Just as in the year the time of greatest warmth is later than the time of greatest light, in man's life new qualities develop when others decline. Spring contains the sorrow of Lent, autumn the triumph of Michaelmas. And between the rhythms of the day and the year there plays the rhythm of the week, reflecting the great steps of Creation and consecrated again by the deeds of Christ. To understand more deeply what these rhythms mean, and to order our spiritual life in relation to them, is one of the tasks of our age, through which the gap between the spiritual and the material in human life can be bridged. We often notice in practice how difficult it is to bring our ideas and ideals effectively into our habits, our temperament, even our state of health. This depends upon our ability to make friends with time. However long the struggle may be to bring regularity and harmonious order into the life of prayer and meditation, there is the great hope that eventually we may bring, when we come at evening and call for the Ferryman, some true gifts from this side to our angel.

Billy Graham and the Religious Situation in Britain

Alfred Heidenreich

Alfred Heidenreich (1898–1961), one of the founding priests of The Christian Community, worked for much of his life in Great Britain, but still found time to establish congregations in North and South America, and later South Africa. In 1955, the American evangelical preacher Billy Graham visited England on a twelve week 'crusade'. During that time more than two million people came to hear him preach. This article is a commentary on Billy Graham's visit to Wembley Arena in London.

Britain has settled down to a period of comfort and prosperity. The austerities of wartime are finally overcome, the revolutionary changes which the Welfare State has brought in its train are digested and adjusted, the fears of poverty through illness, unemployment and old age are banished, the great masses of the people are better off than ever before, and private enterprise has regained sufficient freedom to be attractive to the enterprising. Internationally a progressive relaxation of tension between the two opposing camps is expected. The new government seems to be in the hands of competent and benevolent men, and world markets seem to be reasonably stabilised.

Into this prevailing mental climate, the optimistic approach to the Christian religion that Dr Billy Graham preaches seems to fit very well. He strives for the great good things, peace of mind, good fellowship, a new person, and he promises you that you can lay the unshakeable foundations for all of this in one evening.

There are conditions, of course. You must accept Jesus Christ as your personal Saviour, here and now, and in visible token of your decision, you must come down at the end of the address and stand in the arena. From this beginning you will make a new start in your whole life. You will be asked to give your name. You will then be sent some special literature designed to help you to lead henceforth a Christian life, and your minister will be notified, so that he can make a special effort to assist you in your efforts to live up to your decision.

It was a moving sight on Ascension Day evening, after the sun had gradually set during Billy's sermon, to see several thousands of people in Wembley Stadium congregate on the soft green floodlit turf, which had just recovered from the ravages of the Cup Final. Soldiers, airmen, schoolboys, families, down they all came, and of their need and sincere desire there could be no question. Often, here and there, out of a group of friends, perhaps one girl, having made her decision, rose and walked down, while the massed choir softly hummed a sweet tune.

A few weeks previously I had attended a Billy Graham meeting in the stadium at Aberdeen. The canny Scots had been more reticent. Only a few hundred had come forward, so that Billy Graham fell back on somewhat rougher forms of encouragement, which I did not particularly like. But at Wembley there were more converts than the staff of stewards and counsellors – by no means small – could cope with.

Apart from those who came forward, I believe that very many of the crowd were sincerely impressed. There was something unique in hearing simple evangelical fundamentalism, preached in good-natured and well-spoken terms to an open-air mass meeting of 80,000 people. There is probably no one else in the world at the moment who could do it.

All the same, I could not entirely dismiss certain reminiscences from my mind that were connected with some of the rallies of the Nazi Movement I had witnessed in the early thirties. Of course, the gospel was a very different matter. But there was the same build-up, the same numbers, the same singing, the same magnetic personality, the same persuasive voice, the same appeal to a personal dedication, the same feeling of fellowship and of loneliness conquered. I wonder whether J. B. Priestly had something similar in mind when, in the conclusion of his article 'Thoughts in the Wilderness' in the *New Statesman,* he wrote:

> But the newly arrived British bring with them into this world of mass communications, shows and ballyhoo, a certain innocence, belonging to an earlier age, leaving them unprotected by any rough popular cynicism ... Their minds are wide open as well as being empty. Today it is Billy Graham, old-fashioned fundamental evangelism plus planned public

relations and electronics: no great harm, no great good... But tomorrow who? What? This note sounds a caution.

Billy Graham, of course is convinced that it is God who brought all these thousands to his meetings, and he says so in every address. But is the truth and reality behind it all really as simple as that?

In the Church at Glenilla Road a lively meeting discussed Dr Graham's 'Evangelical Crusade', and a considerable number of people who had attended the meetings gave their impressions and opinions. Several points emerged from the discussion that may be of wider interest.

The religious life in many churches is apparently rather dull and lacks sufficient stimulus to break the uninspiring routine. Billy Graham's crusade supplies an element of excitement, not in itself alien to religion. If religion ceases to be an adventure, it loses something of its essential character. Billy Graham's open-air mass meetings are rare events, particularly for the younger members of the more humdrum Protestant churches. The meetings are something equivalent to that which the Roman Catholic Church provides in its open-air processions. From my schooldays at a predominantly Catholic school I remember how much a big Corpus Christi procession meant to my Catholic schoolmates. A Wembley meeting is not a dissimilar experience.

Again, a public witness and 'acceptance of Jesus Christ as personal Saviour' makes many Protestants feel what a Roman Catholic feels after confession and absolution. It gives him the assurance, which Protestantism does not easily give him in any other tangible form, of a fresh start, with a clean sheet and a new determination. But Catholic experience knows that the new start does not last for very long; and the Catholic religion makes provision for the new start to be repeated time and time again. It is probably one of the major weaknesses of the Billy Graham approach to make people believe that they can keep up their resolve forever; whereas, in fact, it is likely to go the way of all New Year resolutions unless a man is helped very adequately and conscientiously by his minister.

Fundamental and lasting religious conversions do, of course, occur. But they are rather rare and rest on a somewhat unusual karmic background. According to Rudolf Steiner, a fundamental and lasting conversion is possible for a man whose previous life was cut short by a sudden, violent death, and the conversion is open to him at about the same age at which his death occurred in his last life. Naturally, these are considerations still outside the field of vision of the great majority of people at the present time.

The central difficulty, however, is Billy Graham's teaching. I quote an example from a specimen sermon contained in the official half-crown brochure *Billy Graham, the Man and his Message,* which was sold at the meetings:

A lady came here the other night. She was not sure, she was not convinced. She did not come forward. She was still thinking about accepting Jesus as her Saviour when she was struck with a heart attack and the life passed out of her body. And so far as I know, she was not reborn and she must pay the penalty forever – forever! Tonight you have a chance. Why don't you do business with God tonight? He wants you. He loves you. He's patient and He is waiting for you. Come to God tonight in true faith and you live forever. God will not spare you unless you stand clothed in the righteousness of Jesus Christ. You say, 'Well, Billy, what do I have to do?' All you have to do is let Jesus in. You say, 'Is it as simple as that?' It's as simple as A, B, C. It's as simple as falling off a log. You say, 'How long does it take?' Only a second, a twinkling of an eye. Right now where you sit, you can settle it and say 'Yes' to Christ for eternity, and I guarantee on the authority of God's word that you can know before you leave here tonight that you're going to heaven. Utterly sure. You can be certain that you'll escape the judgement of Almighty God. Shall we pray?

This is a typical illustration of a theme that occurs in all of Billy Graham's addresses, whatever the particular variation may be at the time. And I am firmly convinced that this teaching is completely wrong and untrue. The human spirit is not incapable, if we so will, of knowing something of the spiritual realities of the afterlife and of knowing better than this crude doctrine and shock tactics imply. And there is something deeply disturbing in seeing the sacred mystery of spiritual rebirth, to which Christian mystics of all ages have born witness, oversimplified and banalised in this manner. That Billy Graham puts these stories across in a cool matter-of-fact manner aggravates the difficulty still further. It would be far better if he presented them in the emotional hellfire style of the old-fashioned evangelists. Then one could accept them as part of a legitimate dramatisation of his message. But his mode of address is rational and he has been universally commended for it. The emotional hunger of the big audience is met in other ways: by straightforward hymn singing, and by the religious crooning of Beverley Shea, 'America's beloved gospel singer', who has a truly magnificent baritone voice. Billy

Graham himself puts his tenets across with a sober persuasiveness that implies that everything he says is gospel truth and a literal fact.

The problem is, perhaps, even more subtle. A reference to Billy Graham in Sir Stephen King-Hall's *National Newsletter* seems to me to put the finger on the spot. Sir Stephen writes:

> As I had raised certain questions in this correspondence about the American evangelist a newsletter member kindly invited me to meet Dr Graham. I did so and heard him speak. My conviction about his sincerity was reinforced. He preached the simple Christian gospel in a very natural and unemotional manner and quite rightly emphasised that the spiritual battlefield is to be found within each one of us. So far so good, but I must in honesty add that my previous criticism which was, to put it briefly, that Dr Graham may leave many of his listeners with the impression that giving oneself to Christ is as simple and easy an operation as joining Rotary, still held good after I had heard and seen him.
>
> In particular, for example, I was not attracted by a remark he made after saying – I am sure with complete conviction – that he had reached a state of certainty of mind so satisfying about the life to come that death no longer had any terror for him. His remark, which brought me up with a jerk, was to the effect that even if there was not a life hereafter it was very comforting to believe there was such a future life. (*National Newsletter*, May 19, 1955.)

There is no need to draw the uncharitable conclusion from this one remark – astonishing as it is – that Billy Graham indulges in make-believe. But it reinforces the conclusion, which one is compelled to draw from hearing and observing him, that his sincerity rests entirely on his personal and subjective convictions. It is quite misleading to say that his constant references to the Bible provide objective sanction and authority. For it is *his* selection of quotations, indiscriminately lumped together from anywhere in the book, and often taken from their contexts, *his* interpretation of these passages, *his* choice of Christian doctrines that he preaches. Of course, he himself believes tremendously in his message; it gives him power. And he is a very lovable fellow, who has done many people a very good turn, and about whom one hates to say anything but nice things. But a Christianity resting on such very personal foundations and appealing so much to the purely egotistic desire for personal salvation is not the Christianity that can cope with the problems of our age. The mental powers of man need to be Christianised. Otherwise the social, economic, and political problems of our highly mechanised civilisation will drag the world downhill, irrespective of the numbers who felt a sense of personal salvation at Wembley. And the period of comfort and prosperity that is said to be ahead of us may prove an illusion.

Towards the end of the meeting at Glenilla Road the question was raised: What can Billy Graham teach us? One answer from the meeting was: courage. In this he does, indeed, set an example. His courage is a real challenge to other Christians. This ties up with a searching question that was put to us recently by some Anglican theological students who attended one of our Young People's Meetings.

'You seem to have a wealth of knowledge and experience,' they said, 'but what do you *believe*?'

It is easy to reply that the question is wrongly put, and that, in fact, we believe what we know.

But do we?

I can illustrate the problem by a famous historical remark. When the French Revolution broke out, the French King Louis XVI said, 'We have always known it, but we have never believed it.' The world could have said the same about Hitler, and perhaps will have to say the same when the next catastrophe breaks upon us. But this telling phrase can also be applied to positive matters. Christians who have recognised in Rudolf Steiner 'a man sent from God' to help us Christianise the mental powers of man, know a great deal more about the realities of the spiritual world than the majority of other Christians. But has our knowledge really become faith? Do we live by it? Do we stand witness to it with the whole of our being? Do we, in the words of our Communion Service, 'confess unto that which is revealed through Christ' so that he 'takes from us the might of the adversary'? This is a very penetrating question, which in particular the younger generation will put to us. And the fact that among the young people who gave their names at Billy Graham's meetings there were also old scholars of Steiner schools is a timely reminder.

Another answer from the meeting was, he can teach us simplicity of style and direct approach. This may be even more difficult to achieve than courage. But Billy Graham has done us all one great service. It is possible to begin today a conversation on religion with almost anybody. We need only refer to him, mention his name and we have a perfect and simple opening. Let us use it.

True and False Vision
Evelyn Francis Derry

Evelyn Francis Derry (1911–2000) was the first woman priest to be ordained in Britain in 1939. She was a prolific writer and travelled extensively across southern Africa. She worked in London throughout her life and also wrote under the name of Evelyn Francis and Evelyn Francis Capel. In 1954, Aldous Huxley published The Doors of Perception, *an autobiographical account of his psychedelic experience with mescaline. He followed it two years later with the book* Heaven and Hell *in which he elaborated further on his experiences. In this article, Derry compares the visionary experience achieved under the influence of drugs with that achieved as a result of a proper spiritual development.*

On October 28, the *Sunday Observer* reported at length an experiment made some months ago by the MP Christopher Mayhew, and his friend Dr Osmond, with the drug mescaline. The drug is well known to many people by name through two recent books by Aldous Huxley, *The Doors of Perception* and *Heaven and Hell* (Chatto & Windus, 1954 and 1956 respectively). It is not a new discovery. It has been extracted from a type of cactus and used in religious ceremonies by certain tribes of American Indians since ancient times. But it has now been called into use for a new kind of experiment, which Aldous Huxley and certain others have been making on themselves. Mescaline alters the consciousness of the senses without producing oblivion. Drug taking as such always alters a person's consciousness, whether it is done for the sake of supressing pain, inducing sleep and soothing agitation, or for the opposite purpose of stimulating the soul life artificially. People can be drugged today to put them to sleep or to put them into a state of carefree happiness in the face of an unusual strain. Such artificial changes of consciousness are often considered to be on the right side of what is and is not permissible in the use of drugs. Christopher Mayhew, in making an experiment on himself with mescaline, intended to help in research for the relief of 'the vast and growing army of the mentally ill'. His doctor friend believes that this drug has useful properties for medical purposes. Aldous Huxley put forward a different reason for his use of it. He was interested in the change of consciousness for its own sake and believed mescaline to be a safe means of inducing this since it appears to have no after-effects.

His book *The Doors of Perception* describes his first experiment with the drug. In the later one, *Heaven and Hell*, he sets out his conclusions. While admitting that the drug has a varying effect on different people, he found in his own case that it changed the perception of his senses:

> The books glowed when I looked at them, with brighter colours, with a profounder significance. Red books, like rubies; emerald books; books bound in white jade; books of agate, of aquamarine, of yellow topaz; lapis lazuli books whose colour was so intense, so intrinsically meaningful, that they seemed to be on the point of leaving the shelves to thrust themselves more insistently on my attention ... Space was still there, but it had lost its predominance. The mind was primarily concerned, not with measures and locations, but with being and meaning. And along with indifference to space there went an even completer indifference to time.

Along with the change of perception of the external world, he found a psychological change taking place within himself.

> This participation in the manifest glory of things left no room for the ordinary, necessary concerns of human existence, above all for concerns involving persons. For persons are selves and, in one respect at least, I was now a Not-self, simultaneously perceiving and being the Not-self of the things around me. To this new-born Not-self, the behaviour, the appearance, the very thought of the self it had momentarily ceased to be seemed enormously irrelevant ... For the moment, mescaline had delivered me from the world of selves, of time, of moral judgements and utilitarian considerations.

During this state of consciousness, Huxley felt that his perceptions had been released to explore the spheres of awareness usually hidden from ordinary consciousness to which he applied the term 'Mind at Large'. (In the second book, experiments of this nature are described as explorations into the antipodes of the mind.)

While such experiences, which he found very enjoyable, were going on, his will receded out of his reach:

> Though the intellect remains unimpaired and though perception is enormously improved, the will suffers a profound change for the worse. The mescaline taker sees no reason for doing anything in particular and finds most of the causes for which, at ordinary times, he was prepared to act and suffer, profoundly uninteresting. He can't be bothered with them, for the good reason that he has better things to think about.

This aspect of the experiment did not cause him great concern, for the reason, which he later emphasised, that he was in no danger of doing anything offensive or disturbing to others.

Why should anyone wish to put himself out of his ordinary consciousness into such a state? Aldous Huxley found the sights and sounds delightful, the state of Not-self satisfying, but he has not advanced enjoyment as the reason for making such experiments or writing about them. He has put forward the claim that in every age people seek to transcend the limits of their ordinary consciousness in order to achieve spiritual experiences:

> The urge to transcend self-conscious selfhood is, as I have said, a principal appetite of the soul. When men and women fail to transcend themselves by means of worship, good works and spiritual exercises, they are apt to resort to religion's chemical surrogates.

There then follows a long list of such 'surrogates', of which mescaline is claimed to be the least harmful. Christopher Mayhew during his experiment also found himself released from his ordinary consciousness. He noticed especially a changed relationship to time, which greatly intrigued him. At one moment he saw tea being poured from a pot into his cup even though he was already drinking the hot liquid. For a few minutes time went backwards, although on other occasions during the afternoon it was merely jumbled. The state of mind in which a modern intelligent person enjoys experimenting with consciousness in this way is not unlike that of people who relish fun fairs. Most of the devices to be found there give the clients odd experiences of consciousness by throwing them out of the ordinary relation to space, weight and such like. People today are easily bored and enjoy escaping from normal conditions. What is more boring than cane chairs and flannel trousers to the ordinary gaze? Yet Huxley saw them as fascinating objects of art when mescaline had altered the sight of his eyes. He might well wonder, was it not his own eyes that were making him bored? If his sight were changed would the everyday world not seem divine instead of dull?

Although Huxley has obviously found his experiments just amusing at times, he has formulated their deeper issue in both his books. Religion depends on vision greater than the experience of the world, which we get today from the ordinary use of our senses. If we cannot obtain vision by purely spiritual means, we must resort to drugs. Is this a dangerous attitude? The starting point of his argument is so sound that every seeking person could confirm it for themselves. What we perceive, what we think because it is generally accepted around us, is not enough to explain the experiences of life nor to give us our aim in living today. We need more spiritual vision than we have. 'There must be more to it than that' is a popular phrase that would describe the mood in which many people have discovered that they must become spiritual seekers. Does it matter then how the vision is attained? Here, though it means directly contradicting the argument of Aldous Huxley, the answer must be that it does matter very seriously indeed. We need true vision for our spiritual and religious life, not false. It is not possible to have true vision by false means. The vision is affected in its whole nature by the means with which it is attained. If the means are false, the vision will be falsified.

How can we discern the true means from the false? Aldous Huxley has taken the effects as his test. Mescaline, he has argued, is harmless because the taker remains an inoffensive person. He agrees nevertheless that the will of the person under its influence is almost entirely lamed. But what sort of person is one without his will? The mescaline taker has lost his ability to act but kept the consciousness of himself perceiving the world around him. He has preserved his ego-consciousness and mislaid his ego. The substance of our selfhood is in the will which, if we can inwardly free ourselves, can be used in acts of free will. The awareness of our selfhood is given to us through the brain, which mirrors into thought the presence of the will. The self-conscious person who cannot use his will is a ghost, an emptiness, calling himself by an empty phrase. He is no longer a true human self and as such will not be able to apprehend true vision.

Aldous Huxley welcomed the escape from his will because it seemed to release him into oneness with the world. But if a human being abandons his selfhood he is in reality lost in the world. He becomes like a piece of seaweed floating in its ebb and flow. There is another means of transcending the self than by losing it. In *Heaven and Hell* Huxley has himself described at length different kinds of religious art, which, in past ages, stimulated the visionary faculty by form and colour. Today we can no longer do the same, but from a different cause than that which Huxley has put forward. In modern times we need, like people of earlier ages, to transcend ourselves; but we shall fail to do so in fact, if we attempt to revert to old types of consciousness. They can only make us less than ourselves. We need to search among our inner faculties for that which can so develop that a future form of consciousness begins to germinate. We find this when we grasp the nature of our power to think.

As thinking is used in the usual manner nowadays, it enables us to comment on the ordinary world around us, to adjust ourselves to it and to win existence from it. This kind of thinking serves the need of personal selves, which we must transcend when we seek the spirit. But the faculty of thinking has not always been employed in this manner. It belonged originally to divine powers, who exercised it to bring this ordered world into existence out of chaos. It was the property of spiritual beings who exercised it in the universe. Then, in the course of time, it was given over to human beings on earth, by the grace of the divine world. For a certain period they have been allowed to use it for their personal conduct of life. By its own nature, however, it belongs to the world of the spirit. It has in itself the power to lift human minds to the spheres where it once belonged, to help them transcend the limitations of everyday consciousness. Thinking does not become less useful in the ordinary world if it is also used to apprehend the spiritual world. Its capacity enlarges as it is used and developed.

Huxley has recommended a drug for the sake of transcending our present limitations of consciousness. Is it really possible to answer him by pointing to a faculty that people possess today but which they have not yet developed to the full? Can the two be compared? In one respect they are not to be compared. The speed with which results appear is very different. With mescaline curious sense experiences can be attained in one afternoon. The transformation of thinking into an instrument for apprehending the spirit is the work of a lifetime. Long, steady effort of will is required, accompanied by the patience to wait for results that, when they come, will be neither startling nor amusing. But the reward of this slower way is found in what happens to him who takes it. He becomes in all his inner nature, in thinking, feeling and willing, a truer, more spiritual being. The drug taker remains from first to last a drug taker.

In the Act of Consecration of Man we have the true picture for the necessary process of transcending ourselves. The empty cup stands on the altar. It is filled with wine and water during the prayer in which all those present turn willing, feeling and thinking to the Father, the Son and the Holy Spirit. Thereupon it is lifted up as an offering to the divine world. What takes place in the service after this point is the divine answer to this offering. If we so use our power of thinking that our minds become cups lifted in offering to the spirit, our consciousness will become spirit-filled. We shall transcend ourselves, not by laying aside our will, but by using it to raise our thinking. We shall be united with the world, not by dissolving away into what is around us, but by looking up to what is above us. We shall strive, not after the Not-self, but after the true Self, that is to say after the spirit within, which seeks for the divine spirit beyond itself.

Urizen and Los
Adam Bittleston

Adam Bittleston (1911–89) was ordained in 1935 and worked in Leeds and Edinburgh, and in Forest Row, Sussex, where he taught at Emerson College. Here he looks at two figures in the mythology of William Blake: Urizen, the false image of God and representative of fallen thinking; and Los, the prophetic spirit of will that looks ahead to the redemption of human beings.

A great paradox meets us if we try to study William Blake's prophetic books. On the one hand we meet his sense of urgency, his burning desire to communicate his insight: 'Mark well my words! They are of your eternal salvation.' On the other hand we meet what seems to be a private language so opaque and harsh that the reader who cares deeply for Blake's work as an artist and his personality as a man can nevertheless be driven back in despair.

Yet remembering Goethe's words 'God gives us nuts, but He does not crack them for us', we need not draw the conclusion that Blake's prophetic mission has failed, or is failing, because of this obscurity. The very effort to crack these nuts has already meant a great deal in many lives. This was Blake's conscious intention. In a letter to his patron, Reverend Dr John Trusler, dated August 23, 1799, Blake wrote: 'The wisest of the Ancients considered what is not too explicit as the fittest for instruction, because it rouses the faculties to act.' It is just because no one can say with assurance where the study of the prophetic books might eventually lead, that people with diametrically opposed opinions about the world, once they have found something that seems a clue, can work away at them and be enriched. And the conviction soon comes that what Blake wanted to say could not have been said in any other way.

Nevertheless, we have to try to see the relationships between Blake's visions and the thought and knowledge of his day and ours. And I would like to make here some tentative suggestions about figures who play a considerable part in the later prophetic books, figures who must eventually become our friends, so to speak, if the sense of harshness and remoteness is to be overcome.

> Four Universes round the Mundane Egg remain Chaotic,
> One to the North, named Urthona: One to the South, named Urizen:
> One to the East, named Luvah; One to the West, named Tharmas;
> They are the Four Zoas that stood around the Throne Divine.
> (Milton, I, 21.)

'Zoas' refers to the four 'Living Creatures' (Greek, *Zoa*) described in the Revelation of St John 4:6–8: the first like a lion, the second like an ox, the third with the face of a man, and the fourth like a flying eagle. But Blake describes and draws his figures in giant human forms, and nearly always not in the peaceful purity of the vision in the Apocalypse, but as fallen beings. What in Eternity work as creative powers for Man in his heavenly Form, Blake sees as four tragic, heroic figures, often at odds with one another, their primeval universes fallen and shrunk within the form of mortal Man.

In a lecture he gave at The Hague on March 25, 1913, Rudolf Steiner described how it is possible, with spiritually trained vision, to look back at the physical body from the outside. It appears in a great, tragic Imagination as fallen from the original splendour of Paradise and bears within it the shrunken images of the celestial Eagle, Lion, and Bull. The relation of what Blake sees to what is contained in this description does not seem quite simple; for man is a very complicated creature indeed, and we must be careful not to identify anything too quickly. But can we learn anything in this direction, for example about Urizen, who plays so great a part in the prophetic books from *The French Revolution* onwards?

Urizen is the representative of the false image of God to which self-righteous souls look up, the great tyrant of Shelley's *Prometheus Unbound*. Through a conception of the world in which good and evil were seen only in stark contrast with one another, the image of the good had become falsified, tinged with pride and contempt. As Rudolf Steiner pointed out again and again, the good can only be truly seen between two evils, one proudly idealistic, the other material and cynical; and in this connection he spoke specifically of Milton and the German poet Friedrich Klopstock, both of whom described a good that was really Luciferic – proud and contemptuous. Blake loved and suffered through Milton, and William Hayley read Klopstock to him with startling results.

But Urizen is not only the wrong image of God, which Blake regarded as ruling in the churches and philosophical schools of his time. He is the inspirer of that kind of thinking that produces the wrong image. Mr Wicksteed says firmly that his name means 'Your Reason'. Another explanation, suggested by Mr. F. E. Pierce, and quoted by Northrop Frye in *Fearful Symmetry* (Princeton University Press, 1947), his study of Blake's work, is that it comes from the Greek word *horizein*, meaning to fix a limit or to define. It is the origin of our word 'horizon'. There could hardly be a more exact description than this of the gesture made with compasses of light by the sublime figure in the frontispiece to *Europe*, solemnly leaning forward to measure out the world. Blake was an assiduous reader of the Greek New Testament, and this word comes, in the form 'pro-orizo', in a particularly pregnant and relevant passage in Romans 8:29–30:

> We know that in everything God works for good with those who
> love him, who are called according to his purpose. For those whom he
> foreknew he also predestined to be conformed to the image of His Son,
> in order that he might be the firstborn among many brethren.

The word 'predestine' is the hardening, through Latin, of the Greek *pro-orizo* – fore-outline, the drawing in the spiritual world of the frontiers of the archetypal human form. But as the heavenly design becomes in man's mind rigid predestination, so Urizen falls from Eternity to be the sorrowful grim tyrant, 'a self-contemplating shadow'.

Though he has come to have northern qualities of coldness and hardness, his place was once in the south, with the midday sun. Once he was at home in light and moving air, now he is among the rocks and uses for his power the stony tablets of the Law. His fate is a clear picture of the fall of human thinking. It belongs to the essential character of thought that it should be winged and free, moving in the wide spaces of the light-filled air, yet it has come to dwell in the brain, shut up within the dark cell walls of the skull, desiring to impose upon all living things its own chains.

But one day Urizen will take again his true place, with his brothers who have also suffered and struggled:

> Then Albion stretched his hand into Infinitude
> And took his Bow. Fourfold the Vision; for bright beaming Urizen
> Lay'd his hand on the South and took a breathing Bow of
>   carved Gold:
> Luvah his hand stretch'd to the East and bore a Silver Bow bright shining:
> Tharmas Westward a Bow of Brass, pure flaming, richly wrought:
> Urthona Northward in thick storms a Bow of Iron, terrible thundering.
>   (*Jerusalem: The Emanation of the Giant Albion*, 97)

Yet it is not Urizen who came first to meet and help on the infinite work of the redemption of man, or who 'kept the Divine Vision in time of trouble'. The hero among the four is Urthona, whose name in time is Los, who labours continually at his forges, and whose place in heaven is the north. When Jesus appears standing by Albion it is in 'the likeness and similitude of Los'.

When we try to understand the relationship between Urizen and Los with the help of Rudolf Steiner's outlines of cosmic history, we may remember the gigantic periods of evolution that he describes, of which the rhythm of the week is a miniature reflection. He describes a primal world, in which of all the elements only fire existed, and calls it Old Saturn; this is followed by a world of light and warmth and air known as Old Sun; then a world known as Old Moon in which air condensed, as it were, a stage deeper, into water. These are the Saturday, Sunday and Monday of cosmic evolution.

What we have as *thinking* can be seen as a heritage from Old Sun, the universe predominantly formed out of light. And this universe was born from those divine forces represented in the Revelation of St John, among the Living Creatures about the Throne, by the Eagle. Among the starry constellations the direction from which these forces work bears today the tragic name of the Scorpion. Within the most significant period of human history, from the time of the oldest Indian civilisation up to the present time, the Scorpion has changed from a summer sign to a winter one, approximately from July to November. The world direction from which the universe of light once sprang is for us today (in the northern hemisphere) the place of the earthly sun as it approaches the greatest darkness of mid-winter.

As Urizen is Lord of Light and has his true place at the zenith, so Los who is Urthona is at home with the earth-element and at the nadir. In cosmic history, the earth-element originates only with our present universe. In the Cosmic Week, the world which we know has a double character: it is Tuesday-Wednesday,

Mars-Mercury. It is the scene of development for the human individuality, which begins in self-assertion and only gradually learns its mission as Healer. The place for the transformation of the aggressive courage taught by Mars, into the healing compassion taught by Mercury, a transformation we see particularly vividly in the life of St Francis. The great turning-point in world history from a Mars to a Mercury character is the coming of Christ. Since that time all wars are something of an anachronism, the tragic continuation of something that had its place in the education of humanity in earlier times.

In the Revelation of St John, this cosmic change is described in the Letter to Thyatira:

> He who conquers and who keeps my works until the end, I will give him power of the nations and he shall rule them with a rod of iron, as when earthen pots are broken in pieces, even as I myself have received power from my Father; and I will give him the morning star.

The Christian is to have the inner power of iron, the metal of Mars – the mastery over the inherited element, the clay of the Old Adam – and the Mercury power, the morning star. Blake refers to this passage and the corresponding verse in the Psalms (Psalm 2:9) when describing Los:

> Los with his mace of iron
> Walks round; loud his threats, loud his blows fall
> On the rocky Spectres, as the Potter breaks the potsherds,
> Dashing in pieces Self-righteousness.
> (*Jerusalem: The Emanation of the Giant Albion*, 78)

And it is Los who can discern, through all the works of barren intellect, the 'Signal of the Morning which was told us in the Beginning.' The most significant heritage of the first great period of earthly evolution, right up to the Incarnation of Christ, is the prophetic will. Los is for Blake the great representative of this: 'He is the Spirit of Prophecy, the ever-apparent Elias.' (Milton, 4)

In the troubles of time a heroic will develops, which can see in these troubles the 'Mercy of Eternity'. Los is the ploughman, who makes the earth a good field for seeds to grow up into eternity. It is evident to Blake that the prophetic spirit, which comes not from the head but from the region of the will, can show itself in many forms: as the hermit in the wilderness, but also as the artist who may be surrounded by scorn and misunderstanding. Los is very close to him in his own labours.

Urizen cannot redeem himself, nor can he be the first to recognise Christ and lead others to him. It is one in whom the prophetic spirit burns, enkindled among the needs and troubles of earth, who can do these things, and lead towards Urizen's redemption. In the gospels, John the Baptist is the great representative of the prophetic spirit – sacrificing his earthly head while following an immutable path of will.

Our present universe was born out of the cosmic direction from which shine the stars of Taurus, the sacrificial bull. And, though it is possible also to think quite differently about this, we may see something of the polarity between Los and Urizen in the starry polarity of Bull and Scorpion, will and understanding. Both can serve Christ, but only the sacrificing will can bring into human thought the humility and patience it needs before it can really begin to find its way back into the spirit.

As we have a miniature reflection of cosmic ages in the week, we have a more intensive revelation of part of the cosmic process in the seasons of the year. Spring is a renewal of the world-beginnings that were in Old Saturn; summer the splendour of Old Sun; autumn the character of Old Moon. Each winter we pass through the severity and testing that belong to our present universe, Mars-Mercury.

In the flooding light of midsummer we meet the powers of divine thought, of which our own thinking has become so remote and shadowy a reflection. A new kinship between us and the spiritual powers of midsummer depends on the leadership of the prophetic spirit as it lived in John the Baptist: humble, fully aware of human guilt, serving the future.

As we understand Blake better, we may be able to see more and more clearly that he is a companion, in spiritual warfare, of the great forerunner.

The Problem of Community
Kalmia Bittleston

Like her brother, Adam, Kalmia Bittleston (1909–89) was ordained a priest. She worked in Leeds and London. She was always active, particularly in social endeavours, working quietly and in a down-to-earth way. Here she considers different types of communities, from those we are born into to the ones we choose, culminating in a description of the aims of The Christian Community.

From time to time we all hear about the lack of community in the world today. It is pointed out that some people, or classes of people, are selfish, only looking after their own interests, and unconscious of the needs of others. This is certainly often true, but in fact we all belong to a number of circles of community because men and women need each other everywhere in the world, whether they are living the complex life of the cities or struggling with nature in primitive agricultural settlements. Very few people live alone on a desert island, and even the hermits of the Himalayas need a disciple to bring them food. It is not only 'not good' for man to live alone, outwardly it is almost impossible.

Normally we experience two kinds of community in the course of life. In the first people work and live together simply because that is where they find themselves. In the second they are united in a common aim to which all the members subscribe. The earliest community of which the child is aware as he awakens to earthly surroundings is that of the family, and although he has a deep sense of belonging, this is not based on any conscious choice of identity of interests, which may indeed be very different.

Then follows the community of the neighbourhood, either of the street or the village, for children always know each other however indifferent their parents may be. They have one great advantage when it comes to this question of community: they are always interested in the fellow citizens of their world – other children. The purpose becomes all-important as soon as we come to the communities that the individual consciously seeks for himself. These consist of people with like interests. The teenager may join a youth club in order to find dancing partners, or a sports club in order to belong to a team.

Difficulties only arise in any group when people are found to have quite different ideas about the aim for which they are gathered together, or are unable to agree on the way in which this aim is to be achieved. Those who work together should be united in the service of the firm or the factory, but this is usually secondary to the aim of earning their living by taking home a wage. How many are able to consider the people with whom they will have to work when they chose a job? They trust to luck, and if they find their fellow workers too unpleasant then the only thing to do is to look for somewhere else.

There are of course many exceptions to the priority of the pay packet. For most workers in hospitals and schools, and in many working communities large and small, the first aim is the job well done. These people find their work satisfying. They tend to make friends among their fellow workers and to talk shop. These are the fortunate ones who have less need to find a balance to their working life outside it, among circles of people with similar hobbies.

One form of community, however, caters for quite a different aspect of the human being – the needs of his soul and the problems of eternity. This is the religious community, the membership of a church.

Why do people belong to a church? In grown-ups this can only arise out of free choice. Utilitarian interests are not normally served by going to church, although attending a particular church may have indirect results in social life. A religious community states its aims and many churches also lay down the rules by which they are to be realised. The honest member must be in agreement with these aims and, where there are rules, must be willing to keep them. He joins the church because he has recognised the purpose of the church as the aim for which he is striving, and believes that it may be more possible to attain it working with other people than alone.

In a religious community in its strictest sense, the members also live together. They set themselves a high aim and extend the rules by which it is to be attained to include the whole of existence. Such rules may become very complicated over the course of time, and it would be impossible to carry them out except in a sheltered setting especially adapted to such a life. This close and constant contact with other people makes many demands, for it is a strange paradox of present-day human nature that physical nearness can produce spiritual separation. It is as if some inner need for freedom asserts itself. The body is present but the soul escapes.

The opposite is also true. Where a real inner bond exists, then space and separation can be overcome. A modern religious community must be bound together by invisible ties. Ties of consciousness. These are not there automatically. They must often be renewed in thought and prayer. The writer of Revelation refers to the 'angels' of the several churches. It is the way in which people are united together in their consciousness that enables an angel to be present among them.

The Christian Community has no statement of purpose in the form of a written body of dogma or a catechism, but the aims of the Community are clearly expressed in a number of different ways in the wording of the sacraments. To give one example from the Act of Consecration of Man. There the aim is described as 'Walking with Christ' and 'Working from Christ', and the sacrament is a means of attaining this aim. Naturally this represents the highest possible ideal, and the individual members of the Community can only make their own efforts and have sufficient trust in their fellow members to believe that they make efforts too.

If we could even succeed in holding this aim more often before our consciousness we should not need to try and think up other ways of attaining community, it would come of itself. For the Christ, everyone is important and fully understood both in the gifts which they have and the difficulties against which they are struggling. If something can be attained first of all within the setting of a church and with the help of the sacraments, then the members of the community can spread their attitude to the rest of everyday life. The arm of the family, that smallest and most important unit of community, is to make a home, and the purpose of people working together is to do or make something worthwhile. On this basis we could build a happy and stable civilisation for the future.

1960s

the Christian Community

NUMBER 1

JANUARY—FEBRUARY 1968

On 17th January our Editor will be 70 years of age. On behalf of all readers, colleagues and friends throughout the English-speaking world, I should like to extend to him, not only our warmest wishes for many happy returns of the day, but for the 40 years of inspired leadership which we have known and enjoyed under his office.

Although he may climb the stairs more slowly now, from the spiritual point of view he is in the prime of life and doing more than ever before.

A short appreciation of Dr. Heidenreich's position, by Oliver Mathews, Lenker in the Community in Britain, follows below.

Irene Taylor

It has become a custom in our movement, to pay our respect to a colleague when he reaches the age of 70. Why wait for such a tribute until he has passed from this life, and is no longer here to receive it, when our appreciation given now for a lifetime's achievement may help to renew his strength for many years to come?

Shakespeare and the Realm of the Dead

Adam Bittleston

Adam Bittleston (1911–89) was ordained in 1935. His love and knowledge of Shakespeare was equal to that of an academic, and in his lectures and articles, no matter how remote the subject, he almost always managed to show the relevance of the Bard.

In recent years it has been noticeable that the most fruitful commentators of Shakespeare have been those who observe how, from play to play, certain themes reappear and develop. The more deeply we enter into his work, the more plainly it reveals itself as a unity; although we cannot encompass in our generalisations the abundant variety of his moods and themes, they continually interpret and illuminate one another.

It has been said that Shakespeare was concerned with *this* world and not with the eternal destinies of his characters. And yet if we look at plays written at very different stages in his life, we can find that his treatment of the relationship between those on earth and those who have died underwent a very significant development. We may take as a starting point *Richard III,* a fairly early play written probably between 1593 and 1596, when Shakespeare was about thirty. Here the Duke of Clarence while in prison, shortly before he is murdered, relates his terrible dream. He has fallen overboard from a ship and beholds at the bottom of the sea the bodies of many who have been drowned, with gold and precious stones scattered among them. Some of the jewels gleam from the eyes of skulls. His dream leads him through the agony of drowning into his soul's 'tempest'. His 'stranger soul' meets then the appalling figures of those he has wronged in life. One after the other cries out against him in hatred, calling upon him every torment. Waking, he cannot rid himself of this dream (act I, scene iv, lines 1–74).

Towards the end of the play the figures of those who have died appear once more directly as visions in dream, both to Richard III himself and to his opponent, the Earl of Richmond, afterwards King Henry VII. Upon the murderous Richard the dead pour curse upon curse, bidding him 'Despair and die!' To Richmond, whose destiny is to unite the warring factions of York and Lancaster, they promise triumph. Each of the departed spirits speaks out of his or her own peculiar destiny, still deeply involved in their own griefs and angers.

When Shakespeare wrote *Hamlet*, sometime between 1599 and 1601, he gave us his most famous representation of an intervention from the world of the dead. Here again it is a cry for vengeance: the ghost of Hamlet's father describes how he has been murdered by his brother and calls on his son to avenge him. But there is a significant detail. Hamlet's mother is just as guilty as his uncle, and yet the ghost tells Hamlet to undertake nothing against her.

> Taint not thy mind, nor let thy soul contrive
> Against thy mother aught; leave her to heaven,
> And to those thorns that in her bosom lodge,
> To prick and sting her. (I.v.85)

Hamlet is not to do as Orestes did; he is not even told to do what he actually does, which is to tell his mother that he knows her guilt. And when he does so (III.iv), the ghost appears again. He says he has come to stir Hamlet on to act. But at once he goes on to speak of the queen. Hamlet is to 'Step between her and her fighting soul' (line 112), for the power of imagination works most strongly in weak bodies and the queen is weak.

In his later plays, Shakespeare is very much concerned with the quality of compassion. In *King Lear*, written probably four or five years after *Hamlet*, the terrible almost unbearable events of the play are nevertheless softened by a whole series of people, from Cordelia to Cornwall's nameless servant, who are prepared to risk their lives out of compassion for those who suffer. But in the tragedy of *Hamlet* there is very little compassion to be found. Even the prince shows himself again and again to be markedly ruthless. He can jest with what appears complete detachment about the corpse of Polonius. But in an unexpected place, the fierce ghost himself, we find this hint of compassion, this insight into the tragic relationship of soul and body. Hamlet is not to make the conflict worse than it is. He is to speak to his mother, which the ghost cannot do directly, and, it seems, to speak some comfort, which he is in fact unable to do.

Some seven years later, about 1610, Shakespeare describes in *Cymbeline* another direct intervention from the world of the dead. The heroic Postumus Leonatus is tricked into believing his wife, Imogen, had been unfaithful while he was in exile, and he sends his servant with the commission to kill her. The murder does not happen, but he believes his wife dead. Misery upon misery befalls him, and at last he is in prison, condemned to death. His condition is comparable to that of Clarence in *Richard III*; but Posthumus knows that his prison is not only a bodily one; his soul too is in bonds. He hopes that beyond death he may find freedom. While in prison he dreams. There come with solemn music the souls of his father, who died while Posthumus was in the womb, of his mother, who died at his birth, and of his brothers who fell in battle. And these souls speak, each out of their own destiny, as at the end of *Richard III*. Yet the mood is utterly different. To some these verses have appeared poor, unworthy of Shakespeare, and yet they are an essential part of the play. Their peculiar magic has to be understood. They are a call, from humble and simple souls, for the mercy of heaven on a beloved son and brother. There is no call for vengeance upon Iachimo, the man who deceived Posthumus, for he is only 'a slight thing'. But Jupiter, the thunder-master, is asked to look upon the sufferings and the fundamental goodness of Posthumus, and to help:

> All we poor ghosts will cry
> To the shining synod of the rest
> Against thy deity. (V.iv.92–94.)

And Jupiter himself responds.

When Posthumus wakes, he has a remarkable conversation with his jailer. He still supposes that he will be put to death. He cannot understand the riddle presented to him by Jupiter, which is as obscure as the pronouncement of an oracle. But he is absolutely ready to die. He asserts that the path that leads through death is not so dark as is believed, it is only that men are unwilling to use the spiritual eyes which are in their possession. Though the jailer at first laughs at him, when Cymbeline has been summoned into the presence of the king, the jailer speaks out of the impression that the words of Posthumus have made upon him: 'I would we were all of one mind, and one mind good'. And the next scene does bring about a shared and peaceful mind among the protagonists of the play, restoring all who were lost to those who love them.

In nearly all of the last plays to be written by Shakespeare, the recovery of what has been lost is a dominant theme. His final expression of it is *The Tempest*. The editors of the First Folio put *The Tempest* at the beginning of the whole book, although it was almost certainly either the last or the last but one to be written by Shakespeare. They may have meant that the understanding of this play can give a key to all the rest.

Prospero, Duke of Milan, gave most of his time to study, and entrusted the tasks of rulership largely to his brother Antonio. For Shakespeare, rulership is a sacred duty; to delegate it, or to divide it, leads almost always to misfortune. And so it is here. Antonio acquires the taste for power and conspires with the King of Naples to overthrow Prospero. He is successful, and Prospero and his infant daughter, Miranda, are put into a small unseaworthy boat and left out in the open sea to drown. Twelve years later, the King of Naples is returning from the marriage of his daughter in Africa, accompanied by Antonio. Their ship is caught in a great storm and it is here that the play begins.

The King of Naples and his company are threatened with the death to which they had abandoned Prospero and Miranda, whom they seem to have forgotten. For them this tempest is not an ending, but a beginning – as it has been for Lear, who in his exposure to the storm first learned compassion, and to Pericles, who in a storm at sea learned of his wife's death and his daughter's birth.

Prospero did not perish, however. He and Miranda were cast upon an island and there his study has led to the mastery of good magical powers. Through these he has raised the storm that threatens the Duke Alonzo and his own brother Antonio. But through these he will bring them safely to shore when their ship appears wrecked and guide their further destinies.

The Duke of Naples has a son, Ferdinand. He comes alone to shore and believes that his father and all the rest are dead. He hears music, and a voice singing: it is Ariel, the noble, airy spirit who serves Prospero. Here the theme of the drowned bodies deep in the sea, which Clarence described in his dream, appears once more, but in a very different mood. Ariel sings of precious stones, but they do not mock the dead bodies of men. The bodies themselves are transformed into them, bones to coral, eyes to pearl.

To the precious stones, man has a mysterious relationship. In the book of Nature they are the real parables of what his senses, and indeed his whole physical body, can be like when they recover the purity that God has intended for them.

Thus are the precious stones used in the great Johannine picture of the New Jerusalem. In *King Lear*, a play that has so much to do with blindness in body and in soul, Cordelia's eyes are compared to diamonds that weep pearls. She sees clearly, even in grief; her eyes are those that all men have, but do not have the courage to use. Such powers of vision the father of Ferdinand, the king who was blindly willing to share in the overthrow of Prospero, is now to develop.

What then is Shakespeare describing in the events that happen on Prospero's island? It is a condition that follows the tempest; a realm of incorporeal music, where the soul is born afresh. All that happens after the first scene can be regarded as a reflection of the life of the soul after death.

Prospero has suffered the same kind of fate as Hamlet's father: a trusted brother has taken away his power and intended his death. But he does not seek the destruction of this brother. He does not say, like the ghosts to Richard III, 'Despair and die!' Antonio is to be led upon a different path.

Among the courtiers of the King of Naples there is an old and wise adviser, Gonzalo, who had secretly helped Prospero at the time of his downfall, with food, clothing, and the precious books. After the shipwreck, Gonzalo appears as the only one among those who are in the King of Naples company, who is able to speak with real hope. What he says can indeed appear at first trivial and irrelevant, and the others indeed mock his efforts. He speaks of the freshness of their wedding garments, unspoiled by the storm, of the abundant green grass on the island, and of 'Widow Dido'. In everything that he says he is offering his companions a clue to the experiences that are before them. As an outstanding interpreter of *The Tempest*, Mr Colin Still has pointed out that the King of Naples is upon a journey that takes a similar course to that of Aeneas when he left Dido at Carthage. Before long Aeneas was to descend into the realms of the shades and to see there the silent form of Dido, broken-hearted by his act. The King of Naples and the rest had forgotten that one day they would have to meet those they had injured. Gonzalo seeks gently to remind them.

It is the work of Ariel to face them with the full meaning of what they have done. After long wanderings, the king and his companions see a magical banquet spread out before them. But they are not permitted to partake of it. Food and drink vanish, and Ariel stands before them as a spirit of judgment, denouncing the evils they have done and the evils some of them still intend. These are not injuries only to men; earth, sea and sky have also been outraged by them, and will pursue them with their storms, unless these men change their ways.

Very delicately Shakespeare here approaches the mystery of the Last Supper, in which the living and the dead can join – but which must be preceded by sacrifice, the turning of mind and heart and will in humble self-knowledge towards the Ground of the World.

The king and his companions cannot at first fully understand the great words and pictures with which they are confronted. They are seized by a kind of bewildered desperation, and each of the guilty souls needs another, more peaceful companion, to guard and watch over him. With the name of Prospero thundering in their ears from the realm of the elements, they come into the presence of Prospero himself. By the sight of them Prospero is moved, as Ariel has said he would be, to deep compassion for them. He can solemnly forgive the injuries he has suffered, can reclaim his dukedom, and can restore Ferdinand, now betrothed to Miranda, to his father. As at the end of *Cymbeline*, there is peace and order – with the opportunity for human souls to be released from the prison into which they have made themselves, and to look deeply into the destinies of others. As by the jailer in Cymbeline, a simple but far-reaching summing-up is given by Stephano, the king's drunken butler:

> Every man shift for all the rest, and let no man take care
> for himself, for all is but fortune. (V.i.256)

When destiny is woven in the spiritual world, each soul must concern himself with all the rest and accept the concern of all the rest for him. The illusion of separateness falls away and the individual spirit recognises that he is indeed his brother's keeper.

In what was probably the very last of Shakespeare's plays, though it may not have been written entirely by him, he returned to the history of his own country. Here, in *Henry VIII*, there is no magic, no Ariel, and no Caliban, but men and women who seek to use and master the Ariel and the Caliban within themselves.

Once in this play, however, heaven opens. The rejected queen, Katherine of Aragon, is near to death. She has completely forgiven the king, who has caused her so much suffering, and is even able to wish peace to the soul of Wolsey, whom she has hated most among men. She is lonely, relatively poor, and entirely powerless. She asks for music, and speaks of:

> meditating
> On that celestial harmony I go to. (IV.ii.79)

As the music plays sadly and solemnly, Katherine falls asleep. There come to her six 'Personages' in white robes, with golden faces. They make a dance about her and hold a garland above her head. When they have gone, and she awakens, she calls them 'spirits of peace'. She asks her attendants:

> Saw you not, even now, a blessed troop
> Invite me to a banquet; whose bright faces
> Cast thousand beams upon me, like the sun? (V.ii.97–99)

Here again the spiritual world offers a banquet, and no Ariel need stand in judgment to hinder her from sharing in it.

In such ways do the pictures given by Shakespeare develop, and complete, one another.

The Two Messiahs
Ormond Edwards

Ormond Edwards (1928–2009) was ordained in 1960 and worked in London and Aberdeen. His book The Time of Christ: A Chronology of the Incarnation, *presented the results of his extensive research into the chronology of the gospels. In this article he looks at the Dead Sea Scrolls and the Messianic expectations of the Essenes who were expecting* two *Messiahs: a Messiah of Aaron and a Messiah of Israel, a priestly Messiah and a kingly Messiah.*

It is now ten years since the first translations of the Dead Sea Scrolls appeared. In *More Light on the Dead Sea Scrolls* (Secker & Warburg, 1958), Dr Millar Burrows surveyed the vast field of specialist studies on the finds. When he writes, 'No aspect of the Qumran theology has evoked more discussion than its Messianic beliefs', it would have to be admitted that their great significance has not been widely grasped. In fact, the Messianic expectations of the Essenes supply a vital key to the Christmas stories in the gospels.

The Qumran Community lived in expectation of the coming of two Messiahs preceded by the Prophet: 'until there shall come the Prophet and the Messiahs of Aaron and Israel' (The Community Rule from Vermes' translation of the *Manual of Discipline* in the Pelican series). Dr Burrows suggests that where the Damascus Document speaks three times of a single Messiah of, or from, Aaron and Israel, this may have been an emendation of a later scribe to whom the idea of two Messiahs was not familiar. Most scholars, he continues, agree that there will be two anointed ones and that the terms Aaron and Israel refer respectively to the priesthood and the laity. In other words there will be a priestly Messiah and a lay Messiah, an anointed high priest and an anointed king. In his commentary on the Gospel of Matthew (Peake, Nelson, 1962), Stendahl unequivocally relates the expectation of the Essenes to the genealogy in 1:17, which he says also makes clear Matthew's intention:

> Abraham and David are the significant ancestors. There is no interest in anything beyond Abraham, the father of the Israelites. And Jesus is of royal descent. He is a son of David. Among the three Messianic figures of the Qumran community, the Prophet, the Messiah of Aaron and the Messiah of Israel, the genealogy in St. Matthew identifies him with the last, the royal and Davidic, the non-priestly Messiah.

Elsewhere it has been pointed out that St Luke describes the family of Mary as among the 'daughters of Aaron'. The two nativity accounts correspond exactly to the Qumran expectation of two Messiahs. But before the fact can be accepted that two different events were described by Matthew and Luke, it must be shown how there could be only one Messiah at the Baptism.

Between the nativity and the baptism in the Jordan, the gospels describe one scene and one scene only, that of the twelve-year-old Jesus in the Temple. More precisely Luke describes the happening, whereas Matthew at this point is silent. The dramatic psychological change in the child is certainly consonant with the concentration of the Messianic promise upon him. Thereafter, the gospels are silent on the Messiah of Israel. The Messiah of Israel, in the language of the scrolls, becomes subordinate to the Messiah of Aaron. This was a very well defined expectation of what would take place at the Messianic Banquet.

The gospels show the divine work of the Christ beginning with the baptism. In this sphere the scrolls rise to a new level of comprehension. They speak of a divine begetting of the Messiah, and we are referred to Psalm 2:7 (by Cross): 'You are my son, today I have begotten you.' This reading is a reminder that a similar breakthrough to a universal conception of the Messiah is particularly clearly expressed in some variants of Psalm 110:3. Justin's version reads 'In the splendour of the holy ones before the morning star, have I begotten thee.'

The three stages we have been describing are found in archetypal clarity in Isaiah 11:1–3, a favourite passage within the Essene community:

> There shall come forth a shoot
> from the stump of Jesse
> and a branch shall grow out of his roots.
> And the Spirit of the Lord shall rest upon him.

It could well be that the Essenes shared the later view of Epiphanius that their name was derived from that of the father of David, Jesse, of the town of Bethlehem. Nazareth and Nazarene (Matt. 2:23) both contain the branch (Nazer) that should spring from the axed tree of David and receive the gifts of the Holy Spirit.

To students of Rudolf Steiner's understanding of the gospels, who have long been familiar with this background to the gospels that is now so powerfully corroborated, a puzzle remains. How is it that in the two thousand years of Christianity, apart from a few very interesting pictures, the now traditional content of the Christmas festival, despite its manifold contradictions, has remained undisturbed by vital elements in the Christmas story. K. G. Kuhn in his article 'The Two Messiahs' (*The Scrolls and the New Testament*, S.C.M. Press, 1958) shows the procedure at work. He writes:

> It is exactly this concept that is found in the Testament of the Twelve Patriarchs. The understanding of the messianic concept in the Testament of the Twelve Patriarchs had for a long time been misdirected by the theory of R. H. Charles that the statements concerning a Messiah from the tribe of Levi and a Messiah from the tribe of Judah, both of which are found side by side in the Testament of the Twelve Patriarchs, were two competing concepts ... the Testament of the Twelve Patriarchs shows, with complete unanimity, the expectation of two Messiahs ... The priestly Messiah receives the highest place, the royal Messiah ranks second ... Thus, information about this very form of messianic expectations was available before it was found in the Qumran texts ... Had not Charles been so fully influential in this matter, the additional evidence of the scrolls were hardly necessary.

The finding of the scrolls has induced a standard of scholarship that is cautious of bending the facts to fit preconceived theories. That is their real importance.

The Trinity

Evelyn Francis Derry

Evelyn Francis Derry (1911–2000) was the first woman priest to be ordained in England in 1939. She was a prolific writer and worked in London throughout her life. She later wrote under the name of Evelyn Francis Capel. Here she tackles the difficult subject of the Trinity and monotheism.

When Whitsuntide has come and gone, the cycle of the festivals that are related to the incarnation, death and resurrection of Christ is complete. When we look back upon the picture made by the whole sequence, recognising that his was the deed of God performed among men, we realise that it was as significant for the inhabitants of the heavens as it is for the inhabitants of the earth. When we begin to ponder its heavenly aspect, we encounter the idea of God that has been born in human minds through Christianity: we contemplate the mystery of the Trinity. Today this idea has become a problem for many people, for in the course of centuries it has been made into a point of doctrine calling for explanation. In reality it should be now, as in early times, an idea that can be seen in the light of its own truth. When so seen, it is a source of insight into the meaning of Christ's deed for the divine world, from which he descended into the realm of earth.

To know the Godhead in the three aspects of the Father, Son and Holy Spirit is not a matter of a teaching that can be learnt, but of the mind's power of vision. We are not any of us able to have insight of this nature at all stages of our lifetime. We are incapable of it in childhood, but we develop the necessary powers of mind as a result of the changes that take place in us as we grow up. In other words, insight into the threefold nature of God is possible to all human souls when they have acquired the faculties proper to grown-up people. Little children are by nature full of faith in God and willing to see his handiwork in the abundant world around them. Older people may often learn from them such natural confidence in what is divine. It may disappear later, as the soul grows further into the body and the being of the child descends deeper into existence on earth. Nevertheless, most of the hardened, unbelieving older people have started their lives as natural worshippers of God, whether or not they were reared by God-fearing people. One may well wonder how this comes about, whether little children are born with illusions, which they later outgrow, or whether they have a wisdom at the beginning, which is afterwards lost. Such questions are speculation as long as one assumes that magically, out of nowhere, human souls come into existence at the same moment as their bodies. It is quite another matter if one realises that, when the body is born, the eternal soul passes out of one state of being into another. Before birth, the soul has dwelt among spiritual beings in the spheres of the heavens, from which it must depart when the hour comes to enter the human world on earth. Then one sees the natural awareness of what is divine in little children as the fading remembrance of the other life beyond the gate of birth. They know God, because they have only just left his presence and have not forgotten it, as have those whose childhood is far behind.

The world from which we have come at birth is the same as that into which we shall go at death. But we have forgotten from whence we came, and therefore we look ahead into the unknown as we journey towards the gate of death. In the divine world our souls have experienced, and will experience again, the oneness of God. Therefore, the young child, who is still half in that world, knows the One God. When our souls have entered with their full powers into the world of earth, we can experience the threefoldness of God. Neither is a contradiction of the other, but each is a half of the full cycle of human experience. From above, our souls behold the One God, from below the threefold being of Father, Son and Holy Spirit. Every human being may have both visions in due season, if he is able to pass rightly from childhood into maturity of soul on earth, and out again into the life beyond death.

Every properly grown-up person is capable of apprehending the Trinity but does not necessarily grasp and know the idea. This is in need of being discovered again in the present time because, for some time now, it has, under the influence proceeding from the Protestant Reformation, been more a theological principle than a living experience. During the age of the Reformation a great discovery was made – the value and importance of the single human personality. Previously its worth had been felt but little. Since that time the sense of personality has become increasingly precious to each succeeding generation. As individuals grew aware of their own oneness, they consequently directed their attention to the oneness, of the divine world. Prayer became the experience of the single personality addressing the One God. True as this was, and still is, only one aspect of the whole relationship between God and the human soul can be known after this fashion. It has been the typical Protestant temptation to take the part for the whole. This must inevitably prevent a vision of the Trinity from being found, although the necessary faculties have developed in the mind.

Today the time has come for a new discovery of soul. The image of the threefold Godhead is reflected in the human being. He is one and yet threefold. His self is aware, in the moving life of his soul, of forces of three kinds, those of thinking, feeling and willing. When he knows himself, he sees three spheres interweaving in his nature. In his head he finds the brain and the centre of the nervous system, of which the threads extend throughout his body. Here is concentrated his awareness of thinking. In his heart he feels the pulsing rhythm of his blood and in his breast the in- and out-streaming of the breath. Here he knows the restless surge of his feeling. His limbs are activated with energy that is fed from the centre of the digestive process. Here is the seat of his power of willing that streams through all parts of the body. Thus the onefold being finds himself to be a trinity.

Simple as such a description is, a great reality lies behind it that will have far-reaching consequences when it is discovered. The idea of the Trinity, in divine and human form, is most important to the spiritual understanding of modern people. It has been known, in one or another sense, from the beginning of Christianity. Before that time, the idea of the Godhead took two different forms. The Hebrews were chosen to cultivate and develop the conception of the One God. The divine guide who led them was Yahweh. He was not the ultimate Being who was spoken of by Christ as the Father; he was his representative reflecting the image of the One God whose revelation he made known to the people under his guidance. The other races, who were not Hebrews and who are called in the Bible the Gentiles or the heathens, perceived the manifoldness of God. They were conscious of the divine world, filled with many beings, whose activity created and nourished the life of men and women on earth. Behind these manifold and various gods was hidden the divine Unity, apprehended but known in thought only to the most enlightened among men. In those ancient times, people were commonly aware that they shared their existence with a whole multitude of spirits of varied character and powers. They worshipped the great gods, who from time to time appeared on earth to intervene in human affairs. They were familiar with the crowd of less exalted beings, who enlivened the elements of earth, water, air and fire. They were sensitive to the genius of each river and mountain, each ocean and each land. They honoured with sacred rites the spirits who presided in the households, and the members of the family shared with them the domestic hearth. In parts of the globe beyond Europe, this old consciousness of a world filled with a host of beings, who partake in the community of God's universe, still persists today. Those who practise such belief find themselves in contact with demons as much as with benevolent beings. They have to guard themselves against harmful influences and seek the assistance of those that work for good.

Those ancient people, who recognized the oneness of God, and those who beheld his manifoldness, each saw a part of the world-reality. When the turning point of time was reached and Christ became man, the hour had come for a new birth within evolution. His deed on earth created a reality in the universe that had not existed before. We know it, from our human standpoint, as the Trinity. By transforming the future destiny of the earthly world, Christ has brought about something new in the history of the heavens. Before his coming, the Godhead was not yet threefold. In the beginning, at the creation, the God spoke, pouring forth from the world within that which brought into being the world without. The Word, or Logos, was he whom we call the Son of God. At that time in evolution, the distinction between Father and Son was not yet made. The one was within the other. The Word poured out the divine creating power, in the service of the divine will working through the whole universe. 'The Word was with God.' They were united, indivisible, acting out of the unity of all spiritual beings in the Godhead.

Then the created world fell away from the spheres of the heavens. The presence of God was withdrawn from creation and the princes of evil unfolded their powers in the forsaken place of existence. Human souls found their destiny in this separated world, where death could penetrate into their nature and evil threaten to destroy them. To rescue the lost race of men, it was resolved in the divine world to send the saviour. He came, not to release men from the fallen world, but to bring them the power of his spirit to win from death and evil the fruit of freedom. He came to create within humanity on earth that which could nowhere be harvested in the spheres of the heavens. He came to transform the place of separation into that of opportunity, to change the weak and helpless human souls into sons and daughters of God, in whom death and evil would be overcome. When he descended into the body of Jesus at the baptism in Jordan, he left the divine world and entered the place from which the real presence of God had been withdrawn. Thereby his own being suffered separation, and he was born out of God into independent existence. Having been with God, he became man on earth. Through that event, he came to know himself as the Son of the Father God, who is in the heavens. In one of the gospels, two versions are to be found of the words that were heard from the heavens as the dove descended upon Jesus at his baptism. One of them reads: 'Thou art my beloved Son: this day have I begotten thee.' In the hour of incarnation, the spirit, who had lived at the beginning in the Logos, was born out of the being of the All Father and entered upon his Sonship. That which had been united since before time began was divided for the purpose of bringing salvation to humanity. When he who dwells in the heavens looked down and beheld departing from him the one who, until that hour, had been an innate, indivisible part of himself, he called him 'My Son'. When he who went forth from the realms of his true existence looked back to that from whence he came, he said: 'Father, who art in the heavens.'

After the baptism in Jordan, Christ Jesus walked with men on earth. Throughout this time the spirit of Christ was penetrating by stages into the bodily vessel offered to him by Jesus. As the process of incarnation continued, the Son of God entered further into the loneliness of earth existence. He prayed to the Father, and he taught those who followed him to pray. Only he can pray who recognises that he is separated from the Being to whom his prayer is directed. Where there is no separation, there is no need for prayer. The words recorded in the gospels, which the Son spoke while he was on earth to the Father in the heavens, are a testimony to the relation of the one to the other, which evolved in the course of Christ's life as man. The Son had to become increasingly self-existent. The climax was reached at the crucifixion. In the suffering on the cross, Christ penetrated more deeply than before into the body which he was about to lay aside in death. He reached the most profound experience of man's separation from his heavenly origins. He sank so far into the depths of loneliness from God that he could repeat the words of the despairing psalm which begins: 'My God, why hast thou forsaken me?' This hour of dark experience became illumined by the triumph of Christ's spirit. His strength was sufficient for the struggle. The light of the Son of God prevailed in the darkness. The glory of the Son's spiritual being shone into the land of shadows as he descended into death. Never before had he had to undertake so much out of the might of his self-existence. Another interpretation of the words quoted from the psalm reads: 'My God, how hast thou glorified me.' To what glory had his Sonship flowered! Contradictory as the two interpretations sound, they are actually the shadow-side and the light-side of the same happening.

The Son invaded the realm where death is really present, the place most deeply opposite to the life-filled heights of the heavens. Following the will of the Father, drinking to the end the cup that he had been given (Jn 18), he rose again, uniting his spirit with this world that had fallen under the dominion of the powers he had vanquished. The earthly world became, by his resurrection, the kingdom of the Son. At Eastertime he took up his abode there and entered upon his kingship. After the forty days of the resurrection, those who were with him saw him depart, ascending through the doorway of the clouds into heaven. Though he left their sight, he did not disappear from his kingdom. His spirit expanded from the earth, without leaving it, to unite again with the universe. The Son returned to the Father, having overcome death and saved from destruction man, the lost child of God. He restored the earth to the heavenly community of the stars, from which it had for so long been alienated. The Sonship that had been initiated, tried and made true on earth was confirmed and made real in the divine world. The Son was united again with the Father in the Heavens. One part of the Trinity had become a fact in the universe.

Later, at Whitsuntide, the Holy Spirit was given to the apostles. They were assembled, with Mary, in the upper room on the first day of the week when the Spirit descended in a great cosmic thunderstorm. They heard the rushing wind and saw the tongues of lightning strike down upon every head. The Spirit quickened within every heart, and living words poured from every mouth. The Comforter, the one who had been promised, who had been sent to help, had come. As the Son God had been born in the descent from heaven to earth at the baptism in Jordan, so the Spirit God came forth from the Father when the tongues of fire entered the hearts of the apostles. The third person of the Trinity began his separate existence when he came to make his dwelling in the souls of men.

The Holy Spirit had in earlier times worked among men, sending inspiration from the heavens above where he dwelt. He was closely related to the Son, overshadowing his being during his life on earth. At Whitsuntide a new evolution began within the course of the divine existence. He became the offering made through the Son by the Father to human souls, for the sake of their salvation. Christ had performed the deed that changed history; the Holy Spirit brought the force of enlightenment, through which the minds of men should be enabled to grasp and understand it. Christ had given to human souls the inner power of the true self, by which they should grow, in the course of their evolution, into the likeness of the resurrected man that he had revealed in himself. The Holy Spirit came to give clear vision for the Christian ideal and to kindle the flames of enthusiasm in human hearts.

The Holy Spirit is the helper of human souls. In the beginning, the sons of men were created by the Spirit of God. The power of the creation was sufficient to maintain their existence for part of their history, but not until its completion. Men were weakened by the sickness of sin and infected with the forces of death. A new power of spirit, capable of healing their nature from within was bestowed upon them by the grace of the Father and the Son. A new, living impulse has been sent down from the heights of the heavens, which penetrates into the inmost parts of human souls, overcoming their weakness, healing them from the ills produced by sin and temptation. A wellspring of healing force is hidden within them, poor and weak as they may nevertheless appear on the surface.

At one time the picture for the Holy Spirit was the dove, the pure white bird flying down from the door of heaven, the messenger of divine inspiration. At Whitsuntide he came in the guise of tongues of flame. Since that event he lives on earth as inner light and warmth in human souls. The future picture of the Holy Spirit will be in human form. He is still in the process of becoming one with the being of humanity. The Trinity will come to fruition at the end of time, when Man will have attained resurrection. A part of the history of the Son and a still larger part of the history of the Spirit lie in the future, involved with the coming destiny of humanity. The Son has passed through birth, death, resurrection and ascension. The Holy Spirit has been little more than born. A great unfolding of his power is still to come. The Trinity as a whole is in the process of evolving towards that which shall be in the future.

For the sake of humanity, and so that salvation shall be achieved on earth, the Godhead has become threefold. Father and Son and Holy Spirit have become three in the revelation they have poured out into the world of men. In the life we had before birth, we knew the presence of God, his oneness filling the heavens. Here on earth we see his working in ourselves. In the substance of our existence we recognise the Father. In the creating power within us, we feel the Son. In the light shining in our consciousness, we know the Holy Spirit. We behold in the Trinity the gift of God to humanity on earth. That which exists in us, that which creates in us, that which enlightens us is the divine that has been made Three in One and One in Three for the sake of our salvation. God offers himself to human souls as the Father, as the Son and as the Holy Spirit.

1970s

Abraham Lincoln: Servant of Michael

Donald Perkins

Born in England, Donald Perkins (1903–92) was a minister of the Congregational Church. He was introduced to anthroposophy through hearing Karl König lecture, and this led ultimately to him resigning from his position and becoming a priest of The Christian Community in 1946. He was full of enthusiasm and zest for life, and had a great love of the English language and literature.

At the time of Lincoln's birth America was a new nation. She had declared her independence in 1776, she had been conceived in liberty and was still inspired by the memory of the great Washington. But she was by no means established as a nation and there were alien forces that sought to destroy her. In 1860, when Lincoln was fifty-one, there were thirty-three states, each different from the others, each claiming, in a sense, its own sovereignty. Indeed, the Declaration of Independence stated *not* that 'these united colonies are and of a right ought to be a free and independent *Nation*', but 'free and independent *States*.'

The greatest division, however, was between the North and the South. There were differences of soil and climate. In the North industrial life, which so dominates the America of today, was rapidly developing. Here was a race of embryonic businessmen. In the South were the great plantations, the large houses, the culture of those who loved the easy-going country life. A new world was coming into being which the Northern states had accepted, but which the Southern states had refused even to acknowledge. They were steeped in a tradition of which they were proud. There was no wish to change. Withal, in the South, there were the slaves, imported from Africa, whereas the North was abolitionist. The Northerner looked down on the Southerner and his general dislike tended to focus itself on slavery. The South bitterly resented what they regarded as interference by the North, that is by an alien society, in their way of life. Furthermore, there were eighteen states in the North and fifteen in the South. The South was in the minority within Congress. The election of 1860, it is reported, left the South in the absolute political power of the North. It is not difficult to understand that an increasing number of Southerners came to feel that the only solution to the unbearable situation was separation from the North and the founding of an independent nation.

In 1860 South Carolina passed a formal resolution of secession, dissolving the union of the United States of America. In 1861 Jefferson Davis was elected president of the *Confederate* States of America three weeks before Abraham Lincoln was elected president of the United States in Washington. On April 12, 1861, the South Carolinians fired on Fort Sumter, the 'Stars and Stripes' was pulled down with its surrender and the terrible American Civil War started.

The war lasted four years and is recognised as the greatest and most bloody conflict humanity had then known in the whole course of its history. Over 600,000 Americans died – 360,000 Northerners and 260,000 Southerners. It was a civil war, brother fought brother, and the man who was called by destiny to carry the burden of this terrible struggle was Abraham Lincoln – the man of peace, the deeply compassionate. As Phillips Brooks expresses it:

> The only wonder is that only one brave, fearless man
> came forth to cast himself, almost single-handed, with a hopeless hope,
> against the proud power that he hated,
> and to trust the influence of a soul marching on into the
> history of his countrymen to stir them to a vindication of
> the truth he loved.

It is generally believed that the war was fought for the abolition of slavery. This is not strictly true. Abraham Lincoln fought this war to *preserve the Union.* It was in 1854 that Lincoln made his position clear and he never departed from it. He said then that he did not question the constitutional right of the South to keep slaves, but

... slavery is founded on the selfishness of man's nature, opposition to it on his love of justice. These principles are in eternal antagonism, and when brought into collision so fiercely as slavery extension brings them, shocks and throes and convulsions must ceaselessly follow.

It was much earlier, when he was an unknown lumberman, that on a visit to a certain Southern town he attended a slave market with his companion. He said to his friend, 'If ever I get a chance to smash this sort of thing, I'll smash it and I'll smash it hard.' There is no question concerning Lincoln's attitude to slavery, but during the war, in 1862, he wrote:

My paramount object in this struggle is to save the Union, and is not either to save or destroy slavery. If I could save the Union without freeing any slave, I would do it; and if I could do it by freeing all the slaves, I would do it; and if I could do it by freeing some and leaving others alone, I would also do that. What I do about slavery and the coloured race, I do because I believe it helps to save this Union; and what I forbear, I forbear because I do not believe it would help to save the Union ... I have here stated my purpose according to my view of official duty, and I intend no modification of my oft expressed personal wish that all men, everywhere, should be free.

On November 19, 1863, part of the great battlefield of Gettysburg was dedicated as a military cemetery. The official speech was given by one of America's greatest orators, Edward Everett. The speech, on the subject of rebellion, was 'long, learned and voluminous', and it lasted two hours! Lincoln was present because he was president and, of course, he was expected to speak. He did so when Everett had finished. Here are the words he spoke. Most of us, I am sure, have heard them before; some of us may even know them by heart. In any case it is good that we should be reminded of them:

Four score and seven years ago our fathers brought forth, on this continent, a new nation, conceived in liberty and dedicated to the proposition that all men are created equal. Now we are engaged in a great civil war, testing whether that nation, or any nation so conceived, and so dedicated, can long endure. We are met on a great battlefield of that war. We have come to dedicate a portion of that field as a final resting place for those who here gave their lives that that nation might live. It is altogether fitting and proper that we should do this. But, in a larger sense, we cannot dedicate, we cannot consecrate, we cannot hallow this ground. The brave men, living and dead, who struggled here, have consecrated it far above our poor power to add or detract. The world will little note, nor long remember, what we say here, but it can never forget what they did here. It is for us the living, rather, to be dedicated here to the unfinished work which they who fought here have thus far so nobly advanced. It is rather for us to be here dedicated to the great task remaining before us – that from these honoured dead we take increased devotion to that cause to which they gave the last full measure of devotion – that we here highly resolve that these dead shall not have died in vain; that this nation, under God, shall have a new birth of freedom, and that government of the people, by the people, for the people, shall not perish from the earth.

The words of Everett have been forgotten long ago, but this contribution of Lincoln, so brief, so simple, has become one of the jewels of the English language. The address, its wording, its content, even its brevity, the whole circumstances in which it was delivered, have been the subject of considerable study. But all I want us to notice here is that through this address we are able to see the man, Lincoln, and to hear the voice of Michael.

We learn from Rudolf Steiner that the archangel Michael concerns himself with 'what men create out of the spirit, that he lives with the consequences of all that men create.' Michael is the spiritual hero of freedom. He allows men to perform deeds and then takes what becomes of those deeds. He sternly rejects all that arises out of human heredity, all separating elements such as language, colour, nationalism. Men are human beings, sons of God, whatever their nation, colour or creed, and as human beings they must find individual freedom in unity.

And for what did Lincoln strive? What was the great driving impulse of his whole life? He dreamed of a state, a community, that would be the highest expression of our common humanity, and, because we know that Christ is the spirit of true humanity, we can say a Christian nation, a Christian community of peoples.

George Washington was present at the conception of this nation. Abraham Lincoln brought it to birth. He was born in Kentucky on February 12, 1809, the same day as that upon which Charles Darwin was born. He was the son of Thomas

Lincoln, a backwoodsman. As far as we can judge, he owed little to heredity. He was born in a log cabin and in log cabins he lived through his childhood and youth. His schooling altogether lasted not more than twelve months. In the words of James Bryce:

> Born in rude and abject poverty, he had never any education, except what he gave himself, till he was approaching manhood. Not even books wherewith to inform and train his mind were within his reach ... He knew few authors in general literature, though he knew those thoroughly ... He had only the faintest acquaintance with European history or with any branch of philosophy.

In no sense was he orthodox or traditional. He was no churchman. But let him speak for himself:

> I am not a Christian. God knows I would be one, but I have carefully read the Bible and I do not understand this book. I know there is a God and that he hates slavery. I see the storm coming and I know that his hand is in it. If he has a place and work for me, and I think he has, I believe I am ready. I am nothing, but truth is everything. I know I am right, because I know liberty is right, for Christ teaches it, and Christ is God.

When Lincoln says that he is not a Christian he means that he is not orthodox. There is something reminiscent of John the Baptist, the great preparer of the way for the coming of the Christ in Jesus, who said when questioned: 'I am not; I am not the Christ. I am a voice crying in the desert, crying in the loneliness – prepare ye the way of the Lord.'

'I am not,' says Lincoln, 'I am nothing.' Because this was true he became the channel of the spirit who, in so many of us, despite our sincerity, is impeded by egotism and its many manifestations. 'If he has a place and work for me.' He becomes slowly conscious of the presence of the spirit within his soul. He recognises that what he has received from heredity, from society, from the schools is, indeed, nothing. It does not count or counts very little. It was not through anything he was in himself that he was able to make his way to the White House, and to champion a policy successfully to its recognition and acceptance in spite of the tremendous forces ranged against him, through one of the greatest crises in world history. It was not the man Lincoln whom his opponents found invulnerable, but Michael himself whose servant this man was.

You can read of the trials through which he passed in one or other of the biographies. You can read how he remained through storm and calm, through failure and success, through defeat and victory, calm, confident, immovable, 'his white plume unspotted', his faith unchanged. We may think of Rudolf Steiner's words:

> In the Michael Age men of a pronounced character and personality will have this character and personality through what they bring to expression from their understanding of the spiritual worlds.

'Truth is everything, I am nothing.' We are told by Rudolf Steiner that the meaning of earth existence is in this: that we find our relation to truth. It is interesting to note that Lincoln was never regarded, as far as I know, as being a man of personal ambition. He followed his star. The dragon forces were slain by the sword of his word, by the rapier thrust of his glance; yet, from his eyes, there always streamed the light of understanding and sympathy, of compassion for all men. Through him was prepared not only a new nation, but a new conception of human worth and human community.

I have referred to 'the sword of his word'. Lincoln was not an orator as Everett and many of his colleagues were, yet we feel that his speeches were more than oratory. He once said:

> I do not emit ideas as rapidly as others, because I am compelled by nature to speak slowly, but when I do throw off a thought, it seems to me, that it comes with some effort, it has force enough to cut its way and travel a greater distance.

The Gettysburg speech is, perhaps, the finest example. There is no rhetoric, no striving for effect. The speech is simple, and we can imagine the quiet of its delivery. As James Bryce comments:

> The speech states certain truths and principles in phrases so aptly chosen and so forcible that one feels as though those truths could have been conveyed in no other words, and as if this deliverance of them were made for all time.

Lincoln's speeches were not learned or clever, they were never abstract, but through them flashed the sword of the fiery Prince of Thought who is the silent angel. He speaks very little.

When I say that Lincoln owed little to heredity I do not wish to be misunderstood. He owed his strong, robust body to the healthy pioneer stock from which he came. He became an instrument of the spirit, but this instrument was prepared, forged and tempered through the experiences of his early years in Kentucky, Indiana and Illinois. The poverty, the hard living in log cabins, the heavy manual work which brought him into close contact with nature, the disappointments and the tears – all left their mark. The people with whom he lived and worked and identified himself in those formative years were rude and rough, with neither polish nor culture, but they were real people. 'Had Lincoln been a man of high culture,' wrote Herndon, 'had he been a man of polish and literary taste, he might have been a good country lawyer, that's all.'

I have already likened Lincoln to John the Baptist. Here again there is a striking similarity. He was the rough man of the wilderness. He was a voice crying aloud, to prepare the way:

> I am not a master of language: I have not a fine education; I am not capable of entering into a disquisition upon dialectics, (as I believe you call it), I don't care to quibble as regard to words ... I hope that the lamp of liberty will burn in your bosoms until there shall no longer be a doubt that all men are created free and equal.

Herndon goes on to say:

> Lincoln's perceptions were slow, cold, precise and exact. Everything came to Lincoln clean and clear cut, stripped of all extraneous matter whatsoever. Everything came to him in its precise shape, gravity and colour. No lurking illusion, delusion, error, ever passed unchallenged or undetected over the threshold of his mind. Names to him were nothing and titles nought; assumptions always standing back abashed before his cold glare. In his mental view he crushed the unreal, the hollow and the sham.

Lincoln won a mighty battle against the adversary. He did not defeat him, for as we are fully aware the battle goes on. He freed the slaves, gave them citizenship, and at the same time preserved the unity of a nation, a nation in whose future world role Lincoln believed implicitly. Nothing could resist the sword of Michael and his servant, this gaunt, uncouth, uncultured giant of the wilderness.

After the war he turned to the colossal task of restoring his devastated country. But at the beginning of this task, on Good Friday, April 14, 1865, he was assassinated. On the evening of that day, he and Mrs Lincoln went to the theatre. Here is the brief but moving record of James Adams (from his book *The Epic of America* from which I have already quoted in the course of this article):

> He sat in his box, happy and content, the long vigil ended by the side of his broken Union, now reunited, though with wounds which he intended to heal. All eyes were on the stage. Suddenly a shot rang through the auditorium. Lincoln fell forward, unconscious and dying. A half-crazed assassin, waving a knife, leaped from the box to the stage, shouted '*Sic semper tyrannis*' and fled through the stage door to a waiting horse. The president was carried to a nearby house, laid on a bed, and without regaining consciousness, but with a look of perfect peace and rest on his worn features, passed away in the early morning. The war was won; the Union preserved; but peace and love and honesty and brotherly kindness had fled with Lincoln's soul.

But this must not remain the last word. There has always been in America an element that seeks to practice and develop these qualities, and in this century we have only to remember the supporters of Dr Martin Luther King, whose death, one hundred years later, so nearly resembled Lincoln's own. The outcome of steadfast devotion to the cause of unity and the brotherhood of Man.

The Origins of Celtic Christianity

Michael Tapp

Self-effacing and modest, Michael Tapp (1933–2014) had a penetrating intellect and a capacity to see what was needed in any given situation. Though not a world traveller, and firmly rooted in England, he responded to the initiative of people in Australia and New Zealand by moving there to help found congregations in Sydney and Auckland. In this article he presents a brief history of the development of Celtic Christianity and the influences upon it of two particular streams: the druidic and the monastic stream.

The Dark Ages are aptly named, not because they were in themselves dark but because it is so difficult for us to get a clear picture of them. Such terms as 'tribes' and 'barbarians' leave one with an impression of peoples who were primitive and uncultured with the result that the history of these times has in the past been regarded as an insignificant backwater. This is fortunately no longer the case today and much painstaking scholarship, making the most of the meagre material available, is establishing a quite different picture.

Celtic Christianity is especially difficult to study because of the interrelationship between historical and legendary sources, but no attempt will be made in this article to evaluate legendary sources, not because they are unimportant but because it is useful to see what historical research alone can provide as a picture of those early days. It may be that this historical picture itself helps towards an understanding of those sources that are not immediately acceptable to the historian.

First it is necessary to have an historical framework. This can be brief. Britain, including Wales, but excluding Scotland and Ireland, was part of the Roman Empire from the second half of the first century until the final departure of the Roman armies in 410. These were withdrawn to help cope with the increasingly serious inroads made by people invading from the east, which reached crisis level in 409 with the sack of Rome. Roman civilisation left little impact on Britain apart from roads and what was to be mediated by the Church. The British as a whole had remained Celtic speaking and in Scotland and Ireland had also retained their Celtic kingships. But in England, Celtic civilisation was not to survive. Already before the departure of the Romans, Saxon invaders were appearing on the east coast and by the middle of the fifth century, they were settling and pushing westwards. They were held up for a considerable time by a British general, held to be the historical Arthur, following his victory at the battle of Mount Badon (*c.* 500); but a century later the Saxon settlement was virtually complete.

It is primarily the fifth century in which we are interested. Christianity was already widespread in Britain. A year after the Edict of Milan (313), which established Christianity as a permitted religion, three British bishops are reported to have attended a synod at Aries in Gaul, and there is plenty of other evidence, such as Christian motifs in mosaics in Roman villas, to show the existence of Christianity and also to show that it was in close contact with the church in Gaul. But no exact dates can be put to this evidence.

With the departure of the Roman armies in 410, there appears to have been more traffic between the churches in Gaul and Britain. One particular reason for this was that a British monk had introduced ideas into the church that were pronounced heretical and which led Augustine of Hippo in his last years to formulate more precisely his views on original sin, free will and predestination. The monk was Pelagius. Maybe his ideas became particularly widespread in Britain. Whether this was so or not, the church in Gaul sent the Bishop of Auxerre, Germanus, on a mission to Britain in 429 to combat the heresy. He also proved a useful general in combating the Picts, Scots and Saxons.

This was also about the time that Patrick started his Irish mission. A recent book by R. P. C. Hanson (*St Patrick: His Origins and Career*) makes a thorough study of the problems involved in trying to ascertain the facts of Patrick's work. The only known facts come in Patrick's own writings. He tells us of his father and grandfather, both Christians, and of their well-to-do circumstances, but gives no dates or places. Hanson's conclusion is that Patrick was probably born around 390 and possibly in southwest England. When he was nearly sixteen, the estate was raided by a party of Irish and he was taken away by them and sold as a slave in Ireland. Here he looked after cattle. After six years he escaped. In the past it was assumed he escaped to Gaul, but Hanson argues that this was not the case and that there is every indication that Patrick was purely a product of the British church. He was not well educated, but evidently effective and practical. He was in his forties before he returned to Ireland as a bishop where his work had significant results. He organised the church according to the accepted pattern of Roman government, that is by bishops based on the more obvious population centres (though it would be difficult to speak of these in Ireland as on the Continent). He died about 460. In the years that followed, Ireland was cut off from the rest of Britain by the Saxon invasions. It is in these years that a considerable transformation must have occurred within the Irish Church, for when it reappears, the essentially Roman episcopal organisation has disappeared and in its place we find a host of new monastic settlements, each independent or at the most dependent on a mother house, owing allegiance to an abbot. For most practical purposes, the bishops were secondary to the abbots. It is from this new basis that there develops the Celtic Church as we understand it, with its own characteristic life and culture.

To try and form a picture as to how this could have come about, we have to turn to a study of two particular subjects, the druids and monasticism.

Much detective work has been expended on the sources that give us information on the druids. This has been summarised by Nora K. Chadwick (*The Druids,* University of Wales Press, 1966). There are two main traditions in Latin literature. The first is to be found in the writings of Caesar, Pliny, Tacitus and others, and is essentially rather hostile in that the Romans sought a justification for their own policy of exterminating the druids. No doubt the druids were subversive, but these authors seek to discredit them for other reasons, such as their participation in human sacrifice. None of these authors had any first-hand information or experience of their subject. It appears that they derived their knowledge from Posidonius, the Greek statesman who lived in the first century BC and who himself travelled through Gaul. It is generally admitted that all such knowledge comes from a time when druid culture was in rapid decline and is not representative of the time when their influence was at its height. Even so, the information we learn from these sources is significant.

The different writers who tell us about the druids seem to have had slightly varying approaches, no doubt determined by the nature of their own interest. Pliny, for instance, is particularly interested in the druids as doctors and magicians and describes their medical activities in terms of magical practices. He also emphasises their connection to the world of nature, and the fact that their practices were associated with a forest cult. Caesar refers to the druids as the intellectual class of Gaul who were organised as a national body under an archdruid and who met once a year, probably near Chartres. They did not commit anything to writing in order to preserve their esoteric knowledge and also to keep their excellent memories from deteriorating. They were teachers, judges and prophets (or more properly, diviners). How the druids acted in priestly capacities is not clear. Their position seems to have been more general and all-embracing than what we would understand by priest, and it seems there were others who were more directly concerned with actual ritual practices.

It is with the teaching of the druids that we are mainly concerned here. Caesar tells us of their belief in the immortality of the soul and this is confirmed by other Roman writers who also mention the druids' belief in rebirth. In this, as in other details of the druids' teaching, there is a common link with the teaching of Pythagoras. It is not surprising that our other main source of tradition about the druids is Alexandria, which in the early Christian centuries was the place where the remaining spiritual knowledge of the ancient world and the young Church met, where Clement of Alexandria sought to harmonise the spirit of Greek philosophy with Christianity (as Philo had sought to harmonise it with Judaism earlier), where the revival of Plato's philosophy in its Neoplatonic form took place, and where Origen attempted his superhuman task of integrating the knowledge of the past as a whole with the new Christian message. It was only natural that the spirit of Alexandria would include the druids in its brotherhood. The sources of knowledge of the Alexandrians are older than those of Caesar and his contemporaries and go back possibly to the fourth century BC. The Alexandrians stress that the druids had a body of knowledge which went back far into the past. Clement of Alexandria states that Pythagoras himself gained his knowledge from the Gauls and other barbarians. We may safely deduce that Pythagoras indeed had sources of knowledge beyond the confines of the Mediterranean world and that his teaching represents a far older, more spiritual kind of knowledge in which other peoples also participated. It is clear that the druids, in their relative isolation, kept this knowledge alive and were therefore of special interest to those within the Church who sought to seek an understanding and harmony between their faith and the legacy of the past.

We do not have to agree with Nora Chadwick's conclusion that the ideas of the druids 'could be no more than the outer ripple on the circumference from the great centres of thought elsewhere', but rather imagine that the great teaching centres of the ancient world, among which we would have to include those of the druids, had a common spiritual source accessible to the great seers and teachers, whose knowledge, because of the common source, would be broadly similar. Thus, the similarity of the teaching of Pythagoras and the druids, while by no means excluding some physical transmission or exchange of knowledge, would be a clue to both being derived from spiritual sources.

Now we turn to monasticism. The beginning of the Christian monastic development is normally traced to the conversion of St Antony in 271 and to a literal interpretation of Christ's instructions to his disciples. Antony initiated the settlement of hermits in the Egyptian desert. It was not as lonely a life as one might imagine, but it did entail a rigorous discipline. The hermits had a fair amount of contact among themselves. Indeed, when Jerome visited them he found the over-stimulating atmosphere of the somewhat argumentative Egyptian monks altogether a bit too much, though he was cast in much the same mould himself. The first order for community living was formulated by Pachomius (286–346), who organised considerable communities of monks, also in Egypt. An important figure for our subject is Evagrius of Pontus (345–399) who had been trained in the Eastern Greek-speaking part of the Church and who had accepted a large part of the teachings of the Alexandrians, notably Origen and the Neoplatonists. He joined the monks in Egypt and it was no doubt partly due to him that the Eastern monks became famous for their Origenist leanings, a fact that was later to bring them much trouble when some of Origen's basic ideas (such as the pre-existence of the soul) came to be disputed in the Church. Another Eastern-trained teacher and writer, John Cassian, also spent a number of years in the Egyptian desert and what he learned there he then reported on and taught at the newly founded monasteries at Lerins and Provence in southern France in the fifth century. In his teaching he incorporated much of what he had learned of Evagrius' work. Thus, the teaching of the Alexandrians, related as it was to the older teaching of Pythagoras and the druids, reached southern France within the new monastic movement. This monastic movement was then to spread rapidly north and westwards. We can well imagine the impact this could have had on reaching the far Celtic west, for not only the knowledge, but also the monastic way of life had deep roots in the Celtic character.

That Patrick did not go to Gaul and meet this new wave seems entirely plausible. He was trained in Britain and went to Ireland before it arrived, and whereas the Saxon invasions in England would have prevented the expansion of the Christian life in any form (indeed, the Saxons had to be won for Christianity first), Ireland remained untouched and so, by some means, the new seed was planted on Irish soil, which proved to be immediately and spectacularly productive.

What was different in Ireland also gave Celtic Christianity its peculiar character. It had in common with the particular background of monasticism we have been looking at, the more cosmic outlook on man's nature and development, and the inborn intensity suited to monastic life. In addition, it had the natural separatist and independent attitude which reacted adversely to all forms of central authority, and it also had its own special relationship to the world of nature, which has remained a characteristic trait of the Celtic peoples even into this century.

If we accept that Patrick died about 460 and take into account that John Cassian was teaching in the first half of the fifth century, and that already before Patrick's death the British were becoming increasingly preoccupied with the Saxon invasions, we can see that it is altogether plausible that the new enthusiasm for monasticism would have reached the Celtic west sometime after this. We do not know any details as to when the seed was planted, we know only that from 520 onwards there was a rapid expansion of monastic settlements. Columba was born in 521 and without any warning we are in the age of the great Celtic saints.

1980s

Our Relationship with Those Who Have Died

Stanley Drake

Stanley Drake (1906–86) was ordained in 1939 and worked in London and Forest Row, Sussex. In 1962 he published Though You Die, *a thought-provoking book that dealt with life after death, at a time when the subject of death was rarely spoken about. In this article he looks at our connection with those who have died and how the funeral service of The Christian Community, which addresses itself to the continued existence of the one who has died, can help us orientate ourselves towards that person.*

A man has died. The funeral service has been read. The coffin has disappeared. The mourners – relatives, neighbours, friends, business associates – file out of the crematorium, look at the flowers, chat with those whom they know. A few close friends are invited back to the house for light refreshments. After a while the party breaks up and the widow is left with, perhaps, a sister-in-law, a daughter and a nephew who have come from a distance and stay the night.

But when they are gone the house is empty and the woman feels the full impact of the fact that she is now a widow. A reaction to the emotional strain of the last few days or weeks finally sets in. How is life to go on now? She will need the support of understanding friends to help her through this. If there are children to look after that helps fill the day; if there is a job to go to or a business to run, there is plenty to think about. But these do not answer the question: 'How do I live without my husband?' Or rather, as the question should really be put: 'How do I live *with* my husband now?'

The thought that once the funeral is over there is no more to be said or done is a prejudice that still persists in so many people and is hard to overcome. Even when the idea of a life after death is accepted with the mind, it requires persistent effort on the part of most people to make it a reality in terms of a relationship with one who has died. There are of course some people who by character and temperament and by the intensity of their human and spiritual relationship while alive, can immediately feel the presence of their departed partner in all aspects of their daily life. But all are not like that and in general the establishment of a new relationship on a different basis has to be worked at. Where does one start?

An established practice of prayer and meditation, including intercession for others, will be the way for some. But even that needs extension or intensification to meet the particular needs of personal bereavement.

Many people who attend a funeral service of The Christian Community are struck by the sense of reality it brings: a reality of the nearness of the departed and of the invisible world that they are now entering. Let us see what signposts this service gives us for the development of this new relationship. Firstly, we are reminded that our physical body, like everything else on the earth that has life, comes into existence, lives, and passes away:

> As for man, his days are like grass; he flourishes like a flower of the field;
> for the wind passes over it, and it is gone, and its place knows it no more.
> (Psalm 103)

But it is only the physical body that is like grass, for the soul now moves on to a new place of habitation: 'In my Father's house there are many rooms, if it was not so, I would have told you. I am going there to prepare a place for you.' (John 14:2). The soul is not lost or astray, but has an appropriate place allocated to it in the spiritual world according to the state of development it has reached. It is introduced into this world of 'departed' human spirits, of angels and higher beings, through an experience of the being of Christ.

An experience of light

It has been recorded many times how people nearing death, when the soul has already partly withdrawn from the body, become aware of an intense light. It is different from any earthly light, and at the same time appears to be a presence from which there emanates an atmosphere of love. This experience is described in Dr Raymond Moody's book *Life after Life* (Bantam Books, 1975), and again, most vividly, in Dr George Ritchie's book *Return from Tomorrow* (Chosen Books, 1978). In the latter, Dr Ritchie describes his own experience in a military hospital when, having recognised his own 'dead' body, he became aware of an intense brightness. He continues:

> Now I saw that it was not light, but a Man who had entered the room, or rather, a Man made out of light, though this seemed no more possible to my mind than the incredible intensity of the brightness that made up his form ... I got to my feet, and as I did there came the stupendous certainty: You are in the presence of the Son of God.

Differing descriptions of this experience of light will be given by individuals according to their religious convictions, but it is certainly in some sense a Christ experience. This is suggested too by the words of the Act of Consecration for the Dead (Memorial Service), which speaks of the reception of the soul 'out of the hand of Christ'. It is equally true that those who have stood in a relationship of love to the departing soul are waiting to receive it on the other side. It is not unlike the process of being born, where the birth is long expected, welcomed and rejoiced over.

Such facts are relevant to our relationship to the dead because it is important for us to be clear that an event which seems so dark and depressing for us, is, for the one who has departed, a release into a world of lightness and light. They realise the extent to which the physical body was a prison house. Therefore, while the grief and sorrow at parting is not to be denied and is natural and justified, to prolong this into a chronic state of wanting the other person back again is a drag and a hindrance to the soul in the other world. A new and more spiritual relationship is vital for the well-being of both.

The funeral service also indicates that our thoughts must raise themselves to the place where the soul is and that we follow him or her with our thoughts in their activities. This demands of us that we form some realistic picture of the conditions of existence in the other world.

In the writings of Rudolf Steiner we can find many descriptions of the relevant facts, but this knowledge may remain entirely intellectual. What is required is a vivid imagination that can form pictures of a non-material world in which time and space play no part. What a challenge! The difficulty of doing this is well illustrated in the writings of those who have had direct experience of the spiritual world or who receive messages from the other side. Either the pictures are so vague and misty that they do not mean very much or, if they rely too heavily on earthly imagery, we complain that they are too materialistic. It is an inevitable difficulty.

The dead are with us

Nevertheless the dead are with us, they are not thousands of miles away but infinitely close. In a lecture he gave in Nuremburg on February 10, 1918, Rudolf Steiner said:

> People today still find difficulties in acquiring knowledge of the spiritual world. The difficulties would soon solve themselves if a little more trouble were taken to become acquainted with its secrets. There are two ways of approach. One way leads to complete certainty of the eternal in one's own being. This knowledge ... will certainly be attained by those who have enough perseverance, along the path described in the book *Knowledge of the Higher Worlds* ... The other is what may be called direct intercourse with beings of the spiritual world ... Such intercourse is most certainly possible, but it presents greater difficulties than the first form of knowledge.

A simple start is, however, possible if we pay more attention to those moments when we are perfectly quiet and perfectly relaxed. These are likely to be just before we go to sleep and immediately on waking, before the impressions of the outer world call us back into the world of the everyday. In such moments we are on the borders of the spiritual world, from which indeed we have just come (or which we are about to enter), and not infrequently we have the experience, 'An idea has just come to me!'

Where did it come from?

Almost certainly from a soul with whom we are connected and who wishes to help us or to prompt us to some initiative. Of course, we are quite free to disregard such a 'hunch' (and in fact usually do!) but if we were more sensitive to them and more conscious of their origin, we might be more guided in our lives than we are. It is often by means of these 'hunches' that the sheltering power of the dead works in our lives.

Working in the spirit world

Another thought we may take from the funeral service is that the dead one is working in the realm to which he inclined his thoughts. He has a job. He is given a task in accordance with the talents he has developed on earth.

People often say, 'What a waste that a man with such gifts should die before his time!' In the economy of the spiritual world nothing is wasted. All experiences of an earthly life are fully evaluated and their fruits are applied according to the wisdom of higher beings. If a person has been a doctor or healer on this earth, he will be given healing tasks, if he has been a musician he will be creating music on the other plane, if he has performed some humble service, he will help other souls. This also means that a personality who has been closely identified with a joint work in community with others will have a continuing interest in their further activities. True, he can no longer take part in them, but his thoughts will be directed to them and that in itself may have an influence on those who are responsible for them.

But – and this is important – it is only we on the earth who can open the windows for them, only we who can make possible the lines of communication. All too often the dead would send helpful impulses to us, but we frustrate them because our eyes are so firmly fixed on the ground that we take no notice. We are so busy weeding that we do not see the swarm of swallows swirling over the rooftops.

Consciousness and memory

The need for a relationship with the dead is a two-way one and it depends on states of consciousness, for it is only the difference in our states of consciousness, not distance, that separates us. We do not want to lose the connection with someone with whom we have built up a relationship over the years. Our love and friendship remain but have to operate now on a different wavelength. We share memories with the one who has gone. They are a precious possession in the other world, for the soul lives with them and re-lives them vividly. We must remember the dead and our connection with them. To remember them, if only briefly, day by day in our prayers, is the minimum we can do.

No doubt some will object that all this thinking about the dead is rather morbid. It certainly would be if we fall into a melancholic, self-pitying brooding as a result, but not if it takes its place in a well-ordered balanced way of life. Judged by spiritual standards, our lives are mostly neither well-ordered nor balanced because we do not, or will not, leave enough time for the spiritual.

Angels and archangels

Our relationship with the dead is closely bound up with our relationship to the beings of the spiritual world, with angels, archangels and higher beings, right up to the cherubim and seraphim. These beings are very little in our waking consciousness, though we have very much to do with them when we are asleep, as Rudolf Steiner has described in very many of his lectures. Also, when we want to pray for the dead Steiner indicated that to address our prayer to the guardian angel (or angels) is spiritually correct. (See the meditation 'Spirits ever watchful' in *Verses and Meditations,* p. 205, and note 9 thereto.) To cultivate the thought of our guardian angel can be a step towards building that new relationship to one who has gone from us.

In concluding on this note I cannot do better than quote from Adam Bittleston's most helpful book, *Our Spiritual Companions* (Floris Books, 1980):

> If we on earth develop a clear and lively feeling for the spiritual hierarchies, this can strengthen the relationship between the living and the dead. It is our great task after death to find a right relationship to the beings above who serve the Good: it is not achieved all at once. The puzzling moods and impressions experienced by many people have often to do with this. As on earth, so after death, questions are not always answered at once; the effort to find an answer, the effort to learn, has a value in itself. For those who have died the external circumstances of those they have left behind are generally much less important than the extent to which those on earth grow to maturity.
>
> The dead look into our pain, into our sorrow, into our sense of failure; they watch what happens in us, as we can watch movements in a landscape. They see how in us acceptance of destiny and creative freedom are continually meeting; and they can be comforted by the kinship between their tasks and ours. If we begin to look towards the hierarchies with comprehension for their significance in our lives, we breathe with the dead a common light.

The Voice of Conscience in William Wilberforce

Stanley Drake

Stanley Drake (1906–86) joined The Christian Community in London in the 1930s. As well as many articles on translating the gospels, he wrote widely on English history. Here he looks at the struggles of William Wilberforce who was the driving force that led to the abolition of slavery in Britain's colonies, achieving final success only days before his death.

Conscience is one of the characteristic qualities of the individual human being. When Elijah experienced that the Lord was not in the wind and not in the fire but in the still small voice, he had the first premonition of the God within. Only with the coming of Christ and the giving of Holy Spirit could this become a fully conscious reality, but the working of conscience is so individual. It is related to person's ego, but its expression is modified by all those factors that go to make up a person's character: physical constitution, temperament, heredity, upbringing, religion and all that they bring over from earlier incarnations. The combination of all these factors can, on the one hand, virtually extinguish the effectiveness of conscience or, on the other hand, intensify it to the highest degree.

But corporate bodies, companies, councils, economic or political associations, governments, have no conscience. Their actions are determined solely by the aims for which they have been established. The French term, *Société anonyme*, gives expression to this. In an anonymous society no individual person is ultimately responsible. As such the society has no conscience.

Yet societies are made up of men and women who have consciences. How far can these consciences be made effective in the conduct of such bodies? This is a complicated question. Where decisions are taken by majority vote, the objector(s) on grounds of conscience can be simply outvoted. If decision is by consensus, rather more attention must be paid to them, but they can in the last resort be overruled. Are individuals then powerless? There are examples in history that show that they are not if they possess enough personality, persuasiveness, spiritual and moral courage, and immense determination and energy.

Such a man was William Wilberforce (1759–1833) who died 150 years ago on July 29, 1833. The son of a well-to-do Hull businessman, he was a weak child, tiny, frail and with poor eyesight. His father died when he was nine and he was sent to live with an aunt and uncle in London, who were friends of George Whitefield, the evangelist. When he was thirteen his mother called him back to Hull because she was afraid of his being influenced by his aunt and uncle to become a Methodist. He had musical gifts and a fine voice and already in his teens was growing into a charming young man. When he was seventeen, he went up to Cambridge and entered St John's College where, on the strength of money left to him by his grandfather, he had ample funds and led a life of 'sober dissipation'. His movements were very fast and he was seldom still. His conversation followed the same pattern. He would pick up an idea very quickly, play with it and turn to another, only to abandon it in its turn. All this was done with a speed and pleasure that entranced his listeners. He idled away his years at Cambridge but passed his exams (though without distinction) on the strength of his natural talent and quick mind.

He took an interest in politics and at twenty-one won one of the two parliamentary seats for Hull. It was customary then for candidates to pay their supporters £2 for a vote and a further £2 if they won. This election cost Wilberforce more than £8,000. William Pitt, who was to become his lifelong friend, entered parliament the same year and was Prime Minister by the time he was twenty-four. Pitt said of Wilberforce: 'he has the greatest natural eloquence of any man I ever knew.'

The turning point

An important development in Wilberforce's life took place in 1785 when he was twenty-six. In October 1784 he set out to travel on the continent with the Reverend Isaac Milner, Vice Chancellor of Cambridge University, as well as his mother, his sister and two 'ailing females'. They stayed for some time in Nice. The important thing for Wilberforce, however, was his long talks with Milner, who convinced him of the truth and vital importance of Christianity. Wilberforce took this very seriously and, in short, experienced a conversion that changed him from an easy-going hedonist to a 'serious Christian'. He began the practice of spending the first hours of the day in meditation and prayer.

Now his conscience was stabbed awake, and for more than two years he agonised over his previously idle, frivolous and misspent life. (He kept an intimate religious diary, as well as his ordinary one). He thought at first that he should withdraw entirely from public life but was advised not to do this. He was therefore troubled over telling Pitt about the change he had experienced, since he feared it might upset their friendship. When, however, he did write to Pitt, he received a letter back in which Pitt expressed respect for Wilberforce's religious conviction, which he could not share, but hoped he would continue to have his co-operation in parliament. He signed the letter 'affectionately, unalterably yours.'

Around this time Wilberforce recorded in his diary his two main aims in life: the abolition of slavery and the reform of manners. The slavery issue was not new. The Quakers had been protesting against it since 1724 and, from 1761 onwards, forbade any member of their Society to own slaves. John Wesley had condemned it as 'the execrable sum of all villainy.' It seems surprising to read that there were 14,000 slaves in Britain at that time, but this was a small matter compared with the worldwide slave trade in which Britain played a leading part. This was big business on a huge scale and people of all classes had a hand in it. It was perfectly legal (by Act of Parliament in 1698) and part of national policy. By the Treaty of Utrecht Britain gained the sole right to supply slaves to the Spanish colonies. The planters in the West Indies, who imported thousands of slaves from Africa, controlled a considerable block of seats in Parliament. To achieve his first aim was an immense task and Wilberforce met bitter opposition from the vested interests.

The attack on slavery

Wilberforce's first impulse towards raising the matter in Parliament came through a conversation with Pitt when, on May 12, 1787, they were sitting under a tree at Teston in Kent. 'Why don't you give notice of a Motion for the abolition of slavery?' said Pitt, who promised Wilberforce his support. From then on, and for the next forty-six years, bills to abolish slavery were presented to Parliament at intervals by Wilberforce and his friends. Some were defeated in the Commons, some were thrown out by the Lords, but Wilberforce would not give up. The French revolution and wars with France caused nervousness about taking such a radical step. The first victory for the Abolitionists came in 1807 when a Bill for the Abolition of the Slave Trade was passed in the Commons by 283 to 16 and in the Lords by a majority of 64. However, this only made the buying, selling and transportation of slaves illegal. Even this was difficult to enforce and applied only to Britain and her colonies. The US passed a similar bill in the same year and in 1810 a Treaty with Portugal was made on the same subject.

Wilberforce wrote to Czar Alexander Talleyrand and the Marquis de Lafayette trying to get the illegal trade stopped by treaty at the Congress of Vienna in 1815, but although Lord Castlereagh brought nearly a million signatures on petitions put forward in Britain, the motion was defeated by the French Royalists.

A further step was the passing of a Bill for the Registration of Slaves in 1824.

The Clapham Sect

No account of Wilberforce would be complete without some reference to the so-called 'Clapham Sect', a misnomer and probably a deliberate corruption of the earlier designation as the 'Clapham Set'. This was a group of important personalities centred round Pitt and Wilberforce, including Henry Thornton the banker, Zachariah Macaulay, philanthropist and father of Lord Macaulay, and Hannah More, writer. They built themselves houses on a plot of land at Battersea Rise, Clapham, sited round a common garden and with free access from house to house. Their community was based not on common religious belief (though Wilberforce and several others were staunch Evangelicals) but on a shared conviction of the need for social reform, along the lines of Wilberforce's *Reformation of Manners.* The need for this was flagrantly obvious in a society of which it was said that 'the statesmen sailed on a sea of claret and the poor floundered in an ocean of gin.' Crime was a major problem, yet Pitt's Metropolitan Police Bill (1785) was overwhelmingly defeated.

In 1787 Parliament re-issued the Proclamation for the Encouragement of Piety and Virtue and for the Preventing of Vice, Profaneness and Immorality, which had been issued on the accession of George III, twenty-seven years earlier. This was to encourage magistrates to be stricter against brothels and pornography, among other things. Wilberforce founded the Proclamation Society to back this up, having in mind especially the profligacy of the upper classes. He also wrote and published in 1797 a 500-page book on *The Practical View of the Prevailing Religious System.* It went through five editions in the first six months and proved a bestseller for fifty years. The Clapham Set was the source of many societies for social reform and laid the foundations for the stricter morality of the Victorian era and for the creation of innumerable voluntary societies on whom rests, even today with the Welfare State, a great deal of the social work of the country.

Wilberforce, as an earnest Christian belonged to the Evangelical Movement within the Church of England, which was the Church's response to the Wesleyan revival. They were sometimes confused with the Methodists, a name which, for many people at that time, was almost a term of abuse. A marked feature of it was that the leaders of the Movement were lay people, and chief among these were the members of the Clapham Set. Wilberforce's advice was sought by men of all parties whenever any idea was afloat for the general welfare, and when he died the whole country mourned the loss of his boundless sympathy.

Freud's Picture of Man
Tony Brown

Tony Brown (1954–2015) studied philosophy and became a high school teacher at the Waldorf schools in Kings Langley and Michael Hall in Sussex. His great love of ideas and books led him to work for Rudolf Steiner Press and Floris Books, as well as Anthroposophic Press in the United States. He spent the last years of his life in New Zealand. In this article he outlines the work of Sigmund Freud, one of the seminal thinkers of out times along with Charles Darwin, Karl Marx and Albert Einstein. Whatever one thinks of his theories regarding the nature of our mental functioning, it is important to grasp, if only in outline, the fundamental tenets of psychoanalysis if one wishes to understand the intellectual and cultural currents of the twentieth century.

Because of the nature of his discoveries, especially those concerning the role of sexuality in the life of the young child and in the origination of neurosis, it was inevitable that Freud encountered hostility and incomprehension among his contemporaries. For example, at one congress of German neurologists and psychiatrists meeting in Hamburg in 1910, when Freud's theories were being mentioned, a professor interrupted the proceedings by banging his fist on the table and exclaiming, 'This is not a topic for discussion at a scientific meeting: it is a matter for the police!' A professor at a Canadian University commented, after reading Freud's *Five Lectures on Psycho-Analysis*, which were delivered at the University of Worcester, Massachusetts in 1909, 'An ordinary reader would gather that Freud advocates free love, removal of all restraints, and a relapse into savagery.'

Such comments show the extent to which his contemporaries were shocked and disturbed by Freud's findings. The anti-Semitism that also prevailed in Vienna, where Freud spent most of his working life, was another factor that alienated Freud and prevented him from gaining adherents to his views. It wasn't until a number of Swiss psychiatrists, among them Eugen Bleuler and Carl Jung, began to support him from 1906 onwards, that Freud gained a measure of intellectual recognition in more orthodox medical circles. Even then, however, as Jung relates in his autobiography, *Memories, Dreams, Reflections* (Vintage, 1961), he was jeopardising his career by taking such a step.

What then was so disturbing about Freud's investigations? In a short article of this nature, it is not possible to summarise in any detail all aspects of his work. Rather I intend to sketch some of the fundamental postulates of psychoanalysis, examine the importance Freud placed on sexuality in coming to an understanding of the aetiology of the neuroses, and outline the hypothesis Freud developed towards the end of his life of a threefold structure in the 'psychical apparatus' (Freud's words), namely, Id, Ego and Super-Ego, which he believed helped explain the conflicts and tensions of our mental life. Such an examination will give us some insight, I hope, into the underlying image of man that stands behind psychoanalysis.

Fundamental principles

It is a measure of the revolution that Freud has caused in our thinking about the mind, that we, living in the twentieth century, find it hard to comprehend how nineteenth-century thought had failed really to acknowledge the existence of an unconscious level of our mental life. Nietzsche had used the concept of the unconscious philosophically, but to the majority of orthodox scientists and thinkers it was almost a definition that anything 'mental' must be conscious. Freud was led into his investigation by the unconscious study of the problem of hysteria.

Hysteria and its associated symptoms were a puzzling challenge to nineteenth-century orthodox medical thought. How was it, for example, that a hysteric might be suffering from a severe paralysis of the arm, when there was nothing wrong with them physiologically? Most hysterics had been dismissed as hypochondriacs who were wasting the doctor's time. Freud's early medical training had been in neurology and neuropathology. Around 1885 he went to study in Paris under the great neurologist, Charcot, who was demonstrating that hysterical symptoms could be induced in patients under hypnosis. For Charcot the explanation of such a fact could probably be found in some structural defect of the nervous system, but Freud asked whether these hysterical symptoms were not the result of powerful mental mechanisms working at an unconscious level. On his return to Vienna he began an initially fruitful collaboration with the physician Josef Breuer who had used hypnosis to alleviate some of the symptoms of hysteria. Their joint work, *Studies on Hysteria*, published in 1895, heralded the beginnings of psychoanalysis.

Here in this work Freud and Breuer announced that the cause in most cases of hysteria must be sought for in psychological, rather than physical, factors. Distressing and disturbing experiences – a Greek word *trauma* (wound) was used – could often be the start of a hysterical illness. Such experiences are so distressing, evoking fear, anxiety or guilt, that they are banished from consciousness into an unconscious 'area' of our mental life. This process Freud called repression: it is the unconscious forgetting of unbearable, threatening or disturbing experiences. In their work with hysterical patients, Freud and Breuer recognised that most patients do not wish to bring into the light of consciousness these long-buried memories or experiences, and therefore put up an unconscious resistance to ultimate recovery. But when the physician succeeded in bringing to light the memory of the event by which the symptom was provoked and by arousing its accompanying effect or emotion, and when the patient had described that event in the greatest possible detail and had put the effect into words, it was found that the symptom disappeared.

Why was it that the patients put up so much resistance to remembering and re-experiencing this forgotten material? It was at this point that Freud advanced a hypothesis that Breuer was unable to accept and which led to the end of their collaboration. Freud came to the conclusion that the fundamental cause of the great majority of neuroses was the repression of a forbidden sexual wish or experience. Freud discovered in many of his patients buried sexual memories which often took the form of recollections of sexual seduction in infants by parents of the opposite sex. These memories Freud was to call 'screen memories'. They were not memories of what had actually happened but were fantasies of what the patient feared or wished might happen. This discovery was to lead Freud on to the startling concept, which he developed, of infantile sexuality and the Oedipus complex.

However, before going on to examine this, one more fundamental pillar of psychoanalysis needs to be described. This is the concept of 'transference', which can be delineated as the investment of powerful and previously buried emotions by the patient in the physician undertaking treatment. An interesting discussion of it occurs in one of Freud's last works, *An Outline of Psychoanalysis* (Hogarth,

1949). It inevitably occurs that at some point in the process of analysis the patient sees in the analyst the return, the reincarnation, of some important figure out of his childhood or past, and consequently transfers on to him feelings and reactions which undoubtedly apply to this prototype. This can be a great help to the analyst in that the patient becomes keen to win his affection and love, and this provides the true motive force of the patient's collaboration. However, it may well happen that at some stage this positive attitude changes to a negative, hostile one. The patient may act irrationally, feel insulted and neglected, might see the analyst as his enemy and be even ready to abandon the analysis altogether. The analyst must learn to meet these situations with a great deal of tact and careful handling. Freud wisely says, 'In all his attempts at improving and educating the patient the analyst should respect his individuality.'

Transference was such a powerful phenomenon that it proved to be one factor why Freud ultimately abandoned hypnosis and all forms of physical contact between patient and analyst, and developed his technique of 'free association', which was allowing the patient to say, without fear of criticism, everything that they thought of as one association followed another. At some point, Freud believed, the stream of associations would dry up and this would usually be a significant indication that an unconscious resistance had been encountered.

Sexuality

It was in the emphasis that Freud was to place on sexuality in the aetiology of the neuroses, and also in the interpretation of our dream life, that first Breuer and later Jung were unable to accept. Freud made a distinction between the concepts of 'genital' and 'sexual', using the latter in the wider sense of including 'the function of obtaining pleasure from zones of the body', zones that Freud was to describe as 'erotogenic'. Childhood had traditionally been seen as a time of sexual innocence. Only at puberty were sexual drives and urges believed to come to the fore. Freud now advanced the staggering hypothesis that our sexual life is 'diphasic', that is, that it occurs in two waves. Sexual life for Freud begins shortly after birth and reaches a certain peak around the age of five with the emergence and repression of the Oedipus complex. A 'latency period' then follows when our sexual life is relatively quiescent, only for it to have a 'second efflorescence' at puberty.

In the normal course of our sexual development we pass through a number of stages, the first of which Freud describes as 'oral'. The first erotogenic zone is the mouth. The young baby not only derives nourishment from the sucking of the mother's breast, but also a certain satisfaction that can be seen in a wider sense as sexual. The second phase is the 'anal' one, where 'satisfaction is then sought in aggression and in the excretory function'. A child feels pleasure in emptying his bowels and in pleasing his parents by so doing; holding on to the contents of one's bowels can be a way of defying parental authority. The third phase is described as 'phallic', which is a forerunner of what a normal adult achieves in his sexual life. Here the genitals play a large part, the boy in particular discovers that pleasurable sensations are to be gained by a stimulation of his genital organs. The boy now enters the Oedipal phase. His first object of love is his mother, but his desire for his mother's love and complete attention is thwarted by his father whom he now intuitively perceives as a rival. This rivalry with and hatred of his father is accompanied by a fear of castration, a fear based, Freud believed, upon a child's observation of the female genitalia, which provide him with an example of what it would be like not to possess a penis. At this point the child experiences 'the greatest trauma of his life', the Oedipus complex (so named after the Greek king who unwittingly killed his father and married his mother), which is then repressed and which introduces the period of latency (with girls the process is somewhat more complicated; Jung coined the term 'Electra complex' to describe it).

In the normal course of development at puberty the fully developed sexual life of the adult is achieved. However, the amount of sexual energy, which Freud termed 'libido', can often become fixated at a previous stage of sexual development or, under certain conditions of stress, may even regress to an earlier phase. This provides us with an explanation of many neuroses and sexual perversions. In both cases the fixation of the libido inhibits the attainment of full emotional sexual maturity.

The psychical apparatus

In some of Freud's later works, notably *The Ego and the Id* (Norton, 1962) and in particular his last unfinished work, *An Outline of Psychoanalysis*, he outlines his interesting theory of the threefold structure of our mental functioning. The oldest of our 'psychical agencies' is what Freud terms the Id. It contains 'everything that is inherited, that is present at birth, that is laid down in the constitution, above all, therefore, the instincts.' Freud eventually came to assume the existence of two basic instincts: 'Eros', the life instinct associated with the sexual drive, and 'Thanatos', the death instinct, which Freud was first led to postulate in *Beyond the Pleasure Principle* (Hogarth Press, 1922). The death instinct's final aim 'is to lead what is living into an inorganic state.' The instincts are essentially conservative in that they strive for a re-establishment of any disturbed state of equilibrium in the somatic life. The Id follows the 'pleasure principle' in that it seeks only 'the satisfaction of its innate needs.' The fulfilment of such a need is experienced as pleasure, frustration as displeasure. The Id is also, of course, the reservoir for all those unconscious repressed desires and impulses that have been banished from our conscious life.

The Ego is that 'portion of the Id that has undergone a special development' as a result of its contact with the external world. The Ego has the task of 'self-preservation'. Externally, it does this by responding to stimuli from the outside world and by then adapting itself to them or changing them by its own activity; internally, it strives to gain control over the demands of the instincts and decides when such instinctual demands should be allowed satisfaction and when they should be postponed until more favourable conditions in the external world prevail. Although it, too, strives after pleasure and seeks to avoid displeasure, it cannot afford not to take into account external reality. Hence, the Ego could be said to obey the 'reality principle'.

Finally, as a result of the human being's long period of childhood during which one is dependent on one's parents, a 'precipitate' is formed in the Ego of a special agency in which the parental influence is prolonged. This Freud called the Super-Ego. These parental influences include:

> ...not only the personalities of the actual parents but also the family, racial and national traditions handed on through them, as well as the demands of the immediate social milieu which they represent.

The influence of teachers too, for example, also helps to form a person's Super-Ego. Whereas the Id seeks satisfaction of its instinctual needs, the Super-Ego strives to limit instinctual satisfaction. It could be said to follow the 'ideality principle' in that it provides us with a model of what we would like to become and acts as our conscience. However, it is important to realise that both the Id and the Super-Ego are essentially irrational, and both represent the forces of the past: the Id of heredity, and the Super-Ego of what is absorbed from other people and introjected into one's self.

It is increasingly clear then that given this situation the Ego is placed in a position of extreme vulnerability. It has to satisfy the conflicting demands of the Id and the Super-Ego, while taking into account at all times the demands of reality. It is hardly surprising that sometimes the Ego cannot cope rationally with these demands, breaks down, and resorts to what Freud describes as 'defence-mechanisms', such as repression and 'projection', where, for example unpleasant character traits and ways of behaviour that we cannot come to terms with consciously are 'projected' on to other people so that we avoid facing the problem squarely in the face.

Conclusion

Although this exposition of Freud's work is by no means complete, having not mentioned, for example, the important elements of dream interpretation for which Freud is perhaps most popularly known, as well as his stimulating insights into questions of society, religion and anthropology, I would like in this section to draw some of the threads together and try and more sharply delineate what image of man we are left with.

In some respects, it is a rather depressing picture. The rational, civilizing forces of the Ego of man are constantly under attack on the one hand by the powerful irruption into his consciousness of irrational, instinctive desires that are fundamentally aggressive, sexual and anti-social; and, on the other, the Ego is beset by inhibiting, crippling imperatives that have no absolute moral value but which are an amalgam of prejudices unconsciously absorbed from the national racial, religious and cultural milieu in which he happens to live. Between the Scylla of his Super-Ego and the Charybdis of his Id, the Ego's freedom of movement is placed in considerable jeopardy. The unconscious is seen as a cess-pit of disturbing and distressing repressed emotions that conjure up in us feelings of guilt and anxiety; our conscience is, in effect, a moral illusion; civilisation a sublimation of our instinctual life that leads to inhibition and often illness. For Freud the one hope that psychoanalysis offered was to strengthen the Ego, making it more independent of the Super-Ego, and helping it appropriate more and more of our unconscious life, thus bringing it into the light of consciousness. As he puts it in Lecture 31 of his *New Introductory Lectures on Psychoanalysis* (Hogarth Press, 1933), 'Where Id was, there Ego shall be'.

Although in this article I have intended to give a brief exposition of some of Freud's fundamental ideas, rather than a critique of them, I cannot refrain in conclusion from making one or two comments of a more critical nature. In the first place, in Freudian psychoanalysis the Ego of man seems to become unduly passive, deprived of independent and creative initiative, and motivated by forces of which for the most part it remains unconscious. It strikes one as essentially unfree. It is one thing to recognise that one is often impelled by motives that are obscure to us, and quite another to consider, as Rudolf Steiner does in his book *The Philosophy of Freedom*, 'whether motives of action that I recognise and see through' are to be considered as compulsory for me as those actions that I perform in an instinctive, unconscious manner. In other words, can the Ego only repress or sublimate its instinctive life, or can it metamorphose it as a result of its freely creative endeavour?

Secondly, Freud's conception of the unconscious and the emphasis he placed on sexuality as a strongly motivating factor for all that we do, seems unduly narrow and dogmatic. Surely not every endeavour, every aspiration, every achievement, in the realm of art, literature, religion and so on, can be justifiably interpreted as a sublimation of an instinctual sexual urge? Jung was in some senses to reverse the equation and see sexuality as an expression of man's spirituality. Rather than seeing the unconscious as a depository of all our unsavoury infantile and repressed impulses as Freud did, Jung saw it as the creative matrix out of which our consciousness emerges and where the 'archetypes' of humanity's psychic experience arise.

Thirdly, Freud's view of the human conscience is reductive in the extreme and fails to offer, I believe, an adequate explanation of our moral life. It is as if Freud felt humanity to be only open to the forces streaming from below, from the earth, from the animal in us as it were, and refused to recognise that he is open also to forces from above, from the cosmos, from the divine in us, which perhaps provides the archetypal image of man that we are struggling to become as a result of our moral and spiritual endeavours here on this 'fallen' earth. It is here, in the realm of the conscience, that the Christ impulse is at work, helping to transform the influences of heredity and taking us beyond the limiting egotism of the present day, so that we can eventually learn to say along with St Paul, 'Not I but the Christ in me.'

The Mystery of Rebirth in an Esoteric Gospel

Andrew Welburn

Born in 1954, Andrew Welburn was a lecturer at the University of London, has been a Fellow of the Warburg Institute and taught at New College, Oxford, until 2005. He is the author of a number of books on religious subjects, including The Beginnings of Christianity *and* Gnosis: The Mysteries and Christianity.

They arrived at Bethany. And a certain woman, whose brother had died, was there. And coming before Jesus she prostrated herself and said to Him, 'Son of David, have mercy on me.' The disciples rebuked her. But Jesus was angry, and went with her into the garden, where the tomb was. And straightaway a great cry was heard from the tomb. Jesus went and rolled the stone away from the door of the tomb. And straightaway He entered, and there was the youth. He stretched forth His hand and raised him, grasping his hand. And the youth looked at Him, and loved Him. And he began to entreat Him that he might be with Him.

And going out of the tomb, they came to the house which belonged to the youth – for he was rich. And after six days, Jesus told him what to do, and in the evening the youth came to Him, wearing nothing but a linen cloth. And he remained with Him that night. For Jesus taught him the mystery of the Kingdom of God.

And thence arising, He returned to the other side of the Jordan.

The story sounds familiar. At least, the whole first part of it needs only the addition of the name Lazarus to merge into the most familiar and the greatest of the 'miracles' narrated by the gospels. The actual words, however, and the latter part of the episode in particular, may give us pause. The impression of familiarity is checked and undermined.

That is because the story does not come from any of the four gospels in the New Testament, but from one of those 'other' gospels that existed in early Christian times but were rejected by the orthodox Church, one of those known under the name of New Testament Apocrypha or The Apocryphal Gospels, or rather – well, the case is really quite complicated, even scandalously so. Yet it has shed a quite extraordinary light on one of the central events of Christianity, as well as on the activities of the early Church authorities. It has brought into the open a mystery of death and rebirth.

In describing it we shall not be able to avoid some of the scandal, so we may as well face it head-on. The text was recovered as recently as 1958, and fully published as late as 1973, by an American scholar called Morton Smith whose behaviour over the discovery has not always been exemplary. Indeed, there have even been accusations that Smith could have forged the text, but I think we may dismiss these outcries which seem to incline to the hysterical. One can only wish, however, that Smith had behaved a little better and called in corroborative scholarly experts to authenticate the document he found in the Judean monastery of Mar Saba thirty years ago. He didn't, however, and the Archimandrite of the Jerusalem Greek Patriarchate, with jurisdiction over Mar Saba, has not helped things by spiriting away the text to the patriarchal library and thus making it totally inaccessible for the present. Yet it is certain that the text exists. It is certain, too, that the gospel passage we have quoted exists there as it is quoted within a letter from the early Church Father Clement of Alexandria to one Theodore, otherwise unknown. And what Clement says about it is a further scandal. For he counsels Theodore that this is a 'secret gospel', and, when asked about it, '...one should not concede that the secret gospel is by Mark, but should even deny it on oath. For "Not all true things are to be said to all men".'

Readers of Clement will know that this principle is a favourite notion of his. But what is this, 'that the secret gospel is by Mark'?

Clement cites the passage as from the original version of the Gospel of Mark, not from an apocryphal work. Yet this version of Mark is certainly not the one we possess in the New Testament either! In that sense it is most definitely an apocryphal text. The Gospel of Mark accepted by the Church and included in the New Testament canon contains no trace of the Lazarus episode, found otherwise only in the Gospel of John. Over the last fifteen years, since the text was published, scholarly enterprise has tried out most of the possible explanations for the odd state of affairs thus revealed, often with the design of steadying the rocking boat of established traditions. The great Catholic scholar R. E. Brown thought that it was merely a late addition to canonical Mark, written up on the basis of chapter 11 in the Gospel of John to bolster belief in the agreement of all four Gospels, removing the disconcerting silence of three of them over the great event in the fourth. Morton Smith himself advanced a most fantastic and complex family tree for the passage, supposed to reflect the orgiastic practices of Jesus' first disciples, modified in expression by the use of the original Marcan Gospel, so that it is at once primary *and* secondary: a view that has persuaded almost nobody. Time has shown the most simple and coherent explanation to be that the 'secret Mark' is actually the original text of the gospel and not an addition at all. It is the esoteric gospel of which our canonical Mark is a carefully abridged and edited version.

The style of the passage is the same restless, excited Greek as the Gospel of Mark we know. Events happen 'straightaway' or are interrupted by 'and' or 'but' at almost every sentence. The Christ Event cannot be told, in Mark's view, in balanced, formal narrative prose. Christ is a reality constantly breaking in, disrupting the organised order of things to which the Pharisees and the powers of the world adhere. It is as if mundane consciousness sees the surface of things, but behind the surface is the shining light of Christ, and where the surface cracks open we are dazzled by flashes of significance.

Moreover, the passage of the 'secret gospel' fits convincingly into the text of Mark at chapter 10. There we find the appearance, and the even more surprising disappearance, of a rich youth. Coming before Jesus he asks, 'What must I do to inherit eternal life?' Jesus replies, 'Go, sell what you have, and give to the poor, and you will have treasure in heaven; and come, follow me.' But his call is not taken up: the young man's face falls, 'for he had great possessions'. Now if the episode were merely what the textual critics say, a peg on which to hang Jesus' sayings about wealth and the Kingdom of God, that last phrase ('and come, follow me') is redundant, and shows up Jesus with an unfulfilled saying. It would have been enough for him to pronounce 'go sell what you have' and then launch into the saying about the camel and the eye of the needle when the youth slunk off. The next saying makes matters worse. Jesus continues mantically, 'for all things are possible with God.' And yet nothing happens. The youth does not, by divine grace, go through the eye of the needle and become a follower of Jesus – at least not in the canonical Mark. But that is precisely what we do see in the longer, original text. This explains, too, why 'the youth' is introduced in the fragment as if he were already familiar, when all that the 'secret' passage had said of him was an allusion to his being the brother of the woman at Bethany.

The rich youth of Mark 10, in short, turns out to be the figure we know as Lazarus. Far-reaching conclusions can be drawn from that fact alone, but here I want to stay with the Gospel of Mark, chapter 10, where we now insert the longer text after 10:34. With the help of the original gospel, we thus discover that the youth did indeed enter upon the terrible struggle to tear free of the bonds tying him to worldly wealth. In no merely metaphorical sense he had to 'die to the world', so that it had no remaining power over his soul. For a modern man, such a struggle would still be a very difficult one. Yet the crisis for such a man today would be an inner one. What we must appreciate when dealing with the ancient world, however, is that people then felt and experienced things much more as a unity: a crisis of the soul affected them right into their limbs, producing psychosomatic illness. We know from accounts among the Essenes, who put their initiates through similar ordeals, that they went through a bodily as well as psychic collapse:

> I am forsaken in my sorrow,
> and without any strength.
> For my sore breaks out in bitter pains
> and in incurable sickness impossible to stay;
> my heart laments within me
> as in those who go down to Hell.
> My spirit is imprisoned with the dead
> for my life has reached the Pit;
> my soul languishes within me
> day and night without rest.

Thus declares one of the initiation poems from the Dead Sea Scrolls, the writings of the Essene community at Qumran. The rich youth no doubt suffered 'sickness unto death' in his agony of inner transformation; but in the Essene poems too the sickness is not finally unto death, but leads to a new inner birth, a birth to 'eternal life'.

I stress the real, even the physical character, of the young man's death-experience, because the 'secret gospel' goes on to confirm for the first time historically something known to Rudolf Steiner through his spiritual investigations: namely, that the so-called 'miracle' of the raising of Lazarus was an event belonging to the mysteries, a ritual, rather than a literal, death and resurrection. Jesus completes the raising of Lazarus to life with six days of mystery instruction and a rite that is clearly a baptism (also much used by the Essenes). Yet this knowledge of the ritual rather than literal nature of his death and resurrection must not lead us to think it was all some solemn mummery. The ritual completes and heals the wound, the 'incurable sickness' that reached even to the physical body.

The realisation that baptism was involved enables us also to speak, as I have done above, of 'rebirth' as well as of 'resurrection'. For in early Christianity baptism was above all the rite of rebirth. During the early phase of the Church, candidates for baptism into the mystery of Christianity had to undergo a period of fasting and instruction. They were then baptised on the night before the Easter dawn, naked, until they were clothed in white robes, like new-born children or like Adam and Eve in paradise. They were fed on milk and honey, rather than solid food. But these things were only the outer sign, of course, of the rebirth taking place within them. At the same time we need hardly suppose that every initiate underwent the severe trauma of Lazarus. That seems to have been a higher initiation. Indeed, in the Gospel of John it is called a glorification, another term known from the ancient mysteries. But we see that it is no accident to find also in Mark, chapter 10, the famous discourse of Jesus on becoming as little children so as to enter the Kingdom of Heaven.

It is no accident, either, that following the inserted 'secret' text, at the end of chapter 10 we find James and John wishing to enter into Jesus' 'glory'. Jesus in reply asks them, 'Are you able to drink the cup that I drink, or to be baptised with the baptism with which I am baptised?' Many biblical scholars have suspected, from Jesus' words, that he must have performed rites of baptism, though that flies in the face of Church tradition and the gospel texts as they have been transmitted. The 'secret gospel' confirms their suspicion. It shows that the element of the mystery-activity of Jesus has been suppressed from the orthodox text. (And we can see that, in a similar context, the text of the Gospel of John 4:1-2 has been tampered with.) How could this come about?

The loss of the longer text of Mark results from two different factors. Firstly, we must understand the original character of the gospels. They were not published books in the modern sense, available from bookshops and libraries. Their contents were communicated to those entering upon the Christian 'Way', as it was called, as part of their instruction. But full access to the understanding of Christ was possible only to those who, in Paul's words, had been baptised into his death. The evidence is that the secret passage from the original Mark was read to Christian initiates on that Easter night of their baptism. Concerning the highest initiation-baptism performed by Jesus, it was read to them at the most solemn moment of their embarking on the Christian life through inner rebirth. And that was the only time it was read. Its special character thus already separated it from the rest of the gospel, from which readings were made throughout the year.

The second decisive factor, alas, brings us once more into the sphere of scandal. Our information comes once more from the letter of Clement in which the 'secret gospel' is embedded. And it introduces into the story a famous, or infamous, figure: Carpocrates.

Of direct spiritual knowledge, William Blake was to say that 'the righteous will turn it to righteousness, and the wicked to wickedness.' When esoteric knowledge falls into the wrong hands, it is not only likely to be misunderstood, it will have a warped and destructive effect on the soul. There have been without doubt those in the history of Christianity who have grasped at spiritual freedom (that 'freedom in Christ' proclaimed by Paul) who had not developed the inner strength or maturity to be really free. Nevertheless forces were unleashed, and rather than being able to control these forces, such individuals were controlled by them. So-called 'libertine' and orgiastic practices are attested in the second century, with Carpocrates as a leader of the movement connecting them with Christian 'freedom'. Clement adds detail to the reports:

> Since the foul demons are always devising destruction for the race of men, Carpocrates, instructed by them and using deceitful arts, so enslaved a certain presbyter of the Church in Alexandria that he got from him a copy of the secret gospel, which he interpreted according to his blasphemous and carnal doctrine and, moreover, polluted, mixing with the spotless and holy words utterly shameless lies. From this mixture is drawn off the teaching of the Carpocratians.

Clement is rightly horrified that such knowledge should fall into the wrong hands. That is why he advises Theodore to deny any reports about the gospel, even on oath.

But there is an equally horrifying story implicit in what Clement says. The demons after all had their victory. The Church, to fight off the stains of libertine accusation, ended by suppressing the original truth of the gospel. They were manoeuvred into sealing up the esoteric knowledge of Christ, which the event of his death on Golgotha brought into history and briefly opened to the light of day.

1990s

The Body and Its Redemption

Pearl Goodwin

Pearl Goodwin was born in 1937 in Edinburgh. She studied biology and embryology before becoming a priest of The Christian Community in 1977, working in various congregations in England. Here she looks at how our modern obsession with health and physical fitness is perhaps a symptom of a deeper longing for the redemption of the body.

Some thirty years ago the novelist Alan Sillitoe wrote a short story called 'The Loneliness of the Long-distance Runner' which came to have a wide appeal. It is about a young man, seventeen years old, whose Christian name we never learn since his story is told entirely in the first person, he is always 'I'. He is a Borstal boy, remanded for petty thieving for which he remains inwardly unrepentant. The governor of the school discovers in him a talent for long-distance running and places his hopes on him to win at the school's sports day in competition with other schools. The boy has his own kind of honesty out of which he makes the questionable decision to run the race but deliberately lose it as a way of maintaining his own integrity in the face of the patronising attitude of the school. He has come to love running for its own sake, not for the sake of the competition. He has discovered in this sport, and in the loneliness that it engenders, a way of finding himself through a kind of thinking (more like a contemplation) that gives him inner satisfaction and acceptance of himself. But it goes further than that. When he enters into this kind of 'thinking', as he calls it, it reflects back into his body, giving him the ability to run almost effortlessly and without tiring, as if it is no longer his body that runs, but his mind. There is a mysterious interface between his physical organism and his mind or spirit. The young man himself is not a particularly likeable or admirable character, but he nonetheless creates a remarkable focus for his own development out of his own core of integrity.

This was written three decades before the present preoccupation with that interconnection between the body and spirit that we see displayed today in all kinds of sports or exercises. These strengthen, revitalise or beautify the body and at the same time bring about a shift in consciousness, from increased well-being even to the point of radical inner transformation. Much of this is a modern rediscovery in the West of methods and practices long known in the East, where it was common to use the body in such a way that the barrier between consciousness and the deeper, more unconscious aspects of the body was broken through, resulting in an increase of awareness. It was not sport (although all sports may have this as their origin), but well-defined exercises that grew out of deep wisdom about the constitution of man. We can see this in certain kinds of yoga, in particular hatha yoga, and also, in a very intense form, in the Japanese martial arts, which also have some of the physicality and competitive, confrontational quality that we observe in sport. They all have their origin at a time when the human constitution was not necessarily the same as it is now. It is one of the 'blind spots' of contemporary historians to assume that people in ancient times were the same as we are, only less enlightened and quaintly dressed. If one looks at some of the faces in ancient carvings or paintings one sees that they were by no means stupid, but only intelligent in a completely different way. It is not necessarily the same, in its effect, for us to try to influence consciousness through the body, for our whole constitution is permeated through and through with materialism, even if we think otherwise. We are different people, and that difference has to be taken into account.

Today there is an overwhelming abundance of methods to choose from, and an equally overwhelming confusion in this very area of the relation of the body to the spirit. Some are strictly for consciousness, some simply for the improvement of the body, and some are for both. Alongside this profusion has grown up a multi-million-pound industry to supply all the needs for these endeavours: gymnastics and all the machinery that goes with it, medicines that are somewhere between healing and cosmetic, highly specialised clothing (and diets so that we can wear it!), and an avalanche of literature to convince us of their indispensability. Quite often considerable discomfort, even pain, are involved, such as in cycling for miles on a stationary bicycle, or it takes a considerable amount of time, such as jogging or working out for an hour or two each day, to say nothing of the financial outlay that is involved. What is it all for?

Many of the reasons are well-founded, for it is surely sensible to maintain health and physical well-being. But behind that is the awareness that the body will get older, lose its harmony, become ill and finally die, taking us with it. Maybe we can prevent this and return it to an everlasting beauty, life and vigour? It is a wish to redeem the body from this curse and return it to its rightful glory that was spoken over it in a bygone age. It is a wish for resurrection and immortality.

That wish is being taken to absurd lengths in the newly evolving 'science' of cryonics, which claims the ability to deep-freeze a human body in the terminal stage of an illness, with a promise, legally binding, to warm it up again at a point in the future when science shall have found the cure for that fatal illness. There are people who are even now taking this seriously, so deep is the longing for the body to be redeemed from its flawed destiny which ends in inevitable death.

A justified longing

That longing has real and justifiable causes. Deeply embedded in each human soul, deeper even than the egotism that makes one seek for immortality, is the unconscious feeling, even certainty, that we are not yet at the highest point of our evolution as human beings. Whatever the human spirit has achieved it will not feel itself fulfilled until the work of art that is the body is itself redeemed and saved from destruction. It is not surprising that this longing unites itself with our present-day preoccupation with materialism, envisaging the redemption of the body in a material form and resorting to all possible physical methods to bring it about.

Most people in the West know that the theme of redemption of the body, or resurrection, is the central point of the New Testament. Some believe in it, some feel that it is beyond belief, given what we know today about the body. Whether we believe in it or not, it is well beyond our ability to comprehend with our everyday thinking, for the resurrection of Christ was the consequence of a death that truly happened. We can identify with the death, for it seems akin to death as we know it, but we have difficulty imagining a risen body that could appear through locked doors and at the same time have tangible reality. That kind of body seems impossible to us, who know so much about bodies and the matter that constitutes them. So the redemption of the body is envisaged safely within the world of the matter that we do know. Feeling that the resurrection is unattainable, even when not unbelievable, has meant that we take our hopes and longings for such redemption into a sphere where those very hopes become polluted with that same materialism that we are seeking to transcend.

Is it so unattainable? And is it only for the far future? If we return to the story of the long-distance runner, we can see that, for him, his loneliness was the fulcrum of his experience on which everything else was balanced. He did that by simply accepting the inhospitable nature of his situation, and, having done that, he found the lighter, freer side of loneliness which is aloneness. It became a bodily power, an experience in the soul that had an effect on the body. One cannot call it resurrection, only a marginal dissolving of the habitual bodily laws that result in tiredness and need. His body became an instrument rather than a machine.

Examples of this kind are probably known to most of us. They happen whenever we push ourselves, or are pushed, beyond our own natural limits. They can also happen at a much deeper level in the soul when we find ourselves faced with a situation that seems unbearable or hopeless, when we come to the end of our soul's powers, where even prayer cannot help because we cannot find the means with which to pray. That, too, is a kind of fulcrum, a balance point between the laws of this world and the laws of another. It is in this place, which seems so dark because it is between two worlds, that we can truly meet Christ, for that is the space that he inhabited in his passage from the laws of the body into which he gave himself in death, and the laws of the spirit that appeared as the resurrection.

We cannot yet follow his path in its totality, meaning bodily, but we can take certain steps in that direction in our own soul experience. When that point between the familiar and the unknown and dark is accepted, lived with and through and not avoided, then Christ can touch us at the point where he is identical to us: the point of suffering and also its reverse side, redemption. Those who have experienced such things speak of new kinds of strength and life, even in the bodily realm. We will not seek for immortality of the body because we will not mind dying.

That is a direction that can be taken today, quite different to the methods of old. We can begin with consciousness, with our own probably very limited consciousness. We can begin with who we are and hold on to that with integrity and honesty through the hardest passages of life until we touch, and are touched by, the reality that gives meaning to our life and so life to our bodies.

Is Religion Useful?

Tom Ravetz

Tom Ravetz was born in 1964 and was ordained in 1991. Since 2011 he has been Lenker (coordinator) of The Christian Community in Britain and Ireland. In this short article he recalls a significant question that occurred to him when he was a teenager and that led eventually to him becoming a priest in The Christian Community.

When I was about fifteen I discovered that at the end of his life Einstein had said that if he had known what his work would make possible, he would never have embarked on his career as a scientist; he would rather have been a watchmaker like his father. At a time when I was starting to realise that my adult life was about to begin, and that I would have to make choices about what to do with it, this came as a great shock to me. My feeling was, that if one of the greatest geniuses of our time could dedicate his life to research, only to discover that he had not been serving the good but helping a great evil to come into the world, how could I presume to know what would be a worthy cause to dedicate my life to? I didn't feel that anything I had learnt at school so far could answer my question. It was very real to me, and the unwillingness of my teachers to answer it, or even take it seriously as a question, made it difficult to be committed to the idea of studying hard and going along the road that seemed to be mapped out in front of me: taking a university degree and getting started in a career of some kind.

My teachers were frustrated with me. They felt that my attitude was wholly negative, merely a reaction to something not an idea of what to put in its place. They were right, as I discovered after leaving school when I experienced what it meant only to have negative thoughts and feelings about the world. And yet – were they right? Of course, their observation was correct. Teenagers often cannot do much more than react; they can't yet build something up, and instead prefer to rip things down as if that were all that is important. But on a deeper level, I still believe in my question; in fact, I think that it is one of the questions that must be thought about, if not answered, before one can start to do something with one's life.

It was this that was largely responsible for my eventually going to the seminary in Stuttgart and becoming a priest. It was that question that took me off the 'normal' track, which I otherwise would surely have trodden, and, not coming from a Christian Community background, it is very unlikely that I would ever have made contact with the movement. As it was, however, I was casting around for something worthwhile to do, having experienced how terrible it is not to be occupied usefully, no place where one is needed and valued. I came across Botton Village, and it was there that I met for the first time an attitude to life that opened up a whole new dimension to me. The way that people lived, the way they treated the people in their care and the respect they had for the earth, showed their awareness and reverence of the spirit. Just witnessing this attitude as a possible way of being, filled me with hope that there might be another way of seeing the world.

Shortly after I arrived in Botton I stood one evening in the gentle North Yorkshire spring sunshine and was filled with an overwhelming feeling of gratitude, of joyful, stammering thanks, which I had to put into words. Standing alone on the pathway I had to say out loud, 'Thank you!' For the first time in many years I had become aware of God, not as an idea to be discussed, but as a vital factor in life, something that made a tremendous difference to the way one lived and worked and thought.

Some time later I was able to experience the Michaelmas Act of Consecration of Man as an event that went some way to answering the question that had occupied me for so long. In Michael's beckoning gesture, in his bidding humanity to follow him to a new kind of thinking that encompasses God and the Deed of Golgotha, I could feel, if not understand, something that would lead on from the moral dead-end of twentieth-century thought as I had experienced it. If I could see the world permeated by spirit, sustained and revitalised by the sacrifice of the highest divine being, then here would be an orientation for my decisions about life. Here I could find the trust that I would not discover at the end of my life that I had been deluding myself, that I had served evil rather than good.

Imbuing life with this meaning, finding even in the most insignificant things – or, rather, especially there – the reality of the spirit: this belongs to the central tasks of the priest, and indeed of every Christian human being. It is a great joy to me to be allowed to try to fulfil these tasks as a priest. It is especially rewarding to be allowed to work with young people who are confronted with the same questions as I was, to be able to take these questions seriously, not killing them with ready-made answers, and yet speaking out of a conviction that it is possible to discover a spiritual dimension in life, and that this can enable each one of us to find trust in our path through life.

Market Forces and Ethics
Baruch Luke Urieli

Born in Vienna, Baruch Luke Urieli (1923–2014) worked in a kibbutz in Palestine before becoming a teacher. He undertook further training in Camphill in Scotland, and was ordained a priest of The Christian Community in 1975. After working for a time in Edinburgh, he became the first resident priest in Ireland at the Glencraig Camphill Village. In this article, he looks at the corrosive effects economic ideas can have on an ethical view of the human being.

Since 1979 the professed economic objective of our successive governments in Britain has been 'sustained non-inflationary economic growth'. This object has never been achieved, though we have experienced brief periods of growth with low inflation. Since 1990, recession has set in and continues to take its toll, although it appears now to be ebbing. What does not show signs of ebbing, however, is unemployment and especially long-term unemployment. A year ago 38% of the unemployed in the United Kingdom had been out of work for more than twelve months. The figure of long-term unemployed had then approached one million. There is much evidence that indicates that it is the poverty, despair and deprivation accompanying these economic facts that have made parts of our larger industrial cities into unsafe places.

How did this development begin? It started with the ideology of so-called 'monetarism'. This appeared to be an updated version of the teachings of Adam Smith, a modern recipe for increasing the wealth of the nation based on the simplistic assumption that this would be the inevitable result of increased productivity and profit achieved by competing individuals in a free market economy.

J. K. Galbraith, the eminent Scottish-American economist, welcomed the inception of monetarism in Britain, assuming that this new economic ideology would be applied by the government with thoroughness, thereby proving (or rather disproving, as Galbraith thought) before long its real value, of which Galbraith did not have a particularly high opinion. One can now say with hindsight that Galbraith's premonitions were justified, perhaps much more justified than the layman reader would have wished them to be, with all one's sympathy for this highly intelligent, upright and thoroughly practical man.

In 1900 an article by Galbraith commemorating the two hundredth anniversary of the death of Adam Smith, was published in the *Observer* under the title, 'Who is Afraid of Adam Smith?' In it, Galbraith showed how far the views of this man differ from the policies of both those on the right and the left who made him their idol or mascot. Wherein lie the fundamental differences between the ideas, or rather the attitudes, of Adam Smith and the attitudes that characterise the presumed followers of his teachings in the eighties and nineties?

Adam Smith was a member of a society whose moral foundations, though we may consider them somewhat rigid today, were firm and sound. The family was still a strong institution and moral tradition was consequently alive and generally ingrained. The world of the Industrial Revolution was a harsh world rather far from the image of a caring society, but there was a certain uprightness and reliability that ennobled a great many of its citizens. No member of government of that time would have dared to concede being 'economical with the truth' or to claim 'a right to lie'.

Our present industrial society is one where the background of family tradition has collapsed, as have moral traditions and moral values. Consequently 'monetarism' is not, nor can it ever be, a free market ideology in which the gains of the individual form the basis of the nation's wealth. Rather it is a determined search for gain with no holds barred. It should be called 'Mammonism' rather than 'monetarism', and those who serve 'Mammon' serve a God as demanding as the Old Testament Moloch ever was.

There are two factors that make the long-term success of monetarism an impossibility. The first one is that it works in a way similar to chemical fertilisers. At first the investment brings rich returns. After a while, however, as is the case with artificial fertilisers, an ever-increasing investment is necessary in order to keep up the returns, and the remaining choice is either to pull out at the right time or go bankrupt, just like the farmer who has ruined the natural fertility of their land. And just as the destruction of the fertility of the soil creates dust bowls in nature, so does a monetarist economy create social dust bowls.

The second factor preventing the long-term success of monetarism is the fact that since early this century the term 'national economy' has become ever more an illusion. The reality of a national economy has receded while the world economy must be considered as the foremost factor in any economic consideration. Multinational corporations dominate world trade, and day by day an enormous stream of money flows through the stock exchanges of London, New York and Tokyo in this computerised and fax-equipped world. It is no longer possible to reduce the price of goods and rely on vastly increased sales to make a fortune, because before long any gimmick is copied by others and soon enough the initial advantage in sales turns into a loss. As a consequence trade gimmicks have now to be supported by political and even military pressures. What appear at present to be national, ethnic or religious wars are to a great extent hidden attempts to make one population economically subservient to the other, or to free one population from its economic subservience to the other. The wealth of the earth is a basic factor that can only be released through a combination of human work and human ingenuity. It cannot be increased by any measure that robs Peter in order to pay Paul. Sooner or later any such measures will show socially destructive results.

A path of destruction can be perceived that leads from growing unemployment to a growing lack of truth in dealings between people so that a job or business survives. The third step in this battle for survival is the process of so-called rationalisation, which means in fact the weeding out of the weaker members of society from the job and business market. Poverty, destruction and death follow, until eventually the larger part of humanity may have to accept economic slavery, regardless of whatever euphemistic term it may be given by those who have the final word. The final gratification remaining to the degraded human being, even if it is a sham, is sex without love. The 'brave new world' of Aldous Huxley casts its prophetic shadow right into 1994.

There is a grave danger that the proliferation of agribusiness may be followed by the proliferation of andro-business (that is, modern forms of slavery, the buying and selling of human beings) to the great detriment of the earth and humanity. Must this necessarily be so? To borrow from the title of the poem by Robert Frost, is there no 'road not taken' that can be pursued? Perhaps humanity will have to learn that morality is a *practical* necessity. Humanity has increasingly come to regard morality as a kind of sweet-and-sour pickle that is added by old aunts or clergymen to the practical realities of life, a pickle one can in fact do without. But perhaps this God, who was declared dead by many earlier this century, has in fact left houses and churches for the empty spaces of agribusiness and andro-business, and is waiting for humanity to find him there, not as an optional extra but as a practical necessity.

It may be necessary that new attitudes will have to grow in humanity in order to find a way out of the labyrinth of destruction in which we find ourselves today. The Christian development of the last two millennia found its centre in the seven sacraments, which serve to strengthen and sanctify germinal moments in individual human biography. Could not this process of sanctification and strengthening be extended into the working life and the social interrelationships of the human being, so that the God hidden in farming, trade and industry, in fact in any application of human work or intelligence, could also be revealed there?

The first step in such an endeavour would be to realise the sacramental nature of work. This has been attempted time and again in the past by various religious and socialist movements, but always these attempts evaporated amid the so-called realities of life, perhaps because the need was not yet desperate enough and the time was not yet ripe. The trials of our time may give us the opportunity to come to a firm realisation that work is not just a means to earn money or gain a livelihood. Work may be seen as the way by which we can make use of our particular gifts, thereby entering into mutual relationships with our fellow human beings and thus becoming members of human society. Such an attitude to work would eventually reveal its inner relation to the sacrament of Baptism, which has a similar standing in the individual human biography.

A second step in the endeavour to make divinity visible in the activities of humanity, would be the realisation that nothing that is to last in our relationships can be built without the element of truth. We often lie out of our own clumsiness, for instance in not finding the right way to acknowledge the joy of our neighbour or family member about something they have acquired that we personally would not have chosen, say an item of clothing or a new pet. But upon these lies, the small ones and still more the big ones, no future can be built. Only where uprightness prevails can human beings enter into sound relationships with each other. Such an attitude to truth will eventually reveal its inner relationship to the sacrament of Confirmation, which strengthens in the young person that firmness and uprightness that they will need in order to meet the pitfalls of adult life.

A third step in the endeavour to build up a new ethos of active life would be the realisation that generosity is the most creative power in social life. Modern society, which is even more intellectual, has entered deeply into the attitude of rationalisation. Economic investment, human involvement and moral engagement are rationed in order to achieve maximum results with minimum efforts. But where true generosity is present the miracle of Elijah will always repeat itself: the jar of flour will not be spent, the cruse of oil will not fail, the power of life will be renewed (1 Kings 17:8–24). Such an attitude of generosity will eventually reveal its inner relationship to the sacrament of Communion.

These are the first three steps on a 'road not taken' that could bring healing to our relationships with each other and with the earth. We live in a time when we will have to encounter increasingly severe tests. But we may hope that we will find the inner strength to arise out of these trials purified and strengthened.

Counselling and Sacramental Consultation

Tom Ravetz

Tom Ravetz was born in Leeds, England in 1964 and was ordained in 1991. Since 2011 he has been Lenker (coordinator) of The Christian Community in Britain and Ireland. In this article he looks at the problem of sin and how Sacramental Consultation in The Christian Community is a renewed form of the Catholic sacrament of Confession. But instead of absolving a person of their sins, it seeks to give them the strength to deal with them.

I recently asked a group of people interested in becoming members of The Christian Community what their need would be if they came to a priest for the Sacramental Consultation. I did this because I felt it would be important for people to describe the need that Sacramental Consultation seeks to address for them, before telling them about the sacrament itself and risking that they conform their needs to what had been described. I would like to take some of their answers as a starting point in describing aspects of the Sacramental Consultation that are close to the experience of us all.

Balance between extremes

It was clear that the priest should not offer absolution. This could seem surprising, given that the Sacramental Consultation is a renewed form of the sacrament known as Confession in the Roman Catholic Church. But it was clear to the people with whom I was talking that it could no longer be appropriate for modern humanity to be released from sin at the command of the priest: much more important was to be given strength to deal with sin. They did feel that the

Sacramental Consultation had something to do with sin: sin understood in the sense that we had discussed in previous meetings, and as we try to understand it in The Christian Community as the 'sickness of sin' (see for example *The Christian Creed* (Floris Books, 2009) by Hans-Werner Schroeder). They felt that they would wish to be helped to see their destinies from a higher perspective and to find the strength to bring about balance in their lives, which they saw as being in danger of falling into one of two extremes: too 'light' or too 'heavy'. They felt that the help they needed in doing this would be a quality of listening and perhaps also a few well-posed questions.

Most people who know something of the renewed sacramental life of The Christian Community, with its emphasis on the spiritual integrity of the participants in the sacraments, would have similar thoughts. To lead the discussion a stage deeper it was then important to ask the question, why a sacrament? Surely, the qualities of conversation we were describing did not need a priest. One could go and talk to an older, wiser person, one whom one could trust to lead one through a process like the one mentioned above. Or, perhaps even more relevant for today, one could go to a counsellor. I had been at pains to point out to my prospective members that we do not receive a training as counsellors during our training as priests in The Christian Community. Some say we should. Of course, the setting assures certain professional standards: priestly confidentiality is preserved, and the vestments act as a strong 'hygienic' aid, so that the more basic pitfalls possible in the caring encounter can be avoided. But in terms of analysis and diagnosis of psychological situations, to say nothing of prescription of therapy, we are not professionals. Perhaps members and even priests of The Christian Community have sometimes fallen into the trap of thinking that we should be 'competing' with psychotherapists and counsellors of various different schools, or that they are competing with us. Writers in other theological traditions, seeking to reclaim a particular role for the pastoral encounter, have referred to a view, which was widespread in the seventies, that a priest should be little more than a psychotherapist in vestments. I believe this to be a fundamental error.

Priests are not counsellors

To return to the discussion: it was clear that priests are not necessarily counsellors. They all grimaced in agreement when I described to them how hard it is to resist the temptation of giving advice, even of making this into the substance of a pastoral conversation. Of course, it may sometimes be exactly the right thing to do, but it cannot be the principal aim of the Sacramental Consultation. And, although it was harder to find clear concepts at this point, it was also clear that the quality looked for in the Sacramental Consultation would be something different. After all, one would hardly expect a counsellor to start talking about sin, or the healing of sin, although perhaps their task has to do with it.

The quality of the Sacramental Consultation had to do, it was felt, with that part of the Act of Consecration of Man that calls on those present to bring something to the altar, to offer something. It was felt that the priest would give to Christ what had occurred in the conversation, and that the way would then be clearer for this offering to take place in the next Act of Consecration of Man. It was felt indeed that the conversation with the priest should take on the quality of a conversation with Christ, the priest having merely a facilitating role, his primary concern being not to get in the way of what was happening.

All these thoughts then made it possible to describe the Sacramental Consultation, which can be taken as the sacrament of the individual within his or her destiny. In thinking about our destiny we can all experience the reality of sin in ourselves. It is that basic limitation of our human nature, expressed in the passionate cry of St Paul in the letter to the Romans: 'The good that I would do, I do it not!' How often do we have to confess to ourselves that we have failed to notice what was necessary in a certain situation, failed perhaps to meet a fellow human being in the way they deserved, or failed to maintain our own humanity and acted in some way unworthily? And yet we all experience moments, too, when we seem to transcend our limitations: when we are moved by love or compassion or inspiration, and we seem to cast off our limited 'lower' self. In such moments we are aware of our higher self, that self which has chosen the destiny of this earthly life, which wants even the suffering of this life for a very good reason, even if this is hidden from us at the moment.

In the conversation or conversations that precede a Sacramental Consultation, the priest will try to help the one seeking the sacrament to see their life from a different perspective than the normal one. If the reason for the conversations is some period of trial or crisis which that person is going through, then the particular problems that are to be addressed will be in the foreground. But Sacramental Consultation does not have to be given in response to a difficult situation: it can become a regular part of life. As members of The Christian Community we can feel that we are asked to find our own relationship to this sacrament: for some, it is important to come every few months or every year; others will come when they feel a stage of their life has been achieved or is approaching: after a long illness or before marriage. In this way, too, the Sacramental Consultation differs from the counselling or therapeutic conversation, which would be in danger of becoming self-indulgent if it were not clear what particular problem area is to be tackled, and that after something had been achieved the series of conversations should be at an end. In conversations leading up to the Sacramental Consultation, it is not necessary that some particular problem stands in the foreground, nor that, on the most immediate level, any problems that are uncovered be solved.

The Wounded Healer

Henri J. Nouwen, a Reformed theologian and thinker, has described the pastoral encounter in his book *The Wounded Healer* (Doubleday, 1972). His words bear directly on the Sacramental Consultation.

> A minister is not a doctor whose primary task is to take away pain. Rather, he deepens the pain to a level where it can be shared. When someone comes with his loneliness to the minister, he can only expect that his loneliness will be understood and felt, so that he no longer has to run away from it but can accept it as an expression of his basic human condition.

Along with other modern authors on pastoral care, Nouwen stresses the importance of finding a model for the pastoral encounter that moves away from the model of the past, which might be characterised as 'authoritarian': the priest has the answers, the penitent one has only to listen and follow the advice given. With the background of the image of the human being contained in the sacraments of The Christian Community, one can see the rightness in this shift: what is needed for my healing is not something that is intrinsically 'other' than myself, but rather my own essential nature, from which I have become alienated. The healing of my deepest problems will not involve the relieving of symptoms but will involve me in confronting and acknowledging them. Then, in Nouwen's striking phrase, they can be 'shared'.

Everything which has so far been described can make us ask, what would we expect from the sacrament of Sacramental Consultation? Is it just an intensification of what happens or should happen in other human encounters, a kind of 'destiny therapy' or biography work, which, because of the theological background of the 'therapist' and the religious setting, has a particular kind of earnestness about it?

We have arrived once again at the feeling that the group of prospective members had: that there is a relationship between the Sacramental Consultation and the Act of Consecration of Man. In order to understand this relationship we need to understand something of the nature of the sacraments.

Sharing the pain of our destiny

Sacraments always have to do with community, and the essence of community is sharing. In the community of marriage, we share in the realm of life; in the community of a university, we share in the realm of the intellect; the model-railway club is a community of interest. What then is shared in the community of Christians? To take Henri Nouwen at his word it is pain. We could perhaps go further and say that it is the pain of our earthly life that is also its meaning: the pain of our destiny.

Thus, while we have described the Sacramental Consultation as the sacrament of the individual, it is at the same time the sacrament of the community. The priest's presence in vestments makes clear in an image that they are not present in a personal capacity. The priest investments seeks to embody the spirit of their congregation, that spirit which is imbued by Christ.

Here lies the relationship between the Sacramental Consultation and the Offertory in the Act of Consecration of Man. There, in the first part, the 'sickness of sin' is described. In the three qualities of our errings from God, our denials of the divine and our weaknesses, the totality of the symptoms 'sickness of sin' is summed up. All this flows to the Father God – it has already flowed, before the Offertory can take place. In the second prayer we recall the creative deeds of God and turn the highest powers of our soul towards him in devotion, our thinking, feeling and willing. In living with the Act of Consecration of Man, it becomes clear that this is a most important part of the service. The substance of our 'sin', which flows to the altar, is taken up and transformed in the further course of the Act of Consecration. We experience, too, how hard it is really to release this substance and set it free from us. This is where the Sacramental Consultation can be a great help. In beholding one's life from a higher viewpoint, as described above, it is possible to let go of much that has become immobile or stuck, to use the graphic, everyday expression. Our thoughts in particular have this tendency: the ways in which we explain what has happened to us, who we are in relation to the world and our own destinies, become a cherished part of our mental surroundings; we are all too unwilling to let go of it. This 'letting go' as a quality of offering is aided by the verse that makes up the second part of the Sacramental

Consultation. When this has happened, the way is made clearer to find the true source of our will to live: the divine world. In the Sacramental Consultation the process of offering is prepared and practised. What is received as Communion can then be felt to be more personal and individual. At the same time, however, it is an amazing phenomenon that I do not receive 'my' Communion on my own. Offering and receiving are both done in community, so that, regardless of whether I am aware of the particular problems and shortcomings with which my neighbour is struggling, what they can offer is merged with my offering and becomes part of the same transformed substance. Thus the fundamental principle of Christian community is realised: 'Bear each other's burdens, and in this way you will fulfil the law of Christ' (Gal. 6:2).

From consciousness to life

Seen in this way the Sacramental Consultation is first and foremost the sacrament of community, the place where the source of the life of the community is renewed. It has a fundamentally different, complementary direction to the therapeutic conversation, whose aim is to lift what has been lived – illness, trauma and so on – into the light of consciousness. The Sacramental Consultation aims to lead what has been consciously experienced into life, by offering it up to the higher life that animates the congregation and also contains the true life of the individual. It has been called the 'sacrament of rightful forgetting'. Members of The Christian Community, who have lived with it for many years, experience its value at the end of a time of inner trial and conflict, when what has been achieved in thinking something through can be entrusted to the higher world, and new life can begin.

Perhaps these thoughts can make clear the different but (potentially) mutually enhancing roles of counselling and sacrament. The Sacramental Consultation is not a method of therapy independent of the sacramental life of The Christian Community. It leads individuals into a more intense relationship with that life, which, in turn, leads them into a new relationship with themselves.

Forgiving is More Than Amnesia: Reconciliation in South Africa

Julian Sleigh

After working in Camphill, Scotland, Julian Sleigh (1927–2014) went to South Africa to help found Camphill and further its work there. He was ordained in London in 1965 and returned to South Africa where he worked for the rest of his life. Out of his work with the telephone counselling service, Lifeline, he wrote his book, Crisis Points.

It is indeed soul stretching to live in South Africa in these times of transition. But a transition from what to what? That which has been, the apartheid era, is condemned wholesale as having been unjust, bigoted, selective, unfair, immoral and corrupt. The leaders of the now all-powerful African National Congress miss no opportunity to rub in the evil that this period for over forty years inflicted on South African society, for the privilege and benefit primarily of the white population. Throughout these forty years the black population grew in numbers. Today we reckon there must be 32 million black people to the 5.6 million white people and 4.4 million people of colour. The way the white sector retained political power shows how firmly they held onto economic power.

The change began in 1990 with F. W. de Klerk, the then newly installed president, declaring the unbanning of dissident movements, freeing Mandela from prison, and opening the way to negotiations for an interim constitution based on human rights for all citizens. This moved our society towards universal franchise. The election took place in April 1994 for a 'government of national unity', and Nelson Mandela, as leader of the ANC, was inaugurated as president. His influence was, from the beginning, moderating: he was eloquently caustic about the old regime, but advocated that all South Africans, the 'rainbow people', should work together to build a nation free of all forms of discrimination. In its makeup this government reflects the respective strengths of the main parties in Parliament, which was elected on a universal and non-constituency basis; the voting was for parties, not persons, and each party had its list of names to fill the seats allocated according to the number of votes received. This Parliament and government will continue until 1999, when there will be a general election for a Parliament based on a new and final constitution that is being drawn up at present.

There is no doubt that the majority party will then have sole power, and that party, the ANC, could easily win 70% or more of the votes. At that point Mandela (who will be seventy-nine) will almost definitely retire, and his place as president will be taken by one of three likely candidates: Thabo Mbeki, Cyril Ramaphosa or Tokyo Sexwale. All three are persons of moderation, and we hope the spirit of reconciliation will continue.

The divides, the stresses and the possible recriminations are not between blacks and whites. This has always been a dangerously superficial picture of the South African situation. The problems go much deeper and are complex. There are many factions in every racial group and subgroup, often at enmity with each other, and their hostility stems not from racial differences but from deep emotions that belong to the collective unconscious of the retrospective groups. There is also a constant meddling into the relationship between groups, fed by demonic forces. Something similar is happening in many parts of the world.

The need for reconciliation

With these deep-going stresses in our society the only hope is reconciliation, and this has to be deep and true. It also has to reach into the unconscious of everyone who lives in this country. The new government, now in its third year, has embarked on many schemes. The main one is the RDP, the Reconstruction and Development Programme. This aims to reduce the alarming shortage of housing, the inadequacies of the health services, the staggering unemployment and the chaos of education as run by the State.

Another is the Truth and Reconciliation Commission. This Commission of seventeen persons, most of whom are well known in the country, is headed by Archbishop Desmond Tutu, who is much respected for his challenges to the ideology of the past and his continual calling for justice based on Christian love. The Commission has an enormous task: it has to listen to the confessions of all who perpetrated oppressive and morally reprehensible acts in pursuance of any political goal, whether the goal was apartheid and social discrimination or the suppression of dissidence within the ranks of the 'freedom fighters'. All people who have track records of this kind are called upon to submit a confession to the Commission by a certain date, and to be prepared to be questioned on what they did. As Desmond Tutu said recently in an interview: 'The Truth and Reconciliation Commission is the middle path between two extremes.' Here is a quote from a report in the *Cape Times*:

> 'The Truth and Reconciliation Commission is the middle path between two extremes,' says Tutu. 'Some say let us forget the past while others want revenge. We are saying that we are not going to forget and we do not want revenge. Nobody would claim that the Commission is the perfect solution but it is a great deal better than a Nuremburg trial situation.'
>
> Tutu says that the Commission will serve an important function by publicly acknowledging that victims of human rights abuses had their personal dignity violated.
>
> The Commission will have professional mental health workers to counsel victims who come to give evidence.
>
> 'It won't just do for someone to come along and be expected to tell his story and then at the end of the day say goodbye. We are going to have to have a professional support system.'
>
> While acknowledging that the time constraints within which the Commission will be operating – it has 18 months to complete its task with an option to extend that to two years – Tutu points out that it will not be starting from scratch.
>
> 'We have a fair amount of information already through non-governmental organisations and human rights groups. There is also the work of the Goldstone Commission. We are not going into totally virgin territory,' he says.
>
> And to ensure that the Commission works at maximum speed in processing the thousands of cases likely to come before it, its human rights committee will probably operate in three or four centres of the country simultaneously.

The mention of the Nuremburg trials shows that many critics fear a kind of witch-hunt, followed by trials in law courts and heavy sentences. Indeed a much respected young rabbi from Cape Town, Ivan Lerner, wrote to the Cape Town papers to argue the case that the Truth Commission should be stopped. 'The Commission is in my view a tragic mistake.' He feels that, as the difficult transition was achieved peacefully, largely through the leadership of F. W. de Klerk, a general amnesty should be granted for events that took place during apartheid. He questions the value of investigating political and racial crimes going back to 1960. He asks 'how could this help towards reconciliation and unity?' He feels that the Commission will stir up anger and animosity on the part of whites and Zulus; he fears that it will turn into a political circus, making the O. J. Simpson trial seem mild by comparison. Rabbi Lerner recalls how, in 1989, while visiting Jerusalem, Archbishop Tutu told his Israeli hosts that the time was long overdue for Jews to forgive Nazis for the murder of six million of their people, since the Bible advocates and encourages reconciliation and forgiveness.

Rabbi Lerner was answered by Professor Milton Shain of Jewish Studies, University of Cape Town, and two of his colleagues from the faculties of Law and Anthropology. They advocate that coming to terms with the past, 'fronting up' about whatever one did against one's fellow citizens in the name of a particular ideology, is a step towards healing the wounds of the victims. It makes it possible to forgive. Also, within the body politic, the deep layers of guilt and fear on the part of the perpetrators, and the resentment, anger and desire for revenge on the part of the victims, need to be raised to consciousness and expressed in order that our society becomes truly united. Then we can hope for a nation in which the rule of law operates and a culture of human rights can be fostered.

It is a debate between 'forgetting the past' and 'due process'. Professor Charles Villa-Vicencio, of the Department of Religious Studies at UCT, has added his well-respected voice to the discussion: 'True reconciliation is a deeply spiritual exercise that cannot bypass the pain of the past.' He points to the tradition shared by Jew and Christian alike of 'repentance', which involves the acknowledgment or confession of guilt, genuine remorse, commitment to change and restitution. He points out that if the British had publicly acknowledged the suffering inflicted on the women and children in the concentration camps they had set up during the Boer War, 'our history may have been different.' This is a poignant remark, for indeed many of the leaders of the Nationalist Government that took over South Africa in 1948 had been young children with their mothers in those very concentration camps. It was one of them, D. W. Malan, who coined the word 'apartheid', for he and his colleagues were determined to establish Afrikaanerdom as the dominant political, social and ethnic force in South Africa. Their zeal came from an unresolved desire for revenge and a deeply felt need for security on the part of those who had been oppressed. They in their turn then became the oppressors.

'People who have experienced trauma need to tell their stories if they are to move on,' says Mrs Bea Abrahams of the Trauma Centre for the Victims of Torture in Cape Town. It helps the process of healing. Professor Villa-Vicencio rightly points out that if the Commission acts incorrectly and irresponsibly 'it can bleed the nation to death.' But if it does its work wisely 'it can contribute to a national catharsis and a new beginning.'

So the South Africa of today struggles for its health. There are many colossal problems like unemployment and crime, the need for people with professional abilities not to abandon the country, the right use of natural and economic resources, the integration of diverse cultures and languages. But nothing will really work until a healing of wounds takes place, removing the blocks that give rise to insoluble feuds, hatreds and deep-rooted urge for revenge.

What is encouraging about the present transition in South Africa is the way so many people from very different backgrounds are trying to overcome the hurts of the past and learn how to become more decent human beings, free of prejudice, free of grudges and encouraged to accept and enjoy each other's differences. This favourable climate will help the Commission for Truth and Reconciliation to achieve both the expression of truth and the healing powers of reconciliation. The next eighteen months or two years will be critical. We hope and pray that the Commission will succeed.

Finding Stillness in Chaos, Renewal in Decline
Elizabeth Roberts

Born in Yorkshire, Elizabeth Roberts (1949–2014) studied biochemistry and taught in Bristol. After her ordination as a priest of The Christian Community in 1983. she was to work in that city again. In this article, based on a lecture she gave at the Whitsun Congress in Hamburg in 1997, she considers the creative potential that can be found in learning to master the chaos in our lives. and in finding stillness in the midst of the storm.

Nowadays, life brings us ever and again into situations in which we can only exist through what we are – situations that demand that we give up all we have, all that gives us stability and security, everything that we have relied upon. It is as if the ground is taken from under our feet. The characteristic of what we might call 'living on the edge' is that it is precarious, it is a balancing act. We have to keep moving – like riding a bicycle, the faster we pedal the better we can stay upright.

We could describe this condition in terms of our being on a threshold, the threshold from one form of being, of consciousness, to another. The reason why life at the threshold is so unpredictable is that different laws obtain on either side. The laws of the physical world apply on this side. They have enabled us to become citizens of the earth, to feel secure on earth, have given us our three-dimensional, point-centred consciousness. Therefore, because of them our ego has been made to grow in strength, free from destabilising influences; it has gained in dignity and stature; it is able to take hold of the divine.

But these laws have worked so effectively to give us such an egocentric perspective that we feel ourselves to be at the centre of the world. Hence the devastating rise of egotism – on both the individual and the global scale.

However in the course of this century our powers of perception have been broadened. From the 1950's onwards we stand ever more under the laws of the spirit in which the whole realm of the forces of life are at work. To our three-dimensional, point centred consciousness an expanded, peripheral consciousness is added. This gives rise to a consciousness that looks inwards from the periphery, where the laws of counter space or non-Euclidean space apply.

We can learn a lot about such an awareness from autistic people. In extreme cases they say 'I' to everyone else and 'you' to themselves in what is called reverse identification – they find it almost impossible to centre themselves.

As we become more open to what works in from the periphery we notice that what lives in us as a thought or feeling starts to appear in others and vice-versa. In the phenomenon of projection, subject-object boundaries become blurred. This leads to a kaleidoscope of images.

At the threshold conditions from either side pertain, which leads to confusion and provokes reactions with which we are only too familiar – perplexity, outright fear, even mental imbalance. Such conditions are referred to in the 'Little Apocalypse', Luke 21, the Advent Gospel Reading. The surging ocean waves can be seen as an image of the breaking in of the forces of life.

This gives rise to the sense that the whole fabric of society is unravelling. Chaos reigns, both around us and within us. For what rises up from the depths of our being and breaks into social life is ever more chaotic. In this regard we need only think of terrorism, mass exploitation, and fundamentalism.

The word 'chaos' nowadays has two connotations: we might think of anarchy, loss of predictability, confusion or, if we are informed by modern chaos theory, a condition of utter meaningless, sliding into a state where the temperature slowly falls ever lower. Whatever the connotation, despair, helplessness and fear are generated. This leads to the sense that we are like corks bobbing up and down on the water at the whim of every current and breeze. But does chaos have to be like this?

For the pre-Christian cultures, chaos had none of these negative connotations. The Greeks for instance, regarded chaos not as the opposite of order in the narrowest sense. They looked upon it rather as a state of potential into which sensitive and creative influence can flow, and out of which creation becomes actualised or realised. It was for them much more like the *prima materia* of the alchemists, the original and undifferentiated substance, a concept that has largely been lost today and which we need to recover if we are not to fall victims to the turbulence around and within us.

The activity of an artist is creation out of the dynamic of chaos. We can gain a visual impression of this dynamic in the work of painters. At every moment the painter is working with two extremes: with the forces of form and fixity, of completion on the one hand and with the tendencies towards dissolution and dissipation on the other. The real painter sees in the random colours a new relationship that is asking to be born, and it is only the master craftsman who is able to plunge with their ego into that middle realm and work creatively with the tensions that live there. If they manage to use imaginatively the forces streaming from both poles without succumbing to either, they produce what we all recognise as a masterpiece. Fra Angelico and Rembrandt are examples of great artists who lived with this tension with every fibre of their being: Fra Angelico living closer to the form pole, Rembrandt living close to the chaos pole. Today some artists leave areas of 'chaos' in their paintings for the observer to 'order'.

All true artists today know the brink. Nowadays we are all challenged to become artists – not in specialised fields of art or craft, but in everyday life. We have to develop 'brinkmanship' of an order not known before. Our ego has to become Master Craftsman. It has to learn to master the chaos, to transform it and then integrate it.

But that is not all. At the same time as being the artist we are asked to become the medium, the raw materials of the work of art. What does that imply? To allow the chaos to work on us, that is to give ourselves up to it, to be prepared to be at the edge, on the brink. This involves casting away our supports – our possessions, our roles – and staying mobile. But saying 'yes' completely to the chaos entails allowing it to buffet us and empty us, to strip us of 'what we are not'. We all know the pain and anguish this causes; life circumstances today bring us constantly to the threshold of despair.

Within such an enormous tension, how do we hold out at the threshold of despair? Can we so take up the tension that we stand our ground and weather the storm? Very often we learn from meteorological events which take place in the earth's atmosphere about what goes on in our own souls.

When a storm breaks out, particularly in a tropical region, cloud masses suddenly build up, threateningly, randomly. Currents surge and sweep, one over the other. But there is always a region in the cloud that is ordered. At the hub of the cyclone the currents spiral inwards towards a focal point that forms a vortex.

This vortex moves with the mass of the clouds but is an entity within itself. Mysteriously, right at the centre, at the eye, it is still. The eye of the cyclone is in fact a hollow. Occasionally, when the clouds at the centre part slightly, they reveal a small circle of blue sky. The eye opens and the light streams forth.

Just as each of us has known despair and pain amid the chaos, so we have also experienced times of grace when we are mysteriously transported to a place that seems outside time and outside space – a place where we gain unexpected respite and repose. Though outwardly nothing may have changed, from this new vantage point we are utterly at home and at one with ourselves.

Whilst everything around us is restless and turbulent we are completely at rest at this still point. We gain a new perspective on our situation. We see it in a new light, for we see with the eyes of the spirit. At the still point, the oppressive circumstances in which we found ourselves hitherto gain a new meaning; we can cope differently even if outwardly nothing has changed. Through the experience of the still point we begin to develop a new faculty. We learn to be able to feel our way into the complexities of whatever situation we are in, and to empathise with others without losing our centre. In other words, we are able to be peripheral and receptive whilst also remaining fully awake and centred.

These two activities are no longer exclusive. They can occur together without contradiction for Christ has entered into the chaos. He holds the middle ground so that the conditions and laws at work on both sides of the threshold operate together. We move from antithesis to synthesis. A truly magical interplay of opposites is an essential component of the mystery of the Second Coming, for the Son of Man has wrought for us a new existence at the threshold through his ordeal and suffering in recent times. The 'sun-bright realm' is brilliantly bright everywhere, but it is able to be present with the same power just as much in the part as in the whole. In meditation and prayer we wrestle at the threshold and hope to find the still point. In the Act of Consecration of Man, as in other still moments, grace can be given.

The experience of seeing at the threshold is complemented by an experience of hearing. At the still point where we are utterly at rest, at one, the home of our own 'I am' not only unites with us fully, but reveals itself to each of us individually in our daytime state of consciousness. At such times the voice of our self-centred self, who uses others and works through others, is silenced. Out of the silence there speaks the one in us who seeks to work for the sake of others – our own true 'I am'. We become aware of this speaking in different ways: as a thought that 'springs to mind' or as the voice of conscience for example.

As once the 'I am' of humanity spoke to Moses in the flames of the burning bush 'I am the I am', so now it speaks through each individual human being. What it says can be rendered 'The essence of my being lies in my becoming'. Whenever we can take hold of what lives in our true self we become creative. The power of our own origin works to lead us selflessly to originality, because we are in continual becoming.

The Advent Mystery of the present, the Advent of the Second Coming, could be summed up in a single word as: 'become'. There is a moral and social challenge in this, which has a Whitsuntide quality. For it is quite remarkable that we forget how to become creative in this way – we forget that it is out of the still point that we can create new beginnings. We need to be reminded by each other that we have to do it and also how to do it. We require constantly to experience each other courageously overcoming the greatest hindrances in ourselves. We need to be prepared to be examples for each other in this. To see each other not shying away from threshold issues and situations teaches us tolerance and compassion. It also encourages us to face up to ourselves more realistically and with ever less illusion. For, spurred on by our neighbours, we take courage in facing up to what we find hardest to look at in ourselves. And what we are least able to face up to is actually what confuses us most. Here we need each other to ask, out of loving concern, the Parsifal question: 'Brother what ails thee?' Today, in the context we have described above, this question could be reformulated, 'What confuses you the most?'

New social forms – particularly within our communities – will succeed when we approach each other in this way – encouraging each other to become masters of living on the brink by facing up to just those areas in our own destiny where chaos and confusion reign.

2000s

On the 150th Anniversary of Darwin's *Origin of Species*

Pearl Goodwin

Pearl Goodwin was born in 1937 in Edinburgh. She studied biology and embryology before becoming a priest of The Christian Community in 1977. In this article she looks at the impact Darwin's idea of evolution has had on our understanding of the world and ourselves. Despite its narrow focus on a purely physical development, she argues that it can be expanded to include the idea of spiritual *evolution.*

Towards the end of his life, Charles Darwin had a profoundly affecting experience that provides us with some insight into the soul of this man who has had such a mighty impact on Western scientific thought. He fell asleep one day in the woods under a tree, possibly in his own garden at Down House near Lewisham. As he wrote later, in that moment between sleeping and waking he saw nature not as a consequence of the long process of chance evolution, with which his name will be forever connected, nor as an abstraction, but as a being, a presence full of beauty and meaning in itself. It is said that he would have given away all his life's work to have that experience again. As far as can be known, he never did have that experience again. But he had caught a glimpse of reality and he knew that what he had done would forever make that reality less accessible to people. Perhaps it could still be available to artists, but scientists had to live with some colder truths. A wedge was placed not only between art and science, but also between religion and science, for how could God have created a world such as Darwin envisaged?

And yet, what Darwin did was an absolute necessity at that point in history. He introduced to the world a rational principle of evolution into an understanding of nature and the human being. As a young man, he was not academic. He preferred simply to look at and collect things. So he became part of the now famous voyage of the *Beagle* where, on its journey around South America, he painstakingly gathered a vast body of data from his observations of the forms in nature that he came across. He spent years ordering what he had observed. Only much later, in 1859, did his seminal book *The Origin of Species* appear. His ideas about how species evolved broke into the world like a bombshell, not so much because he brought the idea of evolution to the forefront – it was not an entirely new idea – but because of the way, even the mechanism, in which nature would have to evolve to meet what was shouting out at him from all his observations. Two phrases by which Darwinian evolution is characterised have become almost household terms; evolution through natural selection and through the survival of the fittest. In a few words, and much oversimplified: a species of plant or animal undergoes small changes and whichever of these changes can best adapt the organism to its environment or set of conditions will enable it to survive and reproduce, because it is best adapted, or 'fittest', to do so. Those characteristics that adapt it in this way will be passed on to successive generations. They have been 'naturally selected', not through any kind of plan or preference or direction, but because they enable survival.

With one stroke, the creation, which had always been seen as the work of God's hand, was diminished into a soulless consequence of chance change. Whatever one saw in nature, whatever is beautiful and wondrous in nature – a butterfly wing, a cheetah's power, the eyes of a child – or wherever one is bound to think 'that has meaning', one could be answered with a Darwinian certainty: 'That has come about only through millions of years of small changes, selected by the environment. It is beautiful because nature has many tools with which to work, but it is nonetheless devoid of meaning in the sense of being intended by any being, divine or otherwise.' So it is clear that human beings descended from animals and not from God. We are simply a bit cleverer because our brains have evolved further. Darwin was himself convinced of the inevitability of his theory of evolution. He knew that he had brought a dead hand into human culture, but he thought it unavoidable. People continue to think in this way. His work pervades every aspect of our cultural and educational life.

However, one of the most positive aspects of scientific endeavour is that it does not remain stationary. In Darwin's time, no one knew how these small changes took place in an organism that could then be selected. Darwin himself had no idea. He only knew that there must be some means or mechanism by which they occur.

The explanation had to wait for the work of the monk Gregor Mendel, near the end of the nineteenth century in Eastern Europe, and his breeding experiments with sweet peas in the monastery garden. Thus the science of genetics was born. This began to be applied to Darwinian theory only at the beginning of the twentieth century. The small changes were brought about by naturally arising but random mutation in the genetic material, the DNA, of the germ cells of an organism. These would either be selected and become a stable component of the DNA of a species or the mutation would die with the less fit organism. And so there arose the seemingly watertight union of evolution theory and genetics, out of which almost all questions could be answered.

For years this has been at the centre of biological science, adhered to with a kind of misplaced religious conviction. The 'dogma of DNA' as it was called was unassailable and indestructible. This came to be known as the reductionist view of nature when the working of DNA was, and still is, seen as the ultimate explanation for all form and development. Opposed to this is the holistic view that sees the organism itself as the master and DNA in the service to the organism. But what is of greatest interest is that it is the development in genetics itself that might ultimately bring about a real co-operation between these two views, the reductionist and the holistic. There has been a vast development in genetics, in the mapping of the genetic structure not only of human beings but of many organisms. Contrary to what might have been expected, it is becoming clear that the DNA of all species, whether bacteria, plant or animal, is largely similar. The DNA (genotype) of all organisms is not nearly so variable as the appearance (phenotype) of all organisms. A bacterium is certainly very different from a rose, which is very different from a cow or a human being. But they all seem to share a great ancestral past of DNA, with only relatively small differences. What then creates the difference? How does a rose get to look so different from a cow or a human being? It is as if there is something else at work, and the DNA itself can metamorphose in its working according to the needs of this 'something' else, be it the being of a rose or a human being. That means that instead of saying that we are just smarter monkeys, since we share about 98% of our DNA with them, we should be asking about the differences between monkeys and human beings in spite of the genetic similarity. It will be interesting to see how science will find answers to these questions, which are becoming ever clearer. Genetics is going through the eye of the needle. It is the serpent biting its own tail, and it may in the end be the means by which a greater perspective is gained that can understand the form and variety of organisms as well as their evolution. It is always the most powerful thing when reductionism itself gives rise to the opposite.

It will still be a long time before natural science is able to accept the possibility that every species is an 'idea', and that an idea is something spiritual. There is a rose idea, a cow idea, and above all, an idea of the human being. That idea is a reality; it is able to take hold of the DNA and in the co-operation between idea and DNA a rose, a cow, or a human being emerges. The new advances in genetics seem to suggest that this could be an answer to the question of where all the differences (phenotypes) come from. It may take some time, and it may never happen. Other answers, approximations, will be found. But if it could happen, then there could be something like a new renaissance, a healing of the breach between art and science, and between religion and science. Darwin brought the reality of evolution to the world. He brought it in the narrowest form, which mechanised both nature and the human being. But he brought it in its most rigorous form so that it could be thought. Now it is time to expand the ideas of evolution with the same rigour, so that creation is not diminished but enhanced by our being able to think it. Perhaps, if Darwin were alive today and if he were to fall asleep under a tree and waken into that transcendent experience of nature, he would know with his thinking that his experience was not outside of his theory of evolution, but it's very crown.

In Search of the Divine Feminine: The Re-emergence of Sophia in Our Times

Martin Samson

Born in South Africa in 1962, Martin Samson was ordained as a Christian Community priest in 1992 and afterwards worked in Australia. He has studied cross-cultural religion, mythology and cosmology. In this article he explores the idea of the divine feminine as it appeared in ancient cultures as well as in the early days of Christianity before it was suppressed by the emerging Church.

I believe that one of the most crucial tasks of Christian religious expression today is the quest to include the divine feminine once more. The popular appeal of Dan Brown's book *The Da Vinci Code* shows that there is a yearning for a worthy and intellectually attractive renewal of the idea of the divine feminine. Christians over the last century have been awakening to the fact that Mary is more than just the mother of Jesus. Yet, at the same time we have to acknowledge the fact that the divine feminine has been denied, sidelined, suppressed and, in a sense, even killed or crucified by the Christian tradition over the last sixteen centuries.

Is there really only one male God? Where, in the life of The Christian Community, do we address and pray to the divine feminine? This article intends to explore the context of the disappearance and re-emergence of the divine feminine within Christianity. I hope that it will generate a thought-provoking and yet open space for further discussion within our community.

The disappearance of the goddess

In many cultures the language, symbols and images used for the divinity, or God, describe a co-creative relationship between the masculine and feminine aspects of being. In modern paganism it is the lord and lady; Egyptians understood the relationship of Isis and Osiris to be the revelation of divine action on earth; in parts of Aboriginal Australia, Baiame works together with the sun goddess, Yhi, in creation. Many cultures have a pantheon of gods and goddesses. Even in most monotheistic religions the feminine side of God remains robust in the devotional life of the culture and community. In China when Confucianism was establishing a male-dominated official philosophical teaching, the goddess of the West emerged amongst the devout as Kuan Yin, the female Buddha of compassion. Within some Christian traditions Mary has become, along with Christ, the focus of intercession with God. Even in the reigns of the monotheistic periods of Akhenaton in Egypt and Zarathustra in Persia the goddess survived as Isis and Astarte. Yet, within Christianity as a whole, we tend to persist in saying there is only one God and attribute predominantly male characteristics to God's being.

The history of many cultures shows a rise in the patriarchal teachings within the ruling classes from around 600 BC. This includes Egypt, Israel, Persia, India and China. In Judeo-Christian history this moment is marked by the return of the Israelites from their captivity in Babylon. Once the Israelites returned to the Promised Land the Zadokite priesthood focused the nation's religious attention on Jerusalem and the rebuilding of the temple. Through the cultural influences in Egypt and Babylon the emerging Jewish nation had moved from being a polytheistic culture to a monotheistic one. The Jerusalem priesthood had gained an upper hand in establishing a single 'authentic' priesthood and over the next few hundred years began writing and editing the teachings of what became the Jewish tradition.

This traditional interpretation is still representative of what many people understand is portrayed in the Bible. The emerging insights from history and archaeology can prompt us to ask whether our God is a singular male God with three distinct male persons. Is there more to the story than what we have grown accustomed to? For example, there is the story of King Saul who went to visit a woman who could communicate with the dead in order to speak with the spirit of the prophet Samuel. Samuel had died, and the Lord was no longer speaking to Saul in dreams or through prophets (1 Sam. 28). While this is not proof of the feminine aspect of God, what it does show is that the Israelites knew of more deities than Yahweh. Abraham went and honoured the high places of local deities, many of which were those of goddesses, before establishing sanctuaries to Yahweh. In the early days of Israel, Jerusalem was not the uncontested place of the Temple and the only high place of Yahweh. There were many sanctuaries to local deities and the Israelites were part of that religious culture to begin with.

Even the interpretation of the traditional struggle between Yahweh and Baal is changing in its perspective through the discovery of temples dedicated to 'Yahweh and his Ashera'. Ashera is the Palestinian/Canaanite name for Astarte and her consort was Baal. Many thinkers see the battles in the Hebrew Bible as metaphors describing the Yahweh's attempts to usurp Baal's throne as Ashera's consort. In summary, it seems that the journey of the Israelites towards becoming the Jewish people began in a polytheistic tradition when one deity, Yahweh, chose a folk with which to work and bring about a specific revelation of the human self. Once the Israelites realised this they became what is known as henotheistic: they worshipped one particular god among all the gods. In times of struggle the Israelites returned to the indigenous gods, as symbolised by the golden calf. Ultimately, their journey focused their devotion and spiritual aspiration towards the 'I am' god Yahweh. These insights from archaeological and biblical scholarship show that outcomes of history that we may consider to be divinely mediated are by no means inevitable. Historical criticism gives us an opportunity to evaluate how personal destiny, cultural influences and the choices people make are incorporated into the results of evolution. It further challenges us to assess how our own choices in philosophy and lifestyles will write the history of our times.

Through the monotheistic philosophical influences in Egypt and Babylon mentioned above, this worship of one god among many became the conviction that there is *only* one God. The Jewish monotheistic philosophy of the Jerusalem priesthood was established and consequently enforced. Monotheism had become the dominant culture at the time of the life of Jesus Christ. This historical background throws light on his anger at the rigid, exclusive orthodoxy of the religious authorities.

Did Christ reclaim the divine feminine in his teachings? Much of the Hebrew Bible was only finally written down a short time before Christ was born. In fact some of the books of what is commonly still called the Old Testament were written in the first century after Christ. It is relatively easy to read passages of the Hebrew Bible and feel the philosophical understandings of the community that edited those passages.

In particular the question of the authorship of the books of Moses, or the Pentateuch, has come under scrutiny over the last three hundred years. At first it was presumed Moses wrote down the first five books of the Hebrew Bible, but later it became obvious that there were very different styles and sources in the narratives. The repetition of certain stories gave rise to the question of there being possibly more than one author. It has become common to think that the Pentateuch draws upon four different sources, each with a very different cultural and philosophical emphasis. The oldest source, dating back to the tenth century BC, is known as the Yahwist or 'J' source from its use of the name of Yahweh for God. Then, in the eighth century BC, came the 'E' source or Elohist writers, who predominantly use the word Elohim for God. In the seventh century BC other authors and editors wrote the deuterocanonical texts, known as the 'D' source. Finally, one community, whose style some of the authors of the New Testament seem to have taken on, was the Jerusalem priesthood or 'P' source editors, who, in the sixth century BC, wrote some passages that are critical for our understanding of the divine feminine: the creation story in the first chapter of Genesis being a central one. This particular understanding of the origins of the Bible texts opens up a different way of interpreting doctrines derived from certain narratives. For example, the understanding of the first creation story in Genesis 1, written by the priestly source, gives a very different emphasis to our understanding of the feminine side of God than the Yahwist narrative of the same event in Genesis 2. Although it may at first seem shocking to analyse the Bible in this way, we are in fact familiar with the idea that one story can be told in different ways by various authors when we read the four gospels. Here we know that each one is true, and that each opens a unique aspect of the truth for our consideration.

Created in the image of God

Genesis 1:27 has three parts: '(1) God created humankind in his image; (2) in the image of God he created them; (3) male and female he created them.' This way of writing is a classic form of Hebrew poetic repetition designed to impress the hearer with the theology of the narrative. The first two parts repeat the same idea but are arranged in reverse. With the third part there are two ways to read the parallelism of the added information. Each choice determines how the roles and relationships between men and women are interpreted, and, subsequently, what the Imago Dei or being created in the image of God might mean.

One way to interpret the ideas in the third part of the sentence is a progressively parallel development of ideas. This means the ideas of male and female are built onto or added to the ideas of the first two. They may not necessarily refer to the image of God, but only anticipate and prepare us for the next verse and the command for humanity to multiply. This choice is well substantiated by the suspicion that the philosophies of the 'P' source, the Zadokite priestly editors of Genesis 1, were not egalitarian and were thus unlikely to express a view that promoted equality between men and women in society. This choice of interpretation has also been the dominant choice within Christian doctrine between the times of Augustine and Calvin. We still live in the on-going social and spiritual repercussions for women in the wake of the teachings arising from reading the creation story in this way.

Another way to read third part of the sentence is as straight parallelism, which leads to the realisation that the reference to male and female does indeed refer to the image of God. In this form of reading humans are called exclusively and distinctively to create out of and in the image of God. The connection of our gender to procreation we share with the whole of creation and it does not describe our specific task given in the creation story. The writer wants the reader to understand God's self as 'male and female' alike.

Which choice do we make as the reader of this information? How do we, as modern Christians within our own social critique on the role of women in society and their equal ability to fully image God, choose to hear this part of the narrative? It hopefully becomes clearer as to how critical it is for our own philosophical framework to make a stand one way or the other. A lot in our lives and how we live them depends on our conception of God in the light of this verse.

The resurrection of Sophia for the survival of Christianity

In esoteric and Gnostic teaching there is an understanding that the divine works as a syzygy: two aspects that in conjunction or alignment with one another enable the other to be active agents in creation. A passive side enables the active. At times it is the feminine aspect that works in the passive enabling complementary role; at other times it is the masculine that acts as the passive role to support the feminine activity again. Neither part can be seen as the more important. Christ was in some ways 'passive' in death and resurrection, while the Sophian aspect, working through the women, was the active witnessing agent. Sophia played an enabling role in the emergence of the transformed, masculine 'I am' force in the death and resurrection of Christ.

In the meantime, wisdom has died through humanity's history and been entombed in intellectual scientific, utilitarian philosophies and societal norms. As stated before, this suppression of the divine feminine took place in many cultures, not only within Christianity. Wisdom has to be crucified and resurrected through humanity. A new aspect of wisdom can be added to her being through human-wrought wisdom. The masculine side of God had to go through a process of death and resurrection at the hand of humanity in the human being of Jesus Christ, facilitated by Sophia. Sophia experiences her death and resurrection through the 'I am' of each individual human being learning to imbue wisdom into creation in our thoughts, feelings, words and actions on the earth. The masculine 'I am' Self within each one of us is called actively to resurrect the Sophian Wisdom we have crucified.

An indication of this can be heard in the epistle on humanity that we hear in the Act of Consecration of Man between the various festivals. In these times we can allow the resounding spiritual content of each festival cycle to settle further into our humanity. In the third part of the epistle we hear of our working with the Holy or Healing Spirit. If we can experience the work of the 'I am' in each human being, as Christ in us and through us, we can also begin to hear the inner dynamic of the epistle which draws us into the relationship of community of life between divinity and humanity. The ideas connected with 'our beholding' move from beholding the spirit towards a calling to imbue the world around us with the spiritual substance of a spirit-filled human soul. The human activity of beholding acquires awareness that our spirit-filled soul has an activity of awakening the Healing Spirit in all that we behold. This kind of active perceiving of the world allows creation to receive our human wisdom as a transformative deed, born and resurrected of our consecrated humanity.

2010s

Mary, Sophia and the New Advent of Christ

Patrick Kennedy

Patrick Kennedy was born in 1976 and is co-director of the Seminary of The Christian Community in North America. In this article he addresses the theme of the divine feminine in relation to the Second Coming of Christ.

In an open conversation last year someone asked about the nature of the Second Coming of Christ and what connection, if any, this might have with the emerging awareness in our time of the divine feminine, or 'Sophia'. This question touches on the deepest realities of our time and on what must begin to happen within Christianity if it is to have any positive future, so I offered to address it within a longer talk. The few thoughts offered here can only be taken as one aspect of an immeasurably deep subject.

Christ's 'second' coming

First, we need to explore our assumptions about the nature of the second coming, a name or title which itself is very misleading. Why? Because it implies that Christ has left. Yet, if we alone follow what the gospels tell us on this subject, he has not left us at all. In the Gospel of Matthew it is Christ who promised 'I am with you always, even to the end of the age' (Matt. 28:20) or 'wherever two or three are gathered in my name there I am also' (Matt. 18:20). The traditional conception of Christ's 'leaving' – as well as the promise of his 'return' – comes, of course, from the story of his ascension (Acts 1:9–11), where the disciples follow his rising into the clouds and hear the words of the attending angels that he will return in the same way. What can be made of these discrepancies? Either these two parts of the Gospel are in direct contradiction to each other, or we need to gain a different understanding of what is meant by ascension and return.

The essential new understanding, attainable through modern spiritual science, of the meaning of Christ's life, death and resurrection, is that Christ's inmost being was united with the earth's being, with the processes and substances of the earth. This truth is expressed in all the central images of the event of Golgotha itself. On the cross we see his blood flowing into the ground and his body is laid in a cave, into the depths of the earth itself. Why would he come so deep into our experience, into human-ness and the depths of matter, only to abandon the earth for the heavens again? St Paul can provide us with a key to understanding the ascension in a way that harmonises with the comforting words of Matthew: 'I am with you always...'

> In saying, 'He ascended', what does it mean but that he had also descended into the lower regions of the earth? He who descended is the one who also ascended far above all the heavens that he might fill all things. (Eph. 4:9–10)

Through all that happened on Golgotha, Paul leads us to see Christ's ascension into 'heaven' as something that could more accurately be called an 'expansion'. Christ does not abandon the earth, but expands into and permeates all earthly and heavenly spheres. What the gospels and the esoteric teacher we know as St Paul show us – and what the open eyes of the heart can perceive – is that Christ did not abandon us here on the earth; he has simply grown beyond the limits of the human form into a new cosmic level, permeating the earth with heavenly being. Christ is with us, it is just that with his 'ascension' he had simply grown beyond our capacity to 'see' him.

But if Christ is with us, what is meant by the second coming? If he permeates our earthly reality, why is it that so many souls cannot perceive him, acknowledge his presence, or know him? What is it that has left us, what have we lost?

The fall of human consciousness

As a way to illustrate what is now missing for us, that is what we have lost here on earth, one can begin by listing the traditional doctrines and tenets of Christianity and honestly asking: what of these can we understand? Which of these fundamental teachings of Christianity can be comprehended and grasped by modern, Western souls? I did this recently at a talk given on this subject. The list began slowly and then began to pick up pace until the entire writing pad was covered with all the fundamental truths of Christianity. For example:

~ the 'virgin birth'
~ why Jesus has two different lineages in the Bible
~ angels of all ranks
~ any of the miracles – for example, the healings, walking on water, the feeding of the 5000
~ the Trinity
~ the transubstantiation
~ the resurrection – the central truth and signature of Christianity

We had to acknowledge that for the modern soul, Christianity and Christ himself had become incomprehensible, something we simply no longer understand. Clearly what we have lost is our understanding, our knowledge of Christ. What is missing is the 'Sophia' or Christ-Wisdom.

Following the trajectory of human thinking and inner understanding of the nature and reality of Christ over the course of the centuries from the beginnings of Christianity, we see a very clear trajectory. The early centuries reveal a consciousness still very much open to the reality and light of the spirit and of the divine, cosmic dimensions of the being that incarnated in Jesus. By the middle ages the light begins to darken, the doors to heaven begin to close and the church desperately tries to hold onto its truths through the establishment of official dogma. By the nineteenth century, almost everything has been lost and the great theologians of the day can only honestly stand behind the figure of Jesus as the 'simple man of Nazareth' who was deluded that the culmination of time had arrived. Thus, in terms of our consciousness, Nietzsche could honestly declare, 'God is dead'. From the time of Christ's appearance in Palestine to the nineteenth and twentieth centuries we can follow how Western souls are less and less able to recognise, acknowledge or understand the divine reality of Christ or the essence of Christianity. Our minds fell into the darkness of materialistic consciousness; our 'soul eyes' became blind to the presence of Christ.

The fructification of the individual soul by the spirit

So what is it that could bring about the renewal of Christianity? What is it that could bring about a new perception of Christ? Nothing other than a search for the Sophia, the knowledge or wisdom of Christ. This was – and is – the mission of that spiritual movement that goes by the name of Anthroposophy. Modern spiritual science, or anthroposophy, provides the means to comprehend everything that has become incomprehensible in Christianity (including each of the items listed above).

The path to rediscovering the Sophia begins with taking in the fruits of spiritual scientific research on the nature of the being of Christ and his transformative life and death. Thinking these thoughts through with honest reflection and sound judgment begins the process of shaping new eyes for perceiving the reality of Christ. However, higher knowledge of the reality of this being requires more than learning new facts; it requires a total revolution and transformation of the soul.

This soul transformation for the reception of the spirit is often called initiation for it is the process whereby one is led, or initiated, into the knowledge of worlds hidden from the senses. The process of initiation is the process of preparing the soul for the birth of the spirit. This preparation can be achieved through what is sometimes called catharsis or the purification of the soul. Exercises in moral development, meditation and prayer, taking in thoughts of the spirit, of the eternal, work to transform the soul and awaken the slumbering, higher human being within. Ultimately this leads to a transformation of the forces already found in the soul: our thinking, feeling and willing. Before initiation they were haphazardly developed in response to life and directed towards the transitory world of the senses. Through esoteric training these powers are lifted up to the highest, the eternal world of the spirit, and brought under the direction of these spiritual principals.

In the path laid out by Rudolf Steiner in his book *How to Know Higher Worlds*, the student is first directed to wrap their inner life in a mantle of feelings of reverence, wonder and devotion. This comes out of a deep knowledge of the laws of the soul and spiritual worlds. 'Wisdom begins in wonder,' Socrates once explained, and the inner experience of Sophia (Wisdom) is made possible through the cultivation of reverential wonder and devotion.

The next step is to educate carefully the three forces of the soul. Our thoughts are to be brought into a harmonious, logical flow and educated in careful attention. With our feelings we are led to three different qualities that must be developed. We are taught to develop an objective relationship to our feelings, no longer overwhelmed by the highs and lows of our soul, the exaltations and lamentations, but instead developing the power of equanimity. Openness to and a true interest in everything that comes our way and a trust that it is directed by the guiding wisdom of the universe, is a second important quality to develop for our feeling. This is expressed in Mary's words, 'May it come to pass as you have said' (Luke 1:38). A third quality of feeling that we must ever strive to develop is the ability to focus our attention on what is good and true, to focus on the positive. This is a very important quality to develop, for as inner vision develops, more and more of the world begins to reveal itself to the esoteric student. This includes the detailed and easily overwhelming vision of all that is imperfect, untrue, ugly and evil in the world and in other people. It often happens, if the student of the inner path has not attended enough to this exercise, that the person on the spiritual path becomes more intolerant, judgmental and negative than before they started.

In the case of the higher development of our willing, it is to be born anew out of our own direction and guidance, not constantly in reaction to the world nor involuntarily following passions and drives. The esoteric student is called to open their will to the needs of others and of the earth and to give their actions a guidance born of insight and inner wisdom. In summary, if one were to use the words of the Act of Consecration of Man, you could say that the intention of the esoteric student is to develop pure thinking, a loving heart, and willing devotion.

The transformation of the forces of the soul, the purification of our feeling, thinking and willing, is what one can call making one's soul a 'virgin' soul. Now, when the student of the inner worlds approaches the world or another person or a higher thought in meditation and prayer, their pure thinking, loving feeling, and devoted and accepting willing, open the soul up to more than just the abstract truths of existence. They enable an encounter, a moment of fructification. This opening allows a moment of grace to take place, the moment of inner conception. It is a real event in the life of the person on the path in which a new, higher life stirs within the soul. Through the path of intimate careful development, as outlined above, the soul is transformed into a womb, a place in which the delicate development of the spirit can unfold, be nourished and protected by the purified soul.

This event in the life of the initiate has been portrayed artistically over millennia. Think of Isis holding Horus, of images of the Madonna shown with the child, often emerging from an opening in her mid-section. In Mary, the artists depicted the purified soul, expressing pure devotion, openness, equanimity and trust in every gesture and colour. All of these images are a representation of a higher experience of knowing, of inner wisdom being fructified by the spirit. In medieval annunciation paintings, Mary is almost always shown reading a book (the scriptures), meditatively pursuing knowledge. We see her at the moment when this knowledge becomes something much more than what we normally associate with knowing: it becomes new life within. We see her head lifting from the page and a ray of light shines down from the heights and touches her head. It is the moment of the conception of the divine child, the higher human within, the one 'born of God'. These images of Mary are a depiction not only of a historical figure but of the human soul itself, and the Christ child presents to us an image of the eternal human spirit, the higher self. Anyone who seriously and devotedly follows the path laid out in anthroposophy will themselves experience this annunciation moment. It is an intimate but completely real and objective experience of the striving individual that comes as a moment of grace on the path of self-development, where they begin to experience 'Not I, but Christ in me'.

The fructification of the community soul

But how does this relate to the specific mission of The Christian Community? One could say that our mission is to facilitate this spiritual conception, this higher knowing, in community through the Eucharist, the centre of the seven sacraments. There too, it requires a 'Mary-Sophia-Soul' to receive the new presence of Christ. In the service, this higher, generative knowing is spoken of in an amazing way. We follow the movement of the book from the right to the inside left of the altar – from outside to inside – a representation of crossing over from the outer world to the inner world, the crossing of the threshold. There, during the stage of the service traditionally known as the Transubstantiation but perhaps better understood as the Transformation, the priest speaks for the soul of the community, praying that the offering be brought through 'our pure thinking, our loving heart, our willing devotion'. Here the three forces of the soul are attributed to a 'we' not an 'I'. A few moments later, the sacred act of inner knowing is described this way: the congregation knows Christ in freedom.

These thoughts may at first seem abstract. However, when we take them into our souls and enter into the Act of Consecration of Man with this thought: together we are building a higher, community soul, that can receive – as Mary did – the being of Christ, this thought can then open the doorway to whole new experiences in our celebrating together. Through this we can begin to feel into how in the Act of Consecration of Man, we approach the divine Ground of the World through the purified Mary-Soul of the community, which is able to be the 'virgin soul' in which the Christ-Spirit can be born. In the service, it is the community that becomes the bearer of Christ. It is the gathered, devoted community and the eternal forms expressed in the ritual that creates a new vessel for Christ's 're-appearance'.

Human souls are in desperate need of the experience of the one who brings peace to human hearts, strengthens their wills and unites us in a new humanity. This is the deepest longing of every soul. Since the time when Jesus Christ walked the earth, our souls have grown less able to perceive his nearness, his presence. Though he is here, radiant and bright, we have grown blind; we have lost the Sophia who knows Christ in the highest sense. I hope that this article can help us gain a sense of how the power of the Sophia can be found again as the essential, receptive power on the individual path of initiation and on the community path of offering.

Fighting the Stigma of AIDS in Uganda

Deborah Ravetz

Deborah Ravetz, born in 1957, studied English Literature at York, as well as Fine Art and Print Making at Aberdeen. She has been part of the editorial team of Perspectives *for many years. In this article she tells the courageous story of Gideon Byamugisha, an Anglican minister in Uganda who spoke out about his HIV-positive diagnosis.*

The psychiatrist Victor Frankl dedicated his life to the search for meaning. When working with people in crises he suggested that they should ask themselves, 'What is my life asking of me?' Recently I conducted an interview with a man called Gideon Byamugisha. He was the first Anglican minister in Africa to come out publicly as being HIV positive and I wanted to ask him to share with me the process by which he came to terms with what had happened to him. To hear his story was to see the words of Victor Frankl put into practice.

Gideon and his wife, Kellen, were just about to travel to England when his wife became seriously ill and very suddenly died. They had been married for only four years and the shock was profound. Unknown to him, his wife's sister had arranged for Kellen to take an AIDS test before she died. The test was positive but she decided not to tell Gideon until he had completed his exams thinking he would not be able to function with yet more trauma. When she finally told him it took Gideon three months to go and get the test because he was so frightened of the outcome. He finally went, telling himself that if he could survive the death of his beloved wife nothing could destroy him.

The test came back positive. The counsellor who handed him the result looked at his priestly collar and said with mocking contempt, 'What will you do now, man of God?'

Gideon was surprised because up until that moment he hadn't realised how much his clerical collar defined him. Even more shattering was the realisation that he was experiencing a hitherto unknown land, the land of stigma. To have AIDS or test positive for HIV in Uganda meant the end of life as one had lived it prior to the diagnosis. It was seen as an illness contracted by prostitutes, long-distance truck drivers who had many partners, and homosexuals who were considered deviant. It was seen as a curse and a punishment and its one outcome was death. Gideon was a minister and a lecturer in a theological college. He knew from that moment his life was over. The death of his wife had caused huge suffering. He couldn't believe there was more to come.

Sitting in the taxi, he had to consider how he would deal with the news. He knew he could keep quiet and protect his reputation. He also knew that as a man of faith it wasn't part of his value system to lead a double life. This time in the taxi was a defining moment, a spiritual struggle. He knew that he needed support from his fellow Christians and that the only way that was possible was if he was honest. His decision to be open was simply realistic. He had a small salary and there was no health insurance or free medicine. He was completely dependent on support from friends and family. Silence would not only be against his principles as a man of faith, it would also mean death. He decided to put his trust in God and face shame, discrimination and stigma.

Gideon made the decision to tell the principal of his college, the staff and his students, and his wife's sister. The college administration agreed to support him if he didn't bring its reputation into disrepute by going public with his HIV status. Gideon refused. He wanted to talk about his experience and warn other Christians and church leaders that what was being said about AIDS as a disease of deviants, which good Christians had nothing to worry about, was simply not true. When he told his students, there was a stunned silence. One student, who is now Bishop in Northern Uganda, said, 'Let us not be impotent, let us pray for our lecturer.'

That prayer, together with the unconditional support he was getting from his sister-in-law's family, gave him courage to slowly build up a circle of care from among the people who mattered most in his life. There it was possible to learn, explore, teach and be publicly open. This kind of openness has a particular character, for in the process of disclosing a positive HIV status, one can choose to benefit from the confidential support of a close-knit circle of trusted friends and family members without being publicly open.

However, Gideon began to feel he wanted to follow a different path, one that meant being completely open about his condition in order to break the stigma, silence, shame, denial and discrimination that, unfortunately, still surround HIV and AIDS. He said that this kind of openness is not necessary for everyone. The path of complete openness is very tough and demands sacrifice. It is a calling that brings life and health outcomes that one cannot always plan for and guarantee. It means becoming a kind of prophetic voice speaking on behalf of the shamed, stigmatised and misunderstood everywhere, and sometimes prophets pay the price of 'speaking the unspoken' with their own lives. Gideon made the decision to do what it took to rise to that challenge and take up that calling.

As he spoke with me, he told many stories. He told me the many different reactions to his openness. Some people were happy and praised his bravery. They acknowledged the need for more people like him who are willing to be open and to share their pain and vulnerability as a way of encouraging others to face theirs honestly, courageously and with hope. Others were not so enthusiastic about his choice to be publicly open about his condition. They said he was washing his dirty linen in public, seeking undue sympathy and bringing shame onto the Church. Some thought he probably deserved his fate and should be prepared to face the music, while others thought he had made the story up in order to make a living as he didn't look like someone who had AIDS! Some didn't know how to react to his story and often took their lead from the majority opinion of whoever was there at the time Gideon was speaking.

The most beautiful story he told me was about his relationship with his bishop, Bishop Samuel. He went for a job interview with the bishop and omitted to tell him about his HIV-positive diagnosis for fear of not getting the job. He found himself being prompted by his inner spirit to return to the office to tell the whole truth. After he had taken the risk and spoken, he shut his eyes, expecting rejection. As he sat there he felt the bishop put his hands on his head and heard him calling him his son. The bishop was overjoyed that Gideon had found it possible to be open with him and took him into his own home. Gideon described how during that time he became desperately ill and lost 20 kg (44 lbs). The bishop wrote a letter detailing Gideon's dire condition to the Ministry of Health of Uganda whose staff made contact with a friend of theirs in America. This woman got in touch with everyone she knew in America, and people went visiting door to door to find anyone one who would share any medicines they had leftover as a result of switching to better regimens. Through these leftover medicines and the intervention of friends from Uganda, USA, the UK and many other places, Gideon has survived long enough to marry again, produce two amazing children (thanks to the HIV-transmission-prevention science that blocks HIV from positive mother-to-child), see his child from his first marriage grow, and tell me his story!

Listening to Gideon speak had a profound effect on my feelings and my life. It was a healing experience to listen to what had happened to him and how he had dealt with it. He said that there were so many stories to tell about the effect his illness had had on himself and others that it was like the end of the Gospel of St John where the evangelist says that if all the stories about Christ were told there would not be space for enough books to write them down. With complete authenticity and absolute sincerity he went on to say that he really had to thank the counsellor who spoke to him so harshly. Because of that experience he had found his life's work among the stigmatised and, with that, the meaning of his existence.

The Spiritual Hierarchies and Our Relationship to Them

Michael Kientzler

Michael Kientzler was ordained in 1971 and worked in Canada and England before retiring in his native Germany. In this article he looks at the ancient teachings of the spiritual hierarchies and how they found modern expression through the work of Rudolf Steiner and anthroposophy.

At the beginning of the sixth century the teachings on the angelic hierarchies were first published by the one now known as Pseudo-Dionysius the Areopagite. 'Pseudo', because he was not the original Dionysius the Areopagite, the pupil of St Paul, initiate of the Eleusinian mysteries, and founder of the school of esoteric Christianity in Athens. Modern theology does not see that this was not a name but a title (like the title King Arthur in the Britain of the Dark Ages). His book *The Celestial Hierarchy* contains the doctrine of the three ranks of three hierarchies. This teaching was embodied in religious art, particularly in baptisteries such as the one in Florence. This tradition comes to an end in the fifteenth century with the rise of Protestantism.

Then, at the beginning of the twentieth century, we see the emergence of anthroposophy. During the preceding century, the same aggressive atheism that we find in Britain today was present in Germany. Its main representative was Ernst Haeckel, an evolutionary scientist and pupil of Charles Darwin. Rudolf Steiner took him very seriously and even wrote a book about him. In his quest for the truth independent of personal feelings, Steiner felt the discrepancy between his own inner experience of the reality of a spiritual world and its beings and these mechanistic theories about the evolution of mankind. He presented these thoughts as an offering to the spiritual world and received as an answer the contents of *Occult Science*, with its description of the evolution of the world originating with the sacrifice of the Thrones. Evolution could now be seen as the work of spiritual beings who themselves underwent a development through the creative process.

A whole new world view arose. The ranks of the hierarchies are differentiated, meaningful, accessible through thinking and reason. Development and movement are brought into that which had been more static and spatial in the old pictures. This also brought the possibility of understanding the gods of other religions. Spiritual science gives us the possibility of comprehending these older siblings and parental beings in their differentiated roles and tasks in the universe, as well as in the formation of the human constitution and destiny. We can understand them as ranks between which a rising up and falling behind can take place. We can even comprehend them now as individual spiritual beings with names and cosmic individualities.

To get an inkling of the nature of these higher beings we can contrast them with human beings. When we look at humanity we see there are enormous differences in development of consciousness, ego-hood and selflessness, of ignorance, wisdom and creative power in humanity. The average contemporary, whether they be a banker or refuse collector, a member of organised crime or the Gautama Buddha, whether Hitler or one of the Masters of Wisdom and the Harmony of Feelings, all belong to the rank of human being – although it is true that some have surpassed it already having developed the spirit self, the ability to do what they know where knowing and doing are one, which is the state of consciousness of the angels.

But there are also numerous spiritual streams in humanity sometimes opposing each other or co-operating or crossing over after the Mystery of Golgotha. It is no less complex in the world of the angelic hierarchies.

The anthroposophic approach to the spiritual hierarchies has risen from the aspect of form to that of dynamic development (from the Exousiai to the Dynameis). It also became much more complex with evolution and devolution, acceleration and retardation of beings. There is normal development, staying behind and moving ahead. In a way there is even the death and resurrection of worlds. We might liken it to the analogy of a child that has to stay back a year in school and repeat a class or two if they didn't pass their exams. As a result a fifteen or sixteen year old might find themselves sitting with the juniors.

Something like this can happen in the spiritual world too (with apologies for the inadequacy of the comparison). An archai, or time spirit, may receive the task of an irregular folk spirit, a being much older, as it were, than the other folk spirits who all belong to the rank of archangels. This can explain many a phenomenon of our time, such as the influence of certain superpowers.

But there are other qualities to be found in staying behind: sacrifice for instance. From the viewpoint of the highest Trinity, the goal of all evolution cannot be achieved without opposing forces because there is no development without polarity. Beings are ordered to stay behind, as it were, to close something of themselves off rather than sharing it with the cosmos. It becomes instead an expression of self-ness. Light reveals, darkness hides; the onward flow must be interrupted for development to take place.

An example of the sacrificial staying behind is Yahweh, the god of the Old Testament. According to esoteric Judaism and to spiritual science, he was one of the seven Elohim. Whereas the other six choose the sun as their place of habitation with an enormous acceleration of development, Yahweh stays with the moon. The moon-god is a reflection of God the Father. He is not the same being though, which explains the fact that he is connected with the people of Israel in this special way. He is a vengeful god, who orders his people to commit genocide by wiping out a whole nation (the Amalekites). He is a mighty spiritual being, involved in the creation of humanity and the separation of the sexes, but a being of the rank of the Exousiai, the lowest of the second hierarchy, whereas the Trinity is above and beyond all angelic hierarchies.

Now to the beings with an accelerated evolution. When a human being reaches the goal of earthly development, when they attain to spirit self or manas, then the angel watching over that person is freed from their task and can take on a higher responsibility. That was the case when the Bodhisattva who incarnated as Siddhartha Gautama became the Buddha. His angel then achieved the rank of archangel and became a folk spirit. The archangels whose names we know have also moved on to join the ranks of the archai, time spirits who reign over periods of 300–400 years: Michael, Oriphiel, Anael, Zachariel, Raphael, Samael and Gabriel (in the sequence of their reign in history).

Michael is the archangel of the sun, who was able to win victory over the dragon (Revelation 12), a being of mixed satanic and demonic forces who is older than Michael and, in a way, stronger. But still Michael is able to force this being out of the spiritual world onto the earth. Through heightened selflessness Michael has surpassed himself in accelerated evolution. In the past he was the countenance of Yahweh and now he is the countenance of Christ (countenance here means the inward revelation of a being to the outside). In the case of Michael's relation to Christ, he identifies himself with Christ so intensely that he can express the inwardness of the one he serves. It is this selfless connection to Christ that gives him the power against the forces of evil that would otherwise be stronger.

We have used an anthropomorphic approach to the spiritual hierarchies. Now we must ask about the differences to the strata of humanity after all the comparison. The first difference is the unity among the ranks of normally evolved beings. It is what is so powerfully expressed in Genesis 1 where the word Elohim, a plural noun, is combined with the singular verb 'bara', which means 'created'. The seven Elohim created heaven and earth as if they were one being, and in 'Let us create Man…' we see once again their cooperation in total unity and harmony. This selfless cooperation is what ultimately will be the criterion for the rank of human beings, the hierarchy of freedom, to move to the next level. Before that can happen, the next step will be the conscious inclusion and cooperation between humanity and the hierarchies.

As humanity has come of age and turned away from the spiritual world, many members of the higher hierarchies have, in a sense, lost their interest in humanity. It can't be a one-way street. If human beings are not interested in these higher beings they will lose interest in us. We have to take the first steps now, otherwise their interest will express itself in purely destructive forces. Earthquakes, volcanic eruptions, tsunamis, destructive weather phenomena, among other things, are already an expression of that: reactions of the earth and the spiritual forces and beings in and behind it.

From the Exousiai (Elohim) upwards we can speak of gods. Why is that so? Because, at the beginning of our earth evolution, these beings had already gone through their human stage in the sense of acquiring an 'I'. They could directly engage their activity towards creating what was to become the hierarchy of freedom.

In this spiritual evolutionary process the adversary forces play an essential part. They were and are as necessary as those beings who follow a normal development. Not only are they instrumental in the forming of modern humanity's constitution, and thereby also in the creation of all the other kingdoms on earth in their beauty and darkness, but they also play an important role in the forming of our destiny and karma of which we can become so painfully aware.

Above, in and through the three hierarchies wields and works the divine Trinity, forming the world plan. Through the first hierarchy (Seraphim, Cherubim and Thrones) the divine Father works, through the second hierarchy (Kyriotetes, Dynameis and Exousiai) the Logos, the divine Son, and through the third hierarchy (Archai, Archangels and Angels) the Holy Spirit. The latter is most concerned with humanity. The second hierarchy is concerned with nature and our planetary system, including the great changes of the earth, and also with processing our biographies after death. The first hierarchy is concerned with the overall ruling of both humanity and nature and with the weaving of human karma for the future; they are however revealed in meteorological phenomena such as lightning. All this and much more is revealed by Rudolf Steiner in an accessible way from the beginnings of spiritual science.

To be a theologian and to know about the divine or the gospels doesn't necessarily mean to be religious, which is to actively connect with the divine on the level of our will. In the same way, a psychologist does not necessarily have good loving relationships with other people. So the question arises what do we do with this knowledge? Do we try to include it concretely in our lives and to establish a religious relationship to these divine angelic beings, our older siblings and parental beings from the spiritual cosmos?

As humanity matures we are granted greater freedom, and it is now up to us to build up our relationship with the higher hierarchies. If we enter the spiritual world at night filled with purely materialistic thoughts and feelings, having spoken not a single word with a spiritual significance during the day, we will be 'unknown' there, never 'seen' before. How do we become 'visible' again? How do we learn to interact with and include these beings in our lives and even our culture?

We can connect with our angel through the way we prepare for sleep, anticipating our meeting this higher guide of our life. We can also connect with the archangels if we speak some spirit-filled words during the day and try to grasp the true task of our folk spirit in this current age of Michael.

Michael is the ruling time spirit, the true zeitgeist of our age to use a German expression that has found currency in the English language. But what can we do to connect with the being of Michael?

To connect with the true spirit of our age we must rise from the level of the merely national to the universal. We must understand the primacy of the individual over everything that is generic in our time and try to develop the courage to recognise and face the steamroller-like advance of the adversary forces in our declining culture. We must learn to 'think things right', to sharpen and exercise our powers of discernment with increasing selflessness towards everything and everybody.

It is this selflessness, the power of self-sacrifice, that is the driving force of spiritual development. This is how spiritual beings like Michael ascend through the ranks of the hierarchies. This is the power of Christ.

Homosexuality and the Bible

Paul Corman

Born in Texas in 1946, Paul Corman was ordained in 1986 and has worked for many years in Peru. Since retiring he has helped out in various congregations from Britain to Australia. In this article he looks at how passages traditionally cited in the Bible as condemning homosexuality have been misinterpreted and do not refer to loving relationships between consenting adults.

What does Jesus say about homosexuality and about same-sex marriage? And what do you say about them?

Actually, in order to answer the first question, we would have to leave the rest of the space in this article blank. Jesus says absolutely nothing at all about either topic. But in order to help us along with the second question, and at the end of the article to leave us hopefully with a lot more questions, we might well ask ourselves, if Jesus didn't say anything, why all the fuss about the topic in certain Christian circles? One reason is that the Old Testament does seem to have something to say as does seemingly St Paul. The conditional quality of these statements ('seem to', 'seemingly') stems from the fact that the word homosexual is a modern word creation that dates to the end of the nineteenth century. Neither the Hebrew in the Old Testament, nor the Greek of the New Testament knows this word. The 1946 RSV edition of the English translation was the first to use the words homosexual and homosexuality, and these translations are very questionable. We will turn to some of these phrases in just a bit.

A central aspect of the Movement for Religious Renewal is a fresh approach to Bible texts, especially New Testament ones. We try hard usually to look at the aura of the words, the biblical context within which they appear, the social aspects of the times, and the uses of the words in other contemporary sources.

The question of homosexual relationships could be an invitation to examine more closely our thoughts and feelings about these topics, and to see what their foundation is. If the movement enshrined in our name is to work effectively, we need to make sure that we are not reacting to and operating out of old prejudices, 'accepted' norms and moralistic judgments. The Christian Community zealously guards individual freedom of thought, free from social and theological dogmas and traditions. The only area where our freedom is limited is in all that is directly related to the celebration of sacraments and rituals. In that area we agree to abide by the forms accepted by the body of priests, who in turn undertake not intentionally to change anything related to these forms. In every other regard, we support and respect individual choice. I believe that the question of homosexuality and same-sex relationships deserves the same openness, as it may be one of the few topics that will define the course of The Christian Community going forward as a movement for religious renewal, one which prays in every Act of Consecration of Man to join with Christ to unite us with the world's evolving.

As an example of the importance of a new and considered look at the original texts and their translation, I would like to begin with the Old Testament and with the events that occurred in Sodom. Sodomy, used to refer to a sexual practice as such, does not appear in the Hebrew or the Greek text, and the word Sodomite in the original texts only refers to a person born in Sodom. In the twelfth century the hermit monk Peter Damian seems to have been the first to use the phrase to refer to a sexual act between two men. From then on, the concepts of sodomy and sexuality became at the same time more intertwined, but also more diverse in the Church. Sodomy laws have included any non-pro-creative sexual act such as masturbation or oral sex in a heterosexual context. In some parts of the world a sodomite is a homosexual. Be that as it may, the sin of Sodom was not homosexuality, at least not according to other biblical texts that refer to it. In the Old Testament, for example Ezekiel 16:49 says:

> This was the sin of your sister, Sodom: she and her daughters had pride, surfeit of food and prosperous ease, but did not aid the poor and needy.

The Book of Wisdom refers to Sodom's sin as 'a bitter hatred of strangers' and 'making slaves of guests who were benefactors.' Other references appear in Isaiah and Jeremiah, but nowhere is there any mention of any sort of sexuality as the sin of Sodom.

When we look at the overall context, the three men (angels) that appear to Lot in Sodom and seek shelter in Lot's home, have come directly from a visit to Lot's uncle, Abraham, who heartily welcomed and properly received them as was fitting and demanded in those time and in that culture. The Sodomites, however, do just the opposite. The story is dark and difficult to understand, but no matter how you turn it, even if you wish to think of what occurred as homosexual behaviour, the sin was then not necessarily the sex itself, but, as stated elsewhere in the Bible, a lack of respect and inhospitality. And if we do take it as a reference to homosexual behaviour, then we would have to call it rape and in no way a loving or consenting encounter between persons of the same sex. Rape of a woman by a man or vice versa is a dastardly deed, but it does not make all heterosexual encounters bad and sinful. Should it be allowed to define all homosexuality?

The story of Sodom given in Genesis 19:1–9 is one of six biblical texts that are most often used by conservative Christians to 'prove' that homosexuality is not compatible with proper Christian behaviour. The others in the Old Testament are the Creation account of Genesis 1–2; the holiness code in Leviticus 18:22 and 20:13, and, in the New Testament, the three letters of St Paul that reference the holiness code of the Old Testament: Romans 1:24–27, 1 Corinthians 6:9, and 1 Timothy 1:10.

There are many elements in the injunctions of the holiness code. Many things are considered abominations and many transgressions punishable by death. There are some, a few, a very few (two to be exact, Leviticus 18:22 and Leviticus 20:13) that seem to condemn homosexuality. In the letters of St Paul referred to above, there are three mentions of the Old Testament code that are quoted as very harsh condemnations of homosexuality and yet none of them use the word homosexuality or homosexual, but rather odd word groupings in both Hebrew and later in St Paul's Greek that have long been assumed to refer to all sorts of homosexual behaviour. For example, Leviticus 18:22 would have to be literally translated something like, 'And with a male you shall not lay lyings of a woman.' What that really may or may not mean is open to interpretation, and, of course, depending on the thinking that is brought to the text, one will interpret and then translate one way or another. In the New Testament, *arsenkoites*, a Greek noun that literally would mean 'male-beds', is found in Timothy and Corinthians, but the meaning is not clear enough to justify the typical translation of 'sodomite' or 'homosexual'. Another word *malakoi* in Corinthians means 'soft', but again it is unfair to assume that Paul is talking about any specific 'gay' demeanour. Here we can only take a general look at these texts of the holiness code injunctions and St Paul's references to them. First of all there are many different injunctions in both Testaments. Some are called abominations, some punishable by stoning, some called lewd, some ungodly or unholy. But the list, especially in the Old Testament of abhorrent abominations, is quite extensive and includes eating unauthorised foods, sowing different sorts of plants in the same field, using clothing made of cloth woven from two different fibres, and among those acts punishable by death are not obeying one's parents and not keeping the Sabbath. In St Paul's letters there is an injunction about women speaking in the congregations, others about divorce and so on.

If we were to take all these commands and injunctions at face value, there would be no Christian Community, for no woman could be a priest. She would be prohibited from speaking in the congregation. And we would probably have altogether many fewer members and priests, for many of us would have already been stoned to death as adulterers or, at the very least, excluded from the community as divorced individuals, unworthy of God's congregation. It seems quite haughty of us now, centuries later, to choose which injunctions from the list of 'abominations' we wish to throw overboard and which we wish to chastise most gravely. It is remarkable how some Christians who cite the Old Testament as the reason for condemning homosexual acts, are so unaware of the many aspects of their behaviour that would be condemned if the same standard were applied. Examination of the context of every one of these 'anti-gay' injunctions shows that they have nothing to do with loving relationships between two consenting adults, but rather with sexual enslavement practices, using sex to lord over the more vulnerable, or temple prostitution, a common religious practice that the Israelites could in no way be encouraged to follow. The idea of a loving relationship between two adults of the same sex is not contemplated in either Testament, except perhaps the love between King David and Jonathan, which was seen as superior to the love of a woman, although it may not have been a sexual relationship.

The point here is that today we need to be talking about loving relations between two adults, some of whom wish to cement their commitment to one another not just with the civil laws of the society in which they live, but who also wish to profess their commitment to one another within the religious community in which they have found a spiritual home, in front of an altar dedicated to serving Christ Jesus, the God of love. Two individuals of the same sex who so find themselves and who come together in love, recognising that there are deep karmic bonds between them that want to be explored and worked through, should be able to do that in a way that is not just a friendship, not just a sexual-romantic relationship, but in a way that is part of community of life, recognised as such before the eyes of men and women and of God. If we can rise above our long-standing prejudices and traditions, and allow for the validity of such a decision and commitment to find its expression before the altars of The Christian Community, these marriages can bring health and healing and happiness to all of humanity – as is expected of any other community of life that is sealed by the word of the couple in our sacrament of marriage. Our sacrament of marriage is too gender-specific to be used to seal the commitment of persons of the same sex. We are not able to change the words of the sacraments. All priests take an oath to guard against such wilful changes. There may come a time far in the future where the human condition has so evolved that changes to our sacraments will become necessary, but we would still need the aid of an inspired initiate to be able to 'read' those changes in the spiritual world, the source of all the sacraments, and translate them into the corresponding, appropriate human wording. Until such a time comes, indeed in order for that time to come, we have a lot of individual work to do on ourselves and a lot of work to do in community. This does not mean creating now a new sacrament or ritual, but we need a worthy cultic form for individuals of the same-sex to consecrate their community of life before an altar. That possibility already exists within The Christian Community. It can take the form of a Close of Day ceremony, but the content of what that Close of Day type ceremony could be needs to be explored and developed. The social environment of The Christian Community that surrounds homosexuals and same-sex couples also needs to be explored, talked about and evolved. We are just at the beginning of a very necessary dialogue within The Christian Community on these issues.

Why Did God Create Moths?
Yaroslava Black

Born in the Ukraine in 1973, Yaroslava Black has worked in Germany since her ordination in 2005. In this article she takes a light-hearted look at our obsession with acquiring and accumulating stuff and considers the moth as a humble symbol of the impermanence of all things – as well as a reminder to occasionally clear out your wardrobe.

Although they do not sow and do not gather in barns, the birds of the sky have a purpose in the created world. They sing, they pick off insect pests or even mice, they are lovely to look at and put us in mind of heavenly messengers. The lilies of the field admittedly do not drive out the mice, but their beauty and scent are allegedly so delightful that even the glory of Solomon's raiment pales in comparison. Let's not say any more about the scent of lilies just now – after all, scent is basically a matter of personal preference.

But moths? To what purpose did the Creator include the moths in his development plan? They are not beautiful, there can be no question of scent or song, and no treatise has yet been written about their usefulness. Yet somehow the moths have even managed to get into the gospels. And since those days, also into our wardrobes. They have withstood all the turmoil of history, steadfastly defied war and hunger, since they actually don't eat anything at all and only very rarely need water.

Unlike us. We always need a great deal – and then yet more.

We collect stamps, beetles, stones, Meissen figurines, hats, tins, nutcrackers, old plates, and many other beautiful and useless things that enrich our lives but also gather dust. And yet still we want more.

Only on a foundation of prosperity could the collector thrive, for when we were still striking fire from flint and circumspectly consuming the laboriously hunted wild boar, there was of course barely time or energy left over to make a special collection of superfluous things. The first hobby of a female person was probably making a necklace of the teeth of a killed animal, since she, being the weaker member of the family, was left behind to guard the fire, and perhaps out of boredom she polished the teeth of the hunted prey to make a bracelet or drew on the wall with a piece of charcoal. But this collection of pictures did not belong to any one person, it was no one's private property. It could neither be auctioned off nor taken along when moving.

How many packing boxes does a person fill nowadays from a single wardrobe? Perhaps we would not even ask ourselves this question if it were not for the moths. For that is where they lurk in the darkness, munching away and driving us to despair. For behind the closed wardrobe doors so many forgotten treasures lie hidden: little dresses and jackets belonging to the children, Grandma's quaint heirlooms, scarves and hats knitted by old friends, Grandpa's trilby hat, carnival costumes from the best years of our youth, Indian silk, Irish wool. All this is not only our property, it is also loaded with precious memories. It smells of far-distant countries and adventures, declarations of love, tokens of friendship, childhood happiness. And now comes the bitter question of disappointment: when and how on earth did this glory of the past turn into moth-fodder? We don't know. One day we open the wardrobe and look through the holes into the void.

A hole that damages the wholeness of matter and makes it unusable is nothing but a portion of void, created by a foreign, outside force. We must fill it again, or we feel compelled to distance ourselves from the entire hole-structure. Is this merely an encroachment upon the inside of the wardrobe, or is it, in fact, an encroachment upon our very selves?

Along with this feeling of powerlessness, certain wise sayings can pass through our minds. Buddha teaches that anyone wishing to reach the highest stage of human development must not strive after belongings. Meister Eckhart's teaching is that in order to gain spiritual riches we should own nothing, empty ourselves and not stand in our own way with our 'I'. Jesus teaches that we should not gather treasure that can be eaten by moths and stolen by thieves, 'For where your treasure is, there will your heart be also' (Matt. 6:19), and no-one likes to think of their heart being in the wardrobe.

It seems virtually impossible to fulfil these exalted aims nowadays. The 'I' defines itself ever more by property and belongings: I am what I have, what I consume. And therefore I am forced to go on consuming. For soon what I already own no longer satisfies me: I need more. Without noticing it, we are caught up just as much in the wealth of affluence as in the prison of selfishness.

In the course of time, our relationship to the word 'having' has changed. As recently as last century we did not speak so often of 'having'. Instead of saying 'I have a problem' one would say 'I am worried', instead of 'I have a doctor' it would be 'I am a patient of Dr Such-and-such', instead of 'I have a wife' one would say 'I am married'. Nowadays we hear almost exclusively 'have': my wife, my children, my doctor, my salary, my problems.

This gives an appearance of strength: I have someone at hand, somebody to whom I can give orders, and I also have someone I can blame for my misfortune or illnesses. If that is taken away, it leads to the experience of an unbearable emptiness. The 'I am something' disappears and one is confronted with 'I have nothing' like a dark hole. Life seems to have no meaning any longer, for we have been used to measuring the meaning of our life by what we have and not by what we are. That is the great illusion of wealth, of belongings. In reality, nothing of what we think we have belongs to us. Only what we ourselves are belongs to us. If we are in possession of joy, courage, faithfulness, honesty, it means that we are joyful, courageous, faithful, honest.

Great affluence is just as much a great burden as is great poverty. A treasure that can endure both in the desert and in the city is this: to be much and to have little. And the moths help us on the way towards this goal. We open the door and become aware of nothingness gaping at us from the holes. Do we, too, stand there gaping – or do we rejoice at the liberation? Are we reminded by the squeaking of the door of the vow of poverty taken by the noble knights of long ago: we have nothing, yet the world belongs to us?

Who knows? Perhaps those little gluttonous beasties aren't, after all, quite so pointless as they seem. The moths remind us of something: matter is not everlasting. It can be eaten; it is perishable. Hence one cannot possess it. The beauty of childhood memories, the warmth of words of love, the light of insight, the strength of friendship: these are the precious treasures of the heart. They cannot be taken from us. They belong to eternity.

Seize the Day: Reflections on Brexit

Luke Barr

Luke Barr was born in England in 1970 and was ordained in 2014. He has worked in Aberdeen, Forest Row and now in Germany. In this article he considers the opportunity presented to the British people, for better or for worse, by the seismic upheaval of the EU referendum result in 2016.

It is five o'clock in the morning on St John's Day in Aberdeen, Scotland. There is a sudden tremendous thunderclap and the tremors roll steadily across the sky. Thunderstorms are rare in this part of the world. It seems that everyone I spoke to the next day was woken by the roar of the thunder.

Aberdeen is in the north east of Scotland. It is a small oil-city very much affected by the economic vacillations of the world. On the morning of St John's Day, the elements bellow out their presence. These mighty friends and servants of John, who appears like a brief but powerful thunderstorm in the gospels proclaiming the coming of the one who will become lord of these elements, awaken the people of Aberdeen on the morning of a significant potential turning point in the island's history. The elements themselves are affected by the events of that night, when a country's future is being decided. And perhaps it is not simply their own concern that they voice; but they carry the thunder to remind us that this momentous event takes place on the day of John.

A member of the congregation told me that her husband, on being woken by the thunder that morning, jumped out of bed and exclaimed: 'That's the Brexit!'

It seems that the impossible had happened. That which no one had reckoned with has somehow come about. The referendum produced a result that wasn't quite expected. Everyone I spoke to was taken aback by the result, particularly as the result was not generally seen as a favourable one in Scotland. Once more, it seems that the English have dragged the Scots, the Welsh and the Northern Irish with them, wherever they wish to go.

When we Brits want to go abroad to our European neighbours, then we often speak of 'going to Europe'. We don't really see ourselves as being part of the main landmass. Geographically, we are an incontrovertible island. The elements have made us this way, and there is something stubborn in the islander's refusal to be part of the mother continent.

The same day that Brexit was announced, the Prime Minister resigned. I heard this as I was standing amongst the crowd at the original Camphill, watching Karl König's cosmic St John's play being enacted.

Once the shock subsided, life returned to normal. The elementals remained quiet now, watching with interest. Petrol prices rose immediately. We anticipate further such disadvantageous fiscal effects. Everyone is aware that the process still requires time. And as it requires time, it seems that we have entered a temporal window of opportunity. The immediate future is now open. Things are up in the air.

Previously, one had the impression that politically, economically (and culturally), Britain, like much of the Western world, was set on a course that had been designed for it by our political and economic masters. But now those figures, who have been the main actors on the stage up until now, have been cleared away. And one can be sure that the various interested parties with their agendas are grasping at the moment, in order to re-form and reassess their positions, to take advantage of the current chaos.

All of this is because we find ourselves at a moment in time when everything is possible, and the ramifications of the referendum are nowhere near being finalised. Whether Brexit is a good thing or not is really beside the point. It is now a fact – a fact that has entered unexpectedly onto the stage of world history.

It reminds me of the situation in Germany in 1990, when, particularly in the East, there was the unnerving excitement of everything being in flux and chaos. It was a time when anything could happen, and, regardless of what eventually *did* happen, our human souls were given a mighty challenge: to envision and implement new ways forward, ways that broke out of the hitherto usual modes of operation.

The media implied that the major issue of the European referendum concerned the refugee problem in Europe and in Britain. Some newspapers reduced the referendum to a vote for open or closed borders. Where Germany had opened her borders and welcomed the wanderers, Britain appears to have opted for the opposite gesture. Possibly, the majority vote gathered force under the momentum of this particular reason. But for whatever reasons that a majority voted to exit the EU, we now have a great moment of opportunity in Britain.

The opportunity seems to point towards the issue of sovereignty, of self-governance. Perhaps the opportunity here is that the mask of political sovereignty could fall away and reveal the challenge to each individual to find their own inner sovereignty, responsibility and independence. It includes the possibility of creating a new community that bears the signature of the archangel Michael.

Sadly, it is easy to doubt whether we will rise to the opportunity. The British are not radically orientated. We are famously liberal, tolerant and conservative. We don't go in for revolution. And there is the infamous British phlegmatic temperament to take into account. People understandably desire political and economic stability, and the British are a little shocked still to find that they have unleashed the possibility for all sorts of destabilising effects to break into their routines. I cannot see major change happening in Britain. If anything, we may be heading towards the ignominy of becoming something like Airstrip One, which George Orwell demoted us to in his novel *Noneteen Eighty-Four,* with its terrible vision of a future war of 'all against all'. In that scenario, we are ostracised from mainland Europe and have become a tiny, military stepping stone into Eurasia, serving the ominous Leviathan, the sinister Oceania.

But the fact that we, a major European country, have voted to step out of the EU, will cause, like the thunder of that night, tremors throughout Europe. And this may lead to more of the unexpected and unanticipated to enter into the scheme of things. It is as if the folk souls of nations are being given a very particular opportunity by the time spirit, the cosmopolitan Michael, who has precipitated this new age of mass migrations. It is as if we are at a certain turning point in time.

The elementals feel the potential enormity of the imminent future. Human routines have been upset: routines and habits of thinking, perception, and action have been de-railed. When this happens, the elementals take great interest. They themselves may not leave their routines. They are compelled to maintain and fulfil their duties and never deviate from them. Only human souls may do this; only human souls may operate in freedom. And now we have one such opportunity for freedom. We have an opportunity for the folk soul to manifest once more.

Will human beings understand that their opportunity is not to use sovereignty to become insular, but to find a truly cosmopolitan human culture that might surpass the technocratic and diluted impulse of the EU? The elementals will be greatly affected by the decisions of human souls. The ramifications of Brexit will roll steadily across Europeans skies, and further out into the world. All depends on whether human souls are sleeping through events or, as the elementals hope, awaken to their import.

This event also stands under the auspices of St John's Day. As in König's St John's play, he is a macrocosmic figure. He is no longer a human soul on earth, but bears now the spirit of metanoia. John appeared before the great turning point in time, and now his spirit appears again. For we are being challenged at this time by John's mighty spirit: change your ways of thinking and perception. Change radically! For the Christ is coming and it is critical that we awaken to his coming. Otherwise, there will be only the inevitable coming of 'the prince of this world', who renders us incapable of perceiving the Christ (John 14: 30).

It may often seem to us as if politics and economics are the particularly effective tools of the 'prince of this world'. But it need not be so. They are in fact expressions of human beings' striving to manifest the spirits of equality and fraternity. Whatever comes out of Brexit will demonstrate how much human souls wish to act out of liberty; to act out of the spirit of freedom, in order to implement right-seeking political forms and brotherly economic forms.

It is vital what we and the coming generation or two decide how to act. The future of the human being may depend on seizing the spirit of this day.

Bursts of Light in the Darkness: Violence in the Light of Anthroposophy

Michael Chase

Born in Cape Town in 1958, Michael Chase is a drama psychotherapist living in Stroud, England. He has taught drama, mime and mask-making as well as directing theatre In this article he considers from a spiritual point of view the effects of violence both on the victim and the perpetrator.

While working as a psychotherapist with violent prisoners in the Democratic Therapeutic Community (DTC) at HMP Grendon, I have accompanied a number of men in what I can only refer to as their lightning flashes of insight. Following these experiences, the person has always taken bold steps into new regions of their being. I would like to acknowledge the extraordinary bravery of these particular individuals who have been able to overcome not only the horrors of their own offences arising from the debilitating circumstances of their childhood, but who have also been able to transform the lives of others. The DTC practice was started by a number of enlightened psychiatrists in 1947 to support soldiers returning from the war with Post Traumatic Stress Disorder (PTSD). These communities were established in a variety of contexts, including domestic abuse centres, mental health trusts, prisons and addiction groups, in order to support people who had undergone extreme conditions of adversity to recover together. HMP Grendon was established in 1962 and is considered a flagship in its field.

Today, out of the 86,000 prisoners across the 140 prisons in the prison estate in England and Wales, men can volunteer to come to Grendon in order to break the cycles of offending, violence and abuse that they've been caught in for years. A multidisciplinary team works together with the prisoners in order to support insight, catharsis and, grace permitting, to bring about transformation.

What is the darkness in which the light flashes? Gordon (not his real name) was sent to prison for murdering his sister's boyfriend in a psychotic, drug-induced fury. Together, we explored his history of violence. At the age of twenty-four, having been in different mainstream prisons for six years, Gordon was dealing drugs when he got into a fight in his cell. In a bout of rage he knocked out his cell mate and picked up a can of energy drink to pound into his head. His hand stopped in mid-air. He described how the world around him went quiet and how, for a strange and unusual moment, he realised he had a choice. He wondered why he wanted to kill this man, how long he would have to stay in prison for double homicide, and how long he could continue like this before he was killed.

This was the beginning of his journey into breaking the cycle that led to his application to HMP Grendon. After three and a half years this led to him awakening to his deeper inner core and becoming a mentor on the wing who could support others in their process of change.

How can we understand the transition from such evil to becoming a force for good? Psychological explanations have their value, but we may sense that something deeper is at work. I found it remarkable to discover that Rudolf Steiner had described this territory in relation to spiritual development. He described how we all bear within us images from the life before birth, expressions of the noble spiritual aims of our future life. If these aims are blocked, they can turn into counter-images, which are their perverted opposite: 'the noblest intentions of sacrifice can turn into the desire to kill.' In his book *The Effects of Esoteric Development*, Steiner goes as far as to say that a person may feel a kind of relief when committing the crime, because it tears away the shell that has surrounded them and lays foundations for new karma. By murdering his victim was Gordon trying to kill himself? If murder is a result of 'repressed suicide and violent behaviour as repressed self-aggression', as Bernd Ruf writes in his book *Educating Traumatised Children* (Lindisfarne Books, 2013), then by not murdering the second man was Gordon saving his own life, and in so doing the lives of others?

Gordon's flash of insight as he raised his hand to kill brought him to Grendon. At the age of thirty-five, having spent three years looking into his biography and coming to terms with the chronic physical, emotional and sexual abuse that had traumatised his life, he was able to get in touch with something deep within himself. He now teaches meditation to other prisoners. By working with Gordon, I came to understand how breaking the cycle of violence and abuse made it possible for him to achieve a kind of redemption, something which otherwise would have had to wait for his life after death.

Using two more stories, I would like to explore how trauma can annihilate the experience of the self, and how evil deeds can stem from a misplaced longing for the light. Gary was recalled to prison at the age of twenty-four for holding up a taxi driver at knife point. He was sentenced to eight years for stealing his taxi and money. He had only been out of prison five weeks and wanted to buy his son a birthday present but was too proud to ask for money. Gary claimed that there was nothing threatening in his behaviour and that the taxi driver was exaggerating in court. After six months in therapy Gary insisted on exploring his offence in psychodrama using role play. I was reluctant at first, but knowing how this intervention can help when people are cut off from feelings of empathy towards self and others, I agreed to his request. In the role of his victim Gary experienced the knife at his throat and began to tremble. In tears he realised how much he had terrified his victim and probably changed his life forever. He began to wonder how his victim's family would feel. He wondered if his victim woke up at night screaming. He wondered whether his victim still had a job.

Having found a new way of relating to his victim inwardly, Gary wondered how he could have committed this offence and all his crimes. At the age of fourteen, he had been taken hostage by a gang in a rival estate for having hit his girlfriend, a cousin of the hostage taker. He had been stripped naked, dragged around the house, stabbed and violated for most of the day. No one came to his rescue.

Research into the effects of trauma on children indicates that severe trauma in early childhood almost always disrupts the development of the child's individuality. The child's 'I' is damaged. As a consequence, the child's capacity for empathy, for establishing relationships, for developing self-trust and trust in others is impaired and destroyed (see *Educating Traumatised Children*).

In the therapy room, fifteen years after being taken hostage, we began to look at repairing Gary's relationship to his 'I' in some way. My strategy was to give

Gary the experience of justice being done in order to reincorporate his younger self, which had got split off, into his consciousness. Could we create conditions safe and stable enough for his 'I' to return? We created what is called 'a surplus reality scene' in which his five abusers were put 'on trial'. Gary assumed the role of the jury, which represented his adult thinking. He also took on the role of the 'good enough' mother, representing his adult feeling, and the 'good enough' father, representing his adult willing. And most significantly Gary assumed the role of the judge, the 'I' within the system of roles. With this team of developing 'soul forces and higher ego', he sentenced his abusers to prison, putting 'wrong to right' and began establishing order within the kingdom of his soul. A month after doing this work, Gary was able to come to a quiet calm place within himself where he was not running from 'high to high', frightened and angry, but could begin to learn to parent himself.

By paying attention to his 'inner child' and by listening and responding to his subtle needs, Gary was able to develop empathy for himself and other people. When a person's daily life is driven by trauma, they can get caught in displacing the abuse they have suffered onto others, as a normal way of behaving. Moving into the light and letting that go can be a shocking and painful journey.

Dwaine came to HMP Grendon with tough body armour. He was a hulk of a man, braced for any eventuality. He imposed his vigilante aggression on all those who dared to misunderstand, misinterpret or take advantage of him or anyone under his protection.

Dwaine had been a gang leader and was in prison for murdering a drug dealer. A month after he was sentenced to twenty-three years for murder, his son was born.

In order to get to the source of this behaviour, we mapped out his life with other group members taking many roles. When, at the age of four, his father violently removed him and his brother from his mother's home, the resulting grief and loss became replaced by fear and anger. At the age of six a local gangster on the run from the police asked Dwaine to bury a gun in the garden. This gave him an adrenalin rush and a feeling of power and agency that his father had all but beaten out of him. By the age of twelve, a false sense of self began to emerge as Dwaine learned to relish the power of seeing fear in the people he stole from and of anyone who threatened his world. By sixteen, he had left home and was living in a gang house. His move into criminality was in full force. He was a high flyer at eighteen, enjoying a glamorous lifestyle that went to his head. His lack of empathy meant his victims were not real, they were only 'bad men selling drugs'. The night of his offence, his foot soldiers beat a man to death while Dwaine looked the other way, chatting on his phone.

Two and a half years into his therapy, Dwaine reached a turning point. As he looked at what had taken place in his life from early memories to his present time, he slowed down. He chose a mask to represent what he called his demon-self and wrapped it up in a blanket. The realisation began to dawn that without his demon mask, that armoured part of himself, he had feelings that he had never felt before. Feelings flooded into him: sadness for himself and compassion for his victim whose mother he had seen breaking down in court. He could see how he had created more victims than he could have imagined: his wife and son, his mother and father, society as a whole. This brought Dwaine to a place of shame and, eventually, to humility. He realised that in order to live with what he had done, he needed to be humble. He learned to take off his armour, both physical and psychological, to stand down when challenged and to support others even if it meant challenging them to do the right thing.

Once again, it seems that there is a deeper dimension at work that cannot be fully explained by psychology. The armour that Dwaine had acquired has a lot in common with what Steiner calls the double. As we advance on the spiritual path, we become aware of everything that we have not yet understood in ourselves, of everything we have not yet transformed through love. This can become like the thick, dead skin of a snake, waiting to be sloughed off. What is remarkable is that Dwaine, like Gary, was not conscious of being on a path of spiritual development, and yet each in their own way made steps that belong to such a path.

The last thing Dwaine said to me when we were talking about me including him in this article was, 'I am not the person I used to be. It is as if that part of me is a mask I no longer choose to wear. But it is there to remind me of who I was and where I come from, so I don't forget. It reminds me of what I have to do, and not to do, as I get on with the rest of my life.'

A friend once asked me how I can keep doing this work. On the one hand, I am aware of the fine line between some of my own experiences growing up in South Africa in the 1960s and 1970s, and the experiences of some of the men we work with. Additionally, it is always deeply moving to witness the profound nature of suffering and change people can go through.

In her book *A Human Being Died That Night: Forgiving Apartheid's Chief Killer* (Granta Books, 2013), psychologist Pumla Gobodo-Madikizela describes her interview with Eugene de Kock, the serial murderer in the apartheid regime in South Africa. She asked him how, during the Truth and Reconciliation procedures, he had felt meeting the wives of men he had murdered. In tears he said, 'I wish I could do much more than say I'm sorry. I wish there was a way of bringing their bodies back alive...but unfortunately...I have to live with it.' Surprising even herself, Gobodo-Madikizela reached out and touched his hand. When people who have done terrible things get in touch with their humanity and feel for their victims, without defending their deeds or rationalising their behaviour, my heart crosses the line, and I trust I am in the right place.

2020s

Paul and Christ
Cynthia Hindes

Cynthia Hindes was born in 1947 and worked as a priest in Los Angeles and in Pennsylvania before her retirement. In this article she looks at how the transformative encounter that Paul had with the Risen Christ on the road to Damascus, points to a future awakening of the spirit in all of humanity.

The apostle Paul was a contemporary of Jesus. His given name was Saul of Tarsus. He was a Jew educated in the Greek language and thought of his time, and he was a Roman citizen as well. After his experience at Damascus, he took on the name Paul, which means 'little' or 'humble'.

Paul plays an extremely important and powerful role in relation to Christ. At the turning point of time, the spiritual life for the entire future of humanity and the earth was dependent on Paul's contribution. Without Paul's experience at Damascus, Christianity could not have spread, for humanity of his time was not developmentally capable of understanding Christ without an interpreter. The Hebrew people were in a transition out of the old natural clairvoyance based on bloodline and tribe, and into ego-hood, so Saul was called upon to create a bridge between ancient Judaism and Christianity.

Because of his Jewish background, Saul was aware of the subtle connection between the divine 'I am' and the earth. This connection had already been illustrated in the experiences that Moses had with the burning bush and when he struck a rock and a spring of water gushed out. According to Rudolf Steiner, Saul, who had been initiated into the Jewish mysteries, had been able to see into the spiritual world fourteen years before Damascus. At that time, he still saw the sun-being of Christ above, in the spiritual world. He knew of the secret teaching that an individual would appear in the flesh whose life would demonstrate that the spirit lives beyond death. Saul also knew that when the Messiah rose victoriously from death, the spiritual sphere of the world would change.

At the same time, however, Saul also strongly felt that it would have been impossible for those learned in the Law and the prophets to condemn an innocent man to be put to death. Therefore, he was convinced that Jesus, who had been crucified, could not be the Christ, the Messiah. Saul spent three years passionately persecuting the followers of Jesus and was present at the stoning of Stephen, the first Christian martyr.

Then came his experience near the gate of Damascus (Acts 9:3–9):

> As he neared Damascus on his journey, suddenly a light from heaven flashed around him. He fell to the ground and heard a voice say to him, 'Saul, Saul, why do you persecute me?'
> 'Who are you, Lord?' Saul asked.
> 'I am Jesus, whom you are persecuting,' he replied. 'Now, get up and go into the city, and you will be told what you must do.'
> The men travelling with Saul stood there speechless; they heard the voice but did not see anyone. Saul got up from the ground, but when he opened his eyes, he could see nothing. So they led him by the hand into Damascus. For three days, he was blind and did not eat or drink anything.

Rudolf Steiner fills in some of the details and meaning of this event. According to him, Christ, the great creative sun-being, appears to Saul in the clouds, as spiritualised fire in an etheric, living form. Saul saw what Moses had seen in the burning bush, and in the pillar of fire and cloud that guided the Israelites by day and guarded them by night as they wandered through the desert. Shocked, he also saw that the power of the sun that was shining out of the clouds was Christ, who through the Mystery of Golgotha had descended to earth and united with it. The sun now lived on earth as a healing, moral power, bringing the kingdom of heaven close. Saul saw not only a life body but also a fully perfected archetypal human physical body here in the spiritual atmosphere of the earth. He saw that Christ Jesus had risen out of the grave as the supersensible physical human form rescued for the sake of all human beings. He saw that Christ is always here, present in the earth's atmosphere as a light form. This was not the case in pre-Christian times, as Paul well knew. He experienced first-hand the words from the end of Matthew's gospel (28:20): 'And see, I am in your midst all the days until the completion of earthly time.'

Christ was the first divine being to go through death. What was revealed to Paul was that death is now a source of life. Paul was aware that we would have lost our eternal nature had Christ not risen from the dead. What we lost through Adam's Fall, the organisational forces of the archetypal body, we regain through Christ's resurrection as a spiritual body. In 1 Corinthians 15:45, Paul says, 'The first human being, Adam, took on body in a life-bearing soul sheath; the last Adam [Christ] in a life-creating spirit form.' (Madsen translation.) The first Adam gave us the fallen mortal body. Christ, the second Adam, gives us the eternal, immortal body, which can gradually replace the first. The 'new Adam' is a capacity laid into human beings as a potential to become Christ-like. It gives human beings the potential, here on earth, to connect with Christ's overflowing life.

We must do something while still in the body on earth so that we bear something in us in death that can help us maintain our consciousness in the face of the overwhelming abundance of the spirit. Taking Christ's life into oneself, through 'Christ in us', we can gradually make our soul being more and more alive until it is fully living and thus overcomes death. Paul saw that, had Christ not risen, the soul would have been chained to those parts of the body that are scattered to the elements after death. Christ freed human beings from the inevitability of this fate. When it has connected with Christ fully, the soul does not die with the body.

At the same time, however, Paul was the first to experience that as the soul and ego become stronger and more alive, something is necessary to counter the strengthening of the ego so that it does not become dangerous. It is the power of Christ's selflessness within the soul that counters the overly strong ego force.

Rudolf Steiner said, 'We moderns tend to say, "I in me, and Christ as far as I can admit of him."' The secret connection to overcoming egotism and death is expressed in the oft-repeated sentence from Paul's letter to the Galatians, 'It is not I who live, but Christ lives within me.' (Gal. 2:20) Or, as Rudolf Steiner paraphrased it, 'Not I work, but Christ works in me.' As human beings actively work to take Christ into themselves, more and more of our soul content will come from Christ. We find Christ only when he is working within us. He is a helping power within, not merely an external example or role model.

Paul also understood that Christ's blood, the carrier of his pure life and selfless ego, entered the earth at the crucifixion. Christ's blood changed the soul-body of the earth. The seed for overcoming death was taken not only into human beings but also into earth evolution itself. 'Not I, but Christ in me' means that we work, not only for our own redemption but for the redemption of the whole earth. In his letter to the Romans 8:19–22, Paul said:

> All around us, creation waits with great longing that the sons of God shall begin to shine forth in humankind. Creation has become transitory, not through its own doing, but because of him [Adam] who, becoming transitory himself, dragged it down with him. …When the sphere of the spirit grows bright, unfreedom will be replaced by the freedom that is intended for all God's offspring. We know that the whole of creation suffers and sighs in the pangs of a new birth until the present day.

The Damascus experience was given to Paul so that he could stimulate a proper understanding of the Christ impulse. After Damascus, Paul wandered the earth for three years until he was thirty-seven or thirty-eight, in the regions where the olive tree grows. Reaching out especially to non-Jews, he brought the teaching of Christianity into earth evolution. Exoterically he taught from his experience in simple form for the people, much of which is contained in his sometimes simple but powerful letters. He influenced the course of Western theology and Western spiritual experience, stimulating such figures as Augustine, Francis of Assisi and Thomas Aquinas.

Paul also worked esoterically, establishing an esoteric school in Athens. The Greeks were particularly receptive to him because Socrates had prepared the spiritual and philosophical ground. Paul's esoteric school laid the foundation for all of Christian esotericism, many hints of which also appear in Paul's letters. His friend and student Dionysius the Areopagite was a fully rational soul, filled with the Mystery of Golgotha, and was instrumental in preserving this orally transmitted occult knowledge. Our understanding of the ranks of the angelic hierarchies can be traced back to him.

Paul's relationship to Christ also continues to be particularly significant for our present age. Paul was 'a premature birth' also because his Damascus experience was the prototype for something that is happening now and will happen with greater and greater frequency in the future. Beginning in the last century and for the next three thousand years, Christ will appear to human beings as a living form on the soul plane. People will know, as Paul did, that Christ lives in the earthly sphere and is the source for the original physical archetype of the human being, which we received from the beginning, now renewed by Christ, and which we need for our full development. As our life bodies become more and more sensitive, we will experience Christ in the way Paul did, as a kind of natural phenomenon.

Paul's relationship to Christ was both intimate and of world-historic significance. Without Paul there would have been neither an outer exoteric spread of Christianity nor any real understanding of the cosmic and esoteric significance of Christ's deed.

Transforming Evil: Understanding, Confrontation, Redemption

Bastiaan Baan

Bastiaan Baan was born in 1949 and was ordained in 1961. He worked in the Netherlands before becoming director of the Seminary of The Christian Community in North America. He retired in 2019. He has written a number of books, including Old and New Mysteries *and* Lord of the Elements.

Redemption of evil is a far-reaching goal that seems to be unattainable, especially in our time, where evil is omnipresent. In this article, I will nevertheless try to illustrate how we can make little steps to prepare for a future where evil might eventually be redeemed.

The very first step in this long-term process is that we diagnose the nature of evil in order to recognise how it works, like a medical doctor who has to make a diagnosis before developing a therapy. Only with the tools that come from understanding evil will we be prepared to confront these forces. This step – recognising evil – presents us with a huge challenge, because many forms of evil step in at the moment when we are somehow asleep. This is shown by an etching by Francisco de Goya, entitled *The Sleep of Reason Begets Monsters*. The person who is asleep is surrounded and attacked by all kinds of demons.

Indeed, the demons are waiting for the moment when we are not fully awake and conscious. Then they insinuate themselves into our life. Medieval depictions of the Fall often showed Eve in a dreamlike state at the moment when the snake tempted her. A relief in the cathedral of Autun, France, shows this moment of temptation. The snake, hardly visible, offers her the apple from behind, while she looks elsewhere.

In a lecture he gave on January 19, 1915, Rudolf Steiner said:

> We can only develop the right resistance against demons by recognising these forces; that we *know* that they exist. These forces only become destructive when we remain unconscious about them, when we don't know them.

However, we probably all understand that knowledge of evil alone is not enough to withstand these forces – let alone to overcome them. We need a faculty that includes the help of the spiritual world. Our knowledge needs to become wisdom in order to find the right way to encounter evil. In the Jewish culture of the Chassidim, a rabbi asks his students: 'What is the difference between a zaddik (a wise man) and a sinner?' The answer: 'A zaddik knows that he sins as long as he lives. A sinner knows that he lives as long as he sins.' Indeed, with a little bit of wisdom we begin to realise that we are not only surrounded by evil, but that we all have tendencies of evil in us. Regarding evil, we are all in the same boat – at least in our subconscious life. The only relevant question is: are we awake? This insight is the beginning of wisdom. It makes us very modest, and perhaps less judgmental, when we are confronted with crime and violence. When in June of this year the news of the death of George Floyd was released, there was an uproar of horror and protest all over the world for obvious reasons. My wise colleague Jonah Evans, seminary director in Toronto, wrote a contemplation in the weekly newsletter of his congregation, in which he tried to understand from within what had happened:

> As painful as it was to watch the video of the murder of George Floyd, I made myself look in the eyes of Derek Chauvin, the man who knelt on George's neck. And as I looked into his eyes, I saw no shame. No shame. And yet, I also knew in that moment, that I too could do what Derek did. That darkness also lives in me. Derek could be me. This is because I know that there is no evil on earth that is not possible in me.

Evil in us has a name. In psychology, we usually call it the shadow. It is defined as 'suppressed characteristics that are not admitted by a conscious person.' In spiritual language it is called the double or the doppelgänger. Awareness of this spiritual reality can make us even more modest when we think about redeeming evil. Whatever we say about this redemption can lead to delusions.

Our very first little step on this path is what I call 'the royal art of working with evil.' We need to look at it from a higher point of view, so that we are not overwhelmed or paralysed by it. When we have to deal with evil, humour can be an excellent tool that helps us to step back and make ourselves free from its overwhelming power. Humour is a faculty that cannot be conquered by it.

Of course, this little step is again far from redemption, but when we use humour in evil circumstances, we step back from the destructive forces that want to imprison us. In a certain way, we are set free.

People who were able to redeem evil to a certain extent in their own lives sometimes express their hard-won wisdom, as Ita Wegman did, after being the victim of false accusations over many years. When a group of young students asked her 'Why don't you respond to these accusations?', she replied, 'Rudolf Steiner taught me that one should not feed the demons, one should starve them.'

Something similar is expressed in a quote that I once heard in Australia: 'When you are in the zoo, don't feed the animals!' And in Germany, people used to say when confronted with evil: '*Geduld frisst den Teufel.*' Patience consumes the Devil. This can be practised first of all with all forms of evil that live within us. Only with the patience of an angel (or, if you can't manage that, with the stubbornness of a donkey) can we overcome the forces of evil. The Devil is extremely clever, but he has no patience. In the confrontation with evil, all the faculties mentioned above are needed if we are to work with it in a royal way: insight, consciousness, wisdom, self-reflection, humour and patience. Then we might see light at the end of the dark tunnel. A person who went through this tunnel once distilled her experience into a tiny, modest poem:

> When I
> with concentration
> and full of love
> look
> into the darkness
> then I see
> light.

Is the Earth a Living Body? (And If So, Whose Is It?)

Peter Skaller

Peter Skaller was born in 1942. He studied zoology and forestry and lectured in ecology for many years at the University of Pennsylvania. He was ordained in 1978 and has worked in Ontario, Quebec and in New England.

In his first letter to the Corinthians, St Paul's description of the human body emphasised the necessity for different organs and how they form a whole (12:12–21). Today we know that the body's parts are not only complementary in purpose and function, they are also interdependent. The eyes work differently depending on the ear's acuity and vice versa. The working of the heart changes with how the legs are used and vice versa. And the nervous and circulatory systems interconnect and are in turn affected by all the body's parts and processes.

Besides physical organs, a living body must have an etheric body that enables it to grow and function, and for a living body to have conscious experience a 'soul' must also be present. The physical and non-physical members also interact. Physical pain affects the soul, and anxiety impacts the ability of the etheric body to heal wounds. All members of the body are integrated into a unity.

The idea of the body as an entity unto itself has to be modified to account for its continual exchange of minerals, air, water and warmth with the surrounding world. Our spiritual bodies are also affected by, and affect, other beings. Therefore, our body is within, and interacts with, the surrounding world, which as will be shown is another body.

For the parts of a body to function as a coordinated unit directed towards purposeful activity there must be an overarching design, or blueprint, and an implementing builder-coordinator. (It is beyond the scope of this article to talk about the 'template' for this design as described by Steiner; see lecture of October 10, 1911, contained in *From Jesus to Christ*.) R. Buckminster Fuller called the builder-coordinator 'the Phantom Captain', which has 'neither weight nor sensorial tangibility' and without whom the material body would be unable to function properly and would soon crumble.

With the phantom captain's departure, the mechanism becomes inoperative and very quickly disintegrates into basic chemical elements.

The captain's departure also brings about the release of the life-body and soul, but now into the world of the spirit. A seeker of existential truth eventually comes to ask who fashioned the blueprint, and how it is integrated into the larger world around us.

The earth as a body

Ecologists today understand the earth, or biosphere, to be a system comprised of mutually interacting and interdependent domains. In his book *General System Theory* (George Braziller, Inc., 1969) the Austrian biologist Ludwig von Bertalanffy said:

> We are seeking another basic outlook: the world as an organisation. This would profoundly change categories of our thinking and influence our practical attitudes. We must envision the biosphere as a whole with mutually reinforcing or mutually destructive inter-dependencies.
> Bertalanffy also said:
> The mechanistic world view, taking the play of physical particles as ultimate reality, found its expression in a civilization that glorifies physical technology, which has led essentially to the catastrophes of our times … the model of the world as a great organisation can help to reinforce the sense of reverence for the living which we have almost lost in the last … decades of human history.*

As with all systems, the components of the human body or the biosphere can be evaluated at various levels of subsystems. The human body could be

---

* Bertalanffy, L, cited by Rosen, Robert in 'Putting a Science Back on the Track', *Science,* Vol. 164, No. 3880, pp. 681f.

studied at the molecular, cellular and organ levels; the biosphere at the levels of mineralogy, geology, meteorology, botany, zoology, anthropology, or even at the more elemental level of the light, warmth, air, water and mineral realms. At whatever level one looks, the biosphere functions as a body whose parts are so integrated that a change in one part reverberates throughout and changes the entire system.

As was shown for the human body, the biosphere is also in continual exchange with the world around it. The sun, moon and other solar system entities, such as asteroids and meteors, all affect the earth. We can go further out to the stars whose most obvious influence concerns how human star-based navigation altered the entire earthly world. We could also consider the ancient wisdom of astrology.

Except for gravity, today's science may not yet have determined how the earth in turn affects these cosmic entities, but as we increasingly send people, electromagnetic waves and materials into space, and as astrophysics advances, further connections will undoubtedly show themselves. Already there is human garbage and techno-generated electromagnetic fields (EMFs) orbiting the earth. We also should not omit probable far-reaching metaphysical effects of human thinking and feeling as working throughout the cosmos.

Using modes of perception that modern humanity has mostly lost, aboriginal people have since ancient times held that ultimately the earth is part of a system that comprises the entire universe. With today's scientific logic we too can conceive the universe as comprised of a hierarchical arrangement of bodies within bodies within bodies within one great body, like a matryoshka doll. The phantom captain of this great body some call God, and some of its blueprint principles, divined by seers, are suggested in Genesis 1, throughout the modern works of Rudolf Steiner, and by some of today's visionary scientists.

Is the earth alive? The biosphere breathes rhythmically through the daily and seasonal exhaling and inhaling of oxygen and carbon dioxide by the earth's more than three trillion trees, other land vegetation, and by oceanic algae and phytoplankton, while the movement of wind and water functions like a circulatory system. And its wounds can heal through its own activity, for example through the naturally occurring revegetation of strip mines. So the earth exhibits characteristics of life similar to those of the human body. And since it functions as an integrated system, there must also be a blueprint or design with a phantom captain as well.

Is the earth ensouled? That is more difficult to ascertain with normal consciousness. In considering this question, one can ask: How would I know there is a human being standing before me if I were only to perceive a physical body? The self of the other is supersensibly perceived with our 'ego-sense', which becomes the basis for freely willed moral activity, or love. The earth as a 'someone' can be experienced during intimate experiences in a forest, a thunderstorm or hurricane, a rainbow, while watching salmon scale a waterfall, feeling the sun, or even while eating a meal.

Care of the earth

Beginning with any land-use practice, such as farming, waste disposal, fuel burning, mining, drilling, fishing, or building housing, we can follow in detail the interconnected paths of effects and feedbacks. For example, ecologists understand how damming a river affects the oceans, clouds, landforms, air, plants, animals and human beings both near and far. We know how substances introduced at one place, such as through agriculture or manufacturing, impact the biota both locally and in distant regions. But understanding interactions does not necessarily allow for certainty in rendering management decisions. There are many reasons for this:

1. In the material world decisions involve trade-offs based on conflicting needs and values.

2. The intellect is limited in its ability to account for all possible interacting factors. Recent interest in Artificial Intelligence (AI) is based on the notion that computers will outperform people in analysing complex systems and rendering decisions.

3. The discoveries of Werner Heisenberg showed that the universe does not behave as a totally deterministic pool table where Newtonian mechanics rigidly holds sway. He also showed that the mere act of observing a phenomenon alters what is being observed, which plagues ecologists hoping to study natural ecosystems. Edward Lorenz wondered if a butterfly flapping its wings in Brazil could set off a tornado in Texas (the famous Butterfly Effect). His experiments showed how seemingly trivial events can undermine confidence in forecasting weather and ultimately the future of any system. Hence, many think that AI ultimately cannot do what its proponents hope for. (It is worth noting in passing that these recent ideas support 'freedom' as a valid concept in our universe.)

4. As Buckminster Fuller and others have argued, living systems are synergistically more than the sum of their parts. Synergy is the only word in our language that means behaviour of whole systems unpredicted by the separately observed behaviours of any of the system's separate parts or any subassembly of the system's parts. There is nothing in the chemistry of a toenail that predicts the existence of a human being. Or to put it another way, there is nothing in a caterpillar that tells you it's going to be a butterfly.

5. Ultimately, a moral overlay is required in order to choose a course of action in a world of trade-offs and uncertainties. But moral ideas based upon uncertain materialistic principles become so relative and circular as to be essentially irresolvable. Obviously, AI cannot help here. It is significant that the Ten Commandments, the accepted moral fundaments for so many throughout the world, were given as generalised declarative, not relative, statements.

Modernised humanity seems to be seriously deficient in the will to act morally regarding care of people and the earth. Conflicts in resolving trade-offs are overwhelmingly resolved towards acquiring personal power and material advantage, rather than on love. In her book *Braiding Sweetgrass* (Minneapolis, 2013), Robin Wall Kimmerer examines ecological principles from the First Nations' viewpoint that holds that actions towards the earth should proceed not from what we want, but from gratitude for what the earth has given us. In turn, this approach would open paths towards action towards the earth born out of love. Gratitude, or thankfulness, is also the meaning of eucharist, the name of the central sacrament in Christianity. Here, too, gratitude becomes the gate that can open up the possibility of love.

Is there a phantom captain of the earth?

This question is the same as pondering if there is a phantom captain working in one's body or throughout the universe. Of course there is, even if their ways often seem logically contradictory and troublesome. The elements of matter simply cannot arrange themselves into organised material systems, much less into living, ensouled systems, without a blueprint or a design and its creator with the will to manifest it. Religious differences within human culture arise in the naming of this captain and the description of their attributes, not whether the captain exists. Most of the world's religions acknowledge some sort of hierarchy of angelic sub-captains who enact the captain's will within specific subsystems of creation.

In the Christian mystical tradition, the being who carries the world design conceived by the Godhead is called the Word, or the Christ, who creates and lives throughout all the systems in creation including the biosphere. The functioning of the biosphere is under the captaincy of the sun, from whom the Christ's invisible organising intelligence is carried in its light and warmth, along with streaming life-forces that set earth's life into rhythmical activity. But the story doesn't end there. Christian visionaries also stress that ever since the Christ walked, died on, and was buried in the earth, he makes available a new surge of life – for an earth in the throes of illness caused by the loveless actions of human beings – and directly to human beings who, in seeking to open an inner space for him, may also experience healing, eventually manifesting love towards one another and the earth. (John 1: 1–18)

Sources

TC: *Tatchristentum* (German, 1923–24)
CG: *Die Christengemeinschaft* (German, 1924–present)
CCJ: *The Christian Community Journal* (1932–80)
TF: *The Threshing Floor* (1981–86)
P: *Perspectives* (1987–present)

Christ – *TC, April 1923 (translated by Matthew Barton).*
From Buddha to Christ: Repeated Earth Lives – *CCJ, March–April 1956 (excerpt from a 1925 publication).*
An Easter Revelation in the Old Testament – *CG, March 1928 (translated by Matthew Barton).*
Creation – *CCJ, Apr 1933.*
The Name 'Michael' – *CG, October 1932 (translated by Matthew Barton).*
Tobit: An Easter Story – *CCJ, April 1937.*
Human Nature and Morality – *CCJ, July–Aug 1958 (originally published in Czech in 1938).*
The Quaker-Catholic – *CCJ, April 1940.*
The Two Jesus Children – *CCJ, Jan 1948.*
God and the Devil – *CCJ, March–April 1949.*
The Tragedy of Judas – *CCJ, March–April 1952.*
Making Friends with Time – *CCJ, May–June 1952.*
Billy Graham and the Religious Situation in Britain – *CCJ, July–Aug 1955.*
True and False Vision – *CCJ, Jan–Feb 1957.*
Urizen and Los – *CCJ, May–June 1957.*
The Problem of Community – *CCJ, May–June 1958.*
Shakespeare and the Realm of the Dead – *CCJ, Nov–Dec 1964.*
The Two Messiahs – *CCJ, Nov–Dec 1965.*
The Trinity – *CCJ, May–June 1968.*

Abraham Lincoln: Servant of Michael – *CCJ, Jan–Feb 1971*.
The Origins of Celtic Christianity – *CCJ, July–Aug 1971*.
Our Relationship with Those Who Have Died – *TF, Nov 1982*.
The Voice of Conscience in William Wilberforce – *TF, July 1983*.
Freud's Picture of Man – *TF, Aug 1985*.
The Mystery of Rebirth in an Esoteric Gospel – *P, Nov 1988*.
The Body and Its Redemption – *P, Feb 1991*.
Is Religion Useful? – *P, Feb 1994*.
Market Forces and Ethics – *P, 1994*.
Counselling and Sacramental Consultation – *P, Aug 1995*.
Forgiving is More Than Amnesia: Reconciliation in South Africa – *P, June 1996*.
Finding Stillness in Chaos, Renewal in Decline – *P, Dec 1997*.
On the 150th Anniversary of Darwin's *Origin of Species* – *P, Dec 2008–Feb 2009*.
In Search of the Divine Feminine – *P, Jun–Aug 2009*.
Mary, Sophia and the New Advent of Christ – *P, March–May 2012*.
Fighting the Stigma of AIDs in Uganda – *P, Sep–Nov 2012*.
The Spiritual Hierarchies and Our Relationship to Them – *P, Dec 2012–Feb 2013*.
Homosexuality and the Bible – *P, Sep–Nov 2013*.
Why Did God Create Moths? – *P, March–May 2014 (previously in CG Feb 2013)*.
Seize the Day: Reflections on Brexit – *P, Sep–Nov 2016*.
Bursts of Light in the Darkness: Violence in the Light of Anthroposophy – *P, June–Aug 2018*.
Paul and Christ – *P, Dec 2019–Feb 2020*.
Transforming Evil – *P, Sep–Nov 2020*.
Is the Earth a Living Body? (And If So, Whose Is It?) – *P, March–May 2021*.

About *Perspectives*

Perspectives is the journal of The Christian Community in the English language. It is published quarterly in the UK (starting in December) amd contains articles on religious and theological themes as well as news about Christian Community events. The first issue of the year also contains a listing of the Gospel readings for the coming year. It is available in print and as a PDF.

You can view past issues and how to subscribe at *www.perspectives-magazine.co.uk*

You may also be interested in...

Pioneers of Religious Renewal
A History of The Christian Community in the English-Speaking World
Christian Maclean

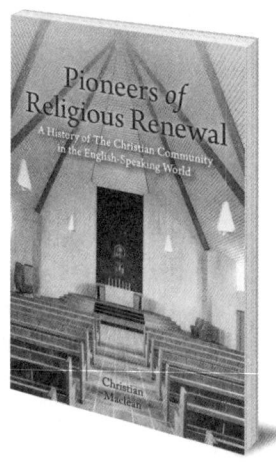

This book looks back to the founding of The Christian Community in 1922, following inspiration from Rudolf Steiner, and especially its beginnings in English-speaking countries.

It includes accounts of the key personalities who brought the organisation into existence, such as Friedrich Rittelmeyer and Emil Bock, as well as the priests and leaders who pioneered it in Britain, North America, South Africa, Australia and New Zealand, including Alfred Heidenreich, Oliver Matthews, Verner Hegg, Heinz Maurer, Julian Sleigh, Eileen Hersey, Michael Tapp and many more.

florisbooks.co.uk

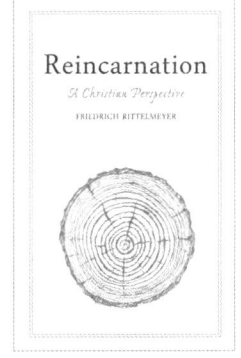

florisbooks.co.uk

For news on all our **latest books**,
and to receive **exclusive discounts**,
join our mailing list at:

florisbooks.co.uk

Plus subscribers get a FREE book
with every online order!

We will never pass your details to anyone else.